DELINQUENT GANGS

A Psychological Perspective

Arnold P. Goldstein

Research Press · 2612 North Mattis Avenue · Champaign, Illinois 61821

Advisory Editor, Frederick H. Kanfer

Cover design by Elizabeth D. Burczy, Chicago, Illinois
Composition by Black Dot Graphics
Printed by McNaughton & Gunn

ISBN 0-87822-324-X
Library of Congress Catalog No. 91-60232

To Donald H. Ford
Very special friend, very special mentor

Contents

Figures and Tables

Preface

Delinquent youth gangs in the United States, as a social (or, better, antisocial) phenomenon, ebb and flow in both their numbers and their societal impact. As the United States enters the 1990s, there seem to be (and are) more gangs, more gang youth drug involvement, and more violence being perpetrated by such youths. This book describes the gang phenomenon and both recommends and exemplifies a strategy for improving the ability to understand, predict, control, and reorient delinquent gang formation and behavior. The strategy is extrapolation—of the findings and insights from diverse fields of psychology to the domain of the delinquent gang.

Part I presents a sense of what the contemporary gang is (chapter 1) and the reasons for its increasing violence (chapter 2). Part II examines and extrapolates from relevant theory and research in clinical (chapter 3), developmental (chapter 4), social (chapter 5), and community (chapter 6) psychology. The reader is invited to share in this process of both reflecting upon such psychological knowledge and seeking to draw from it gang-relevant insights and hypotheses. Portions of chapters 1 and 3 appeared earlier in *Delinquents on Delinquency* (Goldstein, 1990); portions of chapter 5 derive from *Prepare: Teaching Prosocial Competencies* (Goldstein, 1988).

A focal concern of psychology is intervention—preventive, rehabilitative, or other. Intervention targeted at diverse levels (individual, group, community, and state) is the main subject of Part III: Chapters 7 through 10 treat the various levels of intervention, describing the work that has already been accomplished and outlining the research and implementation goals that must be met if gang-related intervention is to be effective.

A closing coda titled "Gangs on Gangs" urges professionals concerned with any aspect of delinquent gang phenomenon—research, theory, prevention, rehabilitation—to recognize the desirability of including gang youths themselves as collaborators in such efforts. Far too often have professionals been talking mostly to each other, to themselves, or to the general public. Far too seldom have their efforts included or reflected open and honest discourse with the object of concern—delinquent gang youths. Such discourse is not easily accomplished, but, as this book seeks to highlight, it is both a valuable and a reachable goal.

My desire to write this book grew from several sources—my career-long concern with juvenile delinquency and with developing means for promoting prosocial behavior among chronically antisocial youths; my felicitous and stimulating involvement with colleagues at the New York State Division for Youth and the New York State Task Force on Juvenile Gangs; my belief in the unity of the subfields of psychology and hence in the value of the extrapolatory process; and my personal belief that ganging in America and its consequences will likely become more serious as the 1990s unfold.

I have been fortunate enough in this effort to benefit from the generous and expert feedback of a number of colleagues who kindly read this manuscript and offered their thoughts and reactions. My special appreciation goes to Donald Ford, Kenneth Heller, Malcolm Klein, Mark Sherman, Irving Spergel, and Shirley White. You each have indeed made this book richer.

PART I

Introduction

CHAPTER 1

Gangs in the United States

DEFINITIONS

What is a gang? This seemingly straightforward definitional question masks concerns of considerable complexity. There is not, nor should there be, a single, acceptable definition of *gang,* any more than a single definition would suffice over many years and across locations for other types of human groups, be they work groups, social groups, organizations, communities, or even nations. Many definitions have been proposed during the past 80 years, and in a real sense all are correct. What constitutes a gang has varied with time and place, with political and economic conditions, with community tolerance and community conservatism, with level and nature of police and citizen concern, with cultural and subcultural traditions and mores, and with media-generated sensationalism or indifference to law-violating youth groups. What is a gang? Chronologically, a gang has been defined as

> for the boy one of the three primary social groups. These three are the family, the neighborhood, and the play group; but for the normal boy the play group is the gang. All three are restrictive human groupings, formed like pack and flock and hive, in response to deep-seated but unconscious need. (Puffer, 1912, p. 7)

> an interstitial group originally formed spontaneously, and then integrated through conflict. It is characterized by the following types of behavior: meeting face to face, milling, movement through space as a unit, conflict, and planning. The result of this collective behavior is the development of tradition, unreflective internal structure, esprit de corps, solidarity, morale, group awareness, and attachment to a local territory. (Thrasher, 1927/1963, p. 46)

> a group of six or more persons who can identify an instigator among their number or who have a group name and who have experienced, as a group, two or more

3

incidents of conflict with other like groups or legal
authorities without openly opposing the moral validity of
the social order or norms. (Arnold, 1966, p. 70)

any denotable adolescent group of youngsters who (a) are
generally perceived as a distinct aggregation by others in
their neighborhood, (b) recognize themselves as a
denotable group (almost invariably with a group name),
and (c) have been involved in a sufficient number of
delinquent incidents to call forth a consistent negative
response from neighborhood residents and/or law
enforcement agencies. (Klein, 1971, p. 111)

a self-formed association of peers, bound together by
mutual interests, with identifiable leadership, well-
developed lines of authority, and other organizational
features, who act in concert to achieve a specific purpose
or purposes which generally include the conduct of illegal
activity and control over a particular territory, or type of
enterprise. (Miller, 1974, p. 295)

an interstitial and integrated group of persons who meet
face to face more or less regularly and whose existence
and activities as a group are considered an actual or
potential threat to the prevailing social order.
(Cartwright, 1975, p. 4)

an organization of young people usually between their
early teens and early twenties, which has a group name,
claims a territory or neighborhood as its own, meets with
its members on a regular basis, and has recognizable
leadership. The key element that distinguishes a gang
from other organizations of young people is delinquency:
its members regularly participate in activities that violate
the law. (Gardner, 1983, p. 5)

a group of juveniles who were linked together because the
police suspected them of committing crimes together.
(Sarnecki, 1985, p. 11)

a group of associating individuals which (a) has an
identifiable leadership and organizational structure;
(b) either claims control over particular territory in the
community, or exercises control over an illegal enterprise; and (c) engages collectively or as individuals in acts
of violence or serious criminal behavior. (California
Office of Criminal Justice Planning, 1987, pp. 3–4)

a group of affiliated individuals who engage in some form
of social behavior which is considered undesirable by
society. (Jetmore, 1988, p. 64)

the most frequently cited elements of a definition for
gang [in their national survey] were certain group or
organizational characteristics, symbols, and a range of
specific and general criminal activities, particularly
violence, drug use and sales. The most frequent elements
used to define a gang member were symbols or symbolic
behavior, self-admission, identification by others,
especially the police, and association with gang members.
(Spergel, Ross, Curry, & Chance, 1989, p. 206)

an ongoing, identifiable group of people (highly organized
or loosely structured) which, either individually or
collectively, has engaged in or is considered likely to
engage in unlawful or antisocial activity that may be
verified by police records or other reliable sources and
who create an atmosphere of fear and intimidation
within the community. (New York State Division for
Youth, 1990, p. 10)

A final definitional perspective will complete the effort to
establish the book's arena through the meanings and perceptions of
others.

The term gang means many things: individuals making
up any group; an elementary, tightly or loosely knit
group of spontaneous origin; a group of congenial
persons with close and informal relations; a group of
persons engaged in improper acts; a group of antisocial
adolescents; a company or organization of criminals.
Definitions of gang have varied over time according to
the perceptions and interests of the definer, academic
fashions, and the changing social reality of the gang. The
gang . . . has been viewed as a play group as well as a
criminal organization (Puffer 1912; Thrasher 1927/1963);
also as malicious and negativistic, comprising mainly
younger adolescents (A.K. Cohen 1955); or representing
different types of delinquent subcultural adaptation
(Cloward and Ohlin 1960). Definitions in the 1950s and
1960s were related to issues of etiology as well as based
on liberal, social reform assumptions. Definitions in the

1970s and 1980s are more descriptive, emphasize violent
and criminal characteristics, and possibly a more
conservative philosophy of social control and deterrence
(Klein and Maxson 1989). The most recent trend may be
to view gangs as more pathological than functional and
to restrict usage of the term to a narrow set of violent
and criminal groups. (Spergel et al., 1989, p. 13)

Miller (1974) surveyed 160 criminal justice and youth service
agencies, inquiring into their respective definitions of *gang*. As
reflected in his definition, presented earlier, six major elements
more or less consensually emerged from this extensive survey:

1. Being organized

2. Having identifiable leadership

3. Identifying with a territory

4. Associating continually

5. Having a specific purpose

6. Engaging in illegal activities

These very features are what most (though not all) of the
foregoing definitions have in common. Thus, in part, the question,
What is a gang? may be answered both longitudinally and cross-
sectionally by reference to these half-dozen qualities. But several
years have passed since the Miller survey. Have other central
dimensions of an accurate and current definition emerged? Reflecting the increasing violence in society at large, definitional inclusion
of violent behavior in considerations of gang-associated youths
appears likewise to have increased in recent years. As society has
increased its involvement in drug use and abuse, apparently so too
have American gangs. Although gang youths still spend a great deal
of their time together "hanging out," currently reported levels of
aggression and drug involvement make older definitions of gang, at
least in part, as a play group, a social group, or an athletic group
seem like quaint, wistful caricatures from a long-gone past. Spergel
et al. (1989) comment:

Some veteran gang researchers have recently changed
their minds as to gang character. Earlier, Miller viewed
the gang as a "stable and solitary primary group

preparing the young male for an adult role in lower-class society" (1958). The gang youth was not particularly aggressive, maintained a versatile repertoire of legal and illegal activities and rarely engaged in lethal activity (Miller, 1962, 1976). More recently, Miller reports that gang members engage individually or collectively in violent or other forms of behavior (1975, 1982). He concludes that "contemporary youth gangs pose a greater threat to public order and a greater danger to the safety of the citizenry than at any other time during the past" (1975, p. 44). (p. 17)

It is not that Miller—or Klein, Maxson, and Cunningham (1988), whose statements reflect a parallel contrast—have changed their minds about what a gang is but, instead, that the character of gangs themselves (even discounting media sensationalism) has substantially changed. They may have structured organization, identifiable leadership, territorial identification, continual associa-tion, specific purpose, and involvement in illegal behavior—as do many of the gangs in California, Illinois, and elsewhere as the United States enters the 1990s. Or, as is rather less characteristic of the typical contemporary gang, they may—as is largely the case in New York City—be loosely organized, have changeable leadership, be criminal-activity and not territorially oriented, associate irregu-larly, pursue amorphous purposes, and engage in not only illegal but also legal activities. Nevertheless, they are more violent and more drug involved, and these two characteristics must also be included in establishing an accurate, contemporary definition of *gang.* How else may the nature of delinquent youth gangs in the United States best be clarified? In the sections that follow we will seek to do so by examining the history of gangs, sketching both early and more recent theories of why groups of delinquent youths engage in criminal behavior, presenting the gang typologies or classification systems that have been put forth, and describing their core demographics.

HISTORY

Delinquent ganging in the 20th-century United States did not emerge de novo but grew from a long and varied tradition of group violence. Between 1760 and 1900, 500 vigilante groups—the Ku

Klux Klan, the White Cappers, the Black Legion prominent among them—appeared in the United States (Gurr, 1989). Whippings, bombings, arson, and murder were among their violent tools for terrorizing ethnic and religious minorities and other targets of their hate. Less organized but directed toward similar violent ends were lynch mobs, responsible for taking the lives of 3,400 Black Americans between 1882 and 1951 (Gurr, 1989). Piracy; banditry; feuding; labor, agrarian, and race riots; and the frequently glamorized marauding bands of frontier outlaws, such as Butch Cassidy's High Five and the Jesse James gang, are all in their own ways ancestors of the contemporary gang (R.M. Brown, 1980). The Forty Thieves, an Irish-American immigrant gang formed in 1820 in the Five Points District of New York City, is cited by the Illinois State Police (1989) as the first modern, adult criminal gang. It gave rise, as did many of the adult gangs that followed, to an "auxiliary" or "subgang" of juveniles, in this instance called the Forty Little Thieves. Other such adult and juvenile gangs quickly followed—the Kerryonians, the Dusters, the Plug Uglies, the Dead Rabbits, and others (Asbury, 1927/1971). The Illinois State Police (1989) write of this early period:

> Most generally it is believed the original gangs were
> formed by young men rebelling against their low social
> status. They came from areas of overcrowded,
> substandard housing, poor or nonexistent health care
> facilities, broken homes, and few economic
> opportunities. . . . Their original intent may have been
> simple camaraderie born of shared frustration at
> perceived social or economic injustices. Whatever the
> reason, their original purpose eventually degenerated to
> social resentment and ultimately they manifested that
> resentment in criminal activity. (p. 2)

As the American population spread westward, so too did the delinquent gang. Some of the early gangs, reflecting the definitions of the day, were largely mischievous play groups, such as W.H. Sheldon's (1898; cited in Furfey, 1926) secret clubs, social clubs, and predatory organizations; Puffer's (1912) clubs and athletic teams; and Furfey's (1926) adolescent groups. But with the passage of time and the growing influence of adult criminal behavior as well as a number of other societal forces, gangs took on increasingly darker tones—as the earlier chronology of definitions revealed. Thrasher's (1927/1963) landmark study of 1,313 Chicago area gangs, anticipating the later emergence of labeling theory, sought to depict how such play groups evolved into delinquent gangs:

> It does not become a gang . . . until it begins to excite disapproval and opposition. It discovers a rival or an enemy in the gang in the next block; its baseball or football team is pitted against some other team; parents or neighbors look upon it with suspicion or hostility . . . the storekeeper or the cops begin to give it shags [chase it]; or some representative of the community steps in and tries to break it up. This is the real beginning of the gang, for now it starts to draw itself more closely together. It becomes a conflict group. (p. 26)

Thrasher's (1927/1963) study was truly seminal, in many instances offering original insights and dimensions of concern that remain key topics in contemporary discussions of gangs and gang behavior. Our own later explorations of the complexity of the roots of gang formation, ganging as a process, situational gang leadership, the influence of community (including physical community) forces on gang organization and behavior, and the role of what came to be called *groupthink* in gang functioning were each anticipated by Thrasher. Other early members of the Chicago school of sociology built significantly upon Thrasher's work. Bolitho (1930), Landesco (1932), and Tannenbaum (1938), for example, each provided further description of the organization and functioning of Chicago's delinquent gangs and further elaboration of several of Thrasher's central conclusions.

Notions about causation—that is, about why gangs form—changed during this early period of gang research. In its beginning, Puffer (1912), reflecting the heavy reliance on both Darwinian theory and instinct as the core explanatory constructs in the behavioral science of the day, asserted:

> We must, then, so far as we are good evolutionists, look upon the boy's gang as the result of a group of instincts inherited from a distant past. . . . [W]e must suppose that these gang instincts arose in the first because they were useful once, and that they have been preserved to the present day because they are, on the whole, useful still. (p. 83)

Thrasher (1927/1963) looked for causative explanation both within the youths themselves and within the community to which they belonged. The typical gang member, in his view, was "a rather healthy, well-adjusted, red-blooded American boy seeking an outlet for normal adolescent drives for adventure and expression" (Hardman, 1967, p. 7). Yet the youth's environment was equally important to Thrasher. Inadequacies in family functioning, schools, housing, sanitation, employment, and other community characteristics combined to help motivate a youth to turn elsewhere—to the gang—for life satisfactions and rewards.

The focus on social causation blossomed fully during the next era of gang research, from the 1930s to the early 1940s, which Hardman (1967) appropriately labeled "the depression studies." It was an era in which social scientists sought explanation for many ills—including delinquent ganging—in "social causation, social failure, social breakdown" (Hardman, p. 9). Landesco (1932) emphasized the effects of conflicting immigrant and American cultures. Shaw and McKay (1942) stressed a more complex combination of slum area deterioration, poverty, family dissolution, and organized crime. Tannenbaum (1938) analogously proposed that the gang forms not because of its attractiveness per se, but because positive sociocultural forces—family, school, church—that might train a youth into more socially acceptable behaviors are weak or unavailable. Wattenberg and Balistrieri (1950) similarly stressed socioeconomically substandard neighborhoods and lax parental supervision. In the same spirit of contextual explanation Bogardus (1943)—conducting one of the first West Coast gang studies— saw the war and the warlike climate in the United States underpinning the formation of aggressive gangs at that time. Dumpson (1949), more multicausal but still contextual in his thinking, blamed the war, racism, and diverse political and economic sources.

Although the social problems of the day have, over the decades, formed the principal basis for explaining why youths form gangs, Miller (1982) offers a more inclusive perspective, which appears to better capture the complex determinants that likely underlie gang formation. Miller observes that

> youth gangs persist because they are a product of
> conditions basic to our social order. Among these are a
> division of labor between the family and the peer group
> in the socialization of adolescents, and emphasis on
> masculinity and collective action in the male subculture;
> a stress on excitement, congregation, and mating in the
> adolescent subculture; the importance of toughness and

smartness in the subcultures of lower-status populations; and the density conditions and territoriality patterns affecting the subcultures of urban and urbanized locales. (p. 320)

A somewhat different but equally comprehensive view of the factors contributing to gang formation is offered by Edgerton (1988) and reflects a causal emphasis on the construct of multiple marginality. Edgerton proposes that the major contributory factors include

residential segregation in low-income areas, poverty, poor school performance, little parental supervision, discrimination, and distrust of law enforcement. In these conditions, young people spent much of their lives together on the streets where a gang served them . . . as surrogate family, school, and police. We also hear from gang members . . . about the appeal that gang membership has for them—friendship, pride, prestige, belongingness, identity, self-esteem, and a desire to emulate their uncles and older brothers who were gang members before them. (p. x)

DELINQUENT GANG THEORY

Until the middle of this century, social scientists' interest in delinquent gangs was largely descriptive. The concern focused on what gangs were and on the societal/familial conditions that spawned and accompanied them. This early era produced little in the way of formal gang theory—that is, conceptualizations of the structural and dynamic variables underlying gang formation, gang structure, and, especially, the delinquent behavior that characterized a substantial amount of gang functioning. This theoretical lacuna was filled—and then some—beginning in the 1950s. As noted earlier, by far the majority of this effort was sociological in nature.

Strain Theory

At the heart of strain theory is the discrepancy between economic aspiration and opportunity, along with such discrepancy-induced reactions as frustration, deprivation, and discontent. Notions of strain theory first appeared in Merton's 1938 article "Social Structure and Anomie," in which he observed:

> It is only when a system of cultural values extols, virtually above all else, certain common symbols of success for the population at large, while its social structure rigorously restricts or completely eliminates access to approved modes of acquiring these symbols for a considerable part of the same population, that anti-social behavior ensues on a considerable scale. (p. 673)

A.K. Cohen's (1955) reactance theory and Cloward and Ohlin's (1960) differential opportunity theory are both elaborations of strain theory. Each seems to enhance that theory's explanatory power, especially with regard to delinquent behavior among low-income youths. Yet such an association between social class and delinquency is inconsistent (Linden, 1978; Rutter & Giller, 1983). Furthermore, most low-income delinquent youths eventually become law-abiding adults, though their economic status often remains unchanged. Hirschi (1969) also marshals evidence indicating that many delinquent youths do not experience the deprivation-induced motivation central to strain theory, and R.E. Johnson (1979) suggests that strain theory holds little explanatory relevance for delinquent acts committed by middle-class youths. These and related caveats notwithstanding, strain theory appropriately survives to this day, its more contemporary versions seeking to respond to both changed socioeconomic forces (Simon & Gagnon, 1976) and evidence indicating that middle-class youths are just as likely as those from low-income environments to aspire beyond their means (Elliott & Voss, 1974). The theory survives not as an all-encompassing explanation of juvenile delinquency in its individual and group or gang manifestations, but as one of several integrated theoretical views on delinquency that acknowledge it as complex behavior derived from a complex of causes.

Subcultural Theory

Subcultural or cultural deviance theory holds that delinquent behavior grows from conformity to the prevailing social norms experienced by youths in their particular subcultural groups, norms generally at variance with those of society at large and including, according to A.K. Cohen (1966), gratuitous hostility, group autonomy, intolerance of restraint, short-term hedonism, the seeking of recognition via antisocial behavior, lack of interest in planning for long-term goals, and related behavioral preferences. Miller (1958) describes these subcultural norms or "focal concerns" as centering on trouble, toughness, (out)smartness, excitement, fate, and autonomy. In this view, the adolescent is "drawn or socialized into law violation in an attempt to live up to the perceived expectations of his or her deviant associates" (R.E. Johnson, 1979, p. 2). Sutherland's (Sutherland, 1937; Sutherland & Cressey, 1974) differential association theory, Miller's (1958) notion of lower class culture as a generating milieu for gang delinquency, differential identification theory (D. Glaser, 1956), culture conflict theory (Shaw & McKay, 1942), illicit means theory (Shaw & McKay, 1942), and what might be termed structural determinism (Clarke, 1977) are the major concretizations of subcultural theory. Of these, differential association theory has clearly been most influential. Delinquent behavior, according to this view, is learned behavior. Further, correctly anticipating evidence that had yet to appear, Sutherland held that the way in which such behavior is learned involves processes no different from the acquisition of any other social behavior.

A substantial number of diverse findings lend considerable credence to the role of such association-engendered learning in the etiology of delinquency, especially gang delinquency. Most delinquent acts are committed by youths in the company of others (Farrington, Gundry, & West, 1975). Youngsters attending a school or living in a neighborhood with high rates of delinquency are more likely to commit delinquent acts than are their counterparts in schools or areas with low delinquency rates (Rutter & Giller, 1983). Males who admit to having delinquent friends are more likely also to admit to delinquent acts than are those who deny having such friends (R.E. Johnson, 1979; Voss, 1963). A youth's likelihood of committing a specific type of delinquent act is significantly correlated with the likelihood of commission of the same act by members of the peer group (Reiss & Rhodes, 1964), and the number of delinquent acts committed by a boy's friends is predictive of his own future convictions (West & Farrington, 1977). Self-report data indicate that, across alternative etiological bases for delinquency (delinquent associates, delinquent values, attachment to school, school performance, parental love, attachment to parents, occupational expectations, perceived risk of apprehension), the strongest covariate by far is delinquent associates (R.E. Johnson, 1979).

Sutherland and Cressey (1974) have criticized differential association theory for omitting consideration of personality traits. Nettler (1974) has noted its disregard for situational determinants of criminal behavior. Nietzel (1979) asserts that the theory reflects an overly simplified view of the learning process, and Wilson and Hernnstein (1985) observe that it provides no explanation for individual differences and hence fails to account for the fact that within a given neighborhood, for example, some youths adopt deviant values and others adopt more conventional ones. Thus, as with aspiration-opportunity-induced strain, it is appropriate to view subcultural influences as but part of the etiological picture— in this instance, however, an especially important part.

Control Theory

Although both strain and subcultural theories seek to explain why some youngsters commit delinquent acts, control theory posits reasons that some youngsters do not. Everyone, it is assumed, has a predisposition to commit delinquent acts, and this theory concerns itself with how individuals learn not to offend. The central construct of control theory, the major mediator of such learning not to offend, is the social bond (Hirschi, 1969). Social bonds grow both from direct social controls (e.g., externally imposed restrictions and punishments) and from internal controls (resulting primarily from affectional identification with one's parents). Social bonds find overt expression, the theory holds, in attachment to other people, commitment to organized society, involvement in conventional activities, and belief in a common value system. Hirschi (quoted in R.E. Johnson, 1979, p. 2) proposes, for example, that "the prospects of delinquent behavior decline as the adolescent is controlled by such bonds as affective ties to parents, success in school, involvement in school activities, high occupational and educational aspirations, and belief in the moral validity of conventional norms."

The weaker the social bonding, thus defined, the greater the purported likelihood of delinquent behavior. Both Hirschi (1969) and Elliott, Ageton, and Canter (1979) have reported evidence in support of this control theory hypothesis. Control theory and its variations (Hewitt, 1970; Matza, 1964; Nye, 1958; Reckless, 1961; Sykes & Matza, 1957) find particular support in the substantial empirical literature convincingly demonstrating the broad and deep influence of family factors upon the likelihood of delinquent behavior. Some of these factors are parental criminality (Osborn & West, 1979; Robins, West, & Herjanic, 1975); parental social difficulties such as excessive drinking, frequent unemployment, and the like (Robins & Lewis, 1966); poor parental supervision and monitoring (Patterson, 1982; H. Wilson, 1980); poor discipline practices—excessive, erratic, or harsh (Deur & Parke, 1970; Sawin & Parke, 1979; Snyder & Patterson, 1987); and, as compared to parents of nondelinquent youths, greater parental reward for deviant behavior, greater likelihood of becoming involved in coercive interchanges, more frequent modeling of aggressive behavior, and the provision of less support and affection (Bandura, 1973; Patterson, 1982; Snyder, 1977). Families of delinquent youths also often display a lack of shared leisure time (Gold, 1963; West & Farrington, 1977), intimate parent-child communication (Hirschi, 1969), and parental warmth (McCord & McCord, 1959; Rutter, 1971). In addition, parental reports suggest lack of attachment to the children and poor identification with the role of parent (Patterson, 1982). The central role of family processes in the social bonding sequence and its consequences for other domains of potential bonding are described well by Snyder and Patterson (1987):

> Inept family socialization practices like poor discipline result in high frequencies of relatively trivial antisocial behavior by the child, like noncompliance, fighting, temper tantrums, petty theft, and lying. These inept practices may also result in poor interpersonal and work skills. Given that the child is antisocial and lacks skills, he is likely to move into the second stage of antisocial training. He is placed at risk for rejection by peers and adults, and for academic and work failure. . . . The rejected child is also likely to associate with other unskilled, coercive children, thereby increasing his opportunities to acquire, perform, and hone antisocial behavior. . . . As the child continues to develop in a family environment with poor socialization practices and to associate with deviant peers, his performance of antisocial behavior becomes increasingly frequent, varied, serious, and successful. (p. 219)

Labeling Theory

In 1938, Tannenbaum described an escalating process of stigmatization or labeling that, he asserted, can occur between young delinquents and their communities. Minor transgressions are met with admonitions, chastisements, and perhaps initial exposure to the police and court components of the criminal justice system. As the transgressive behavior escalates, community response hardens into a demand for suppression:

> There is a gradual shift from the definition of the specific acts as evil to a definition of the individual as evil, and . . . all his acts come to be looked upon with suspicion. . . . From the individual's point of view there has taken place a similar change. He has gone slowly from a sense of grievance and injustice, of being unduly mistreated and punished, to a recognition that the definition of him as a human being is different from that of other boys in his neighborhood, his school, street, community. The young delinquent becomes bad because he is defined as bad.
>
> The process of making the criminal, therefore, is a process of tagging, defining, identifying, segregating, describing, emphasizing, making conscious and self-conscious. The person becomes the thing he is described as being. (Tannenbaum, 1938, pp. 87–88)

Mead's (1934) earlier notion that one's self-concept derives in large part from how others define one lies at the heart of labeling theory. Becker (1963), Hawkins and Tiedemann (1975), Lemert (1967), and Schur (1971) have each explored this notion as it applies to diverse behaviors—including juvenile delinquency—that society at large labels as deviant. It is not the initial act(s) of delinquent behavior (*primary deviance*) that labeling theory seeks to explain, but delinquent acts subsequent to society's official response to the initial act(s) *(secondary deviance).* According to Nietzel (1979), "Persons are pushed to accept and enact these roles because of social expectations which are very difficult to disconfirm. Individuals, ultimately, conform to the stereotypes which have been applied to them" (p. 111). Once the labeling process is under way, Krohn, Massey, and Skinner (1987) note, conventional behaviors performed by the labeled individual may be less likely to receive reinforcement, opportunities to engage in such behaviors may diminish, and impetus to associate increasingly with other similarly labeled persons may increase.

Although labeling theory fails to attempt any causative explanation of prelabeling delinquent acts (primary deviance) and to externalize responsibility completely for the types of delinquent behavior it does seek to explain, it nevertheless quite appropriately signals the likely substantial role of the stigmatizing process in encouraging the very behavior society wishes to reduce. The decriminalization and diversion programs examined in chapter 7 are positive responses by the criminal justice system to this heightened awareness.

Radical Theory

Radical theory, sometimes termed "the new criminology" by its proponents (Abadinsky, 1979; Meier, 1976), is a sociopolitical perspective on crime and delinquency. Its focus is the political meanings and motivations underlying society's definitions of crime and its control. In this view, crime is a phenomenon largely created by those who possess wealth and power. Laws in the United States, radical theorists hold, are the laws of the ruling elite, used to subjugate the poor, minorities, and the powerless. The specific propositions that constitute radical theory (Quinney, 1974) concretize its sociopolitical thrust:

1. American society is based on an advanced capitalist economy.

2. The state is organized to serve the interests of the dominant economic class, the capitalist ruling class.

3. Criminal law is an instrument of the state and the ruling class, which use it to maintain and perpetuate the existing social and economic order.

4. Crime control in capitalist society is accomplished through a variety of institutions and agencies established and administered by a government elite, representing ruling class interests, for the purpose of establishing domestic order.

5. The contradictions of advanced capitalism require that the subordinate classes remain oppressed by whatever means are necessary, especially through the coercion and violence of the legal system.

6. Only with the collapse of capitalist society and the creation of a new society based on socialist principles will there be a solution to the crime problem.

As is evident, radical theory goes far beyond mere matters of social labeling, differential opportunity, or like concerns. Its target is no less than the social and economic structure of society. Although its preferred solutions appear to have little likelihood of becoming reality, the promotion of radical theory has rendered a significant consciousness-raising service resulting in increased awareness within the criminal justice system—and perhaps in society at large—of the degree to which social conflict, racism, exploitation, and related social ills are relevant to the etiology and remediation of criminal behavior.

Little additional strictly sociological theory of delinquent gang development has emerged since the appearance of the perspectives just examined. However, integrative theories combining, for example, constitutional, psychological, and sociological constructs have been put forth. They will be presented in chapter 3, which offers psychology's theoretical efforts to explain gang formation and delinquent behavior.

TYPOLOGIES

This chapter opened with an array of past and contemporary definitions of gang, sketched the early history of gang development, and outlined the major sociological theories of delinquent gang formation and functioning. A further means for understanding what gangs are, who composes them, what they do, and how they are perceived by the surrounding communities is to present the several formal and informal gang classification systems that have been proposed. Table 1.1 shows the diverse schemas suggesting types or typologies of gangs.

Most of the proposed gang typologies, as Table 1.1 indicates, are based on criteria of dominant activity or, closely related, purpose, organizational structure, or level of criminality. In rough parallel with the chronology of gang definitions presented earlier in this chapter, gang typologies chronologically move from inclusion of social and diversely noncriminal categories to more criminal, fighting, and turf themes and, ultimately, to a more contemporary focus on inclusion of serious criminal and violent behavior. The traditional (vertical, area) gang structure appears to be the most common in many locations in the United States. Such gangs involve clusters of age-graded, vertically distinguishable subgroups that typically function as communicating but nevertheless quite separate subgangs—for example, peewees, babies, juniors, seniors, and veterans. Traditional gangs thus defined often exist over many years, even generations; are closely associated with, and in a real sense grow from, neighborhood traditions; have both core and fringe (generally male) members; and, infrequently, have closely associated auxiliary female gangs.

Consistent with this book's overriding purpose—to suggest how psychological research and theory can heighten understanding of the nature and functioning of delinquent gangs—it is worth noting that psychological constructs or categories are employed in none of the proposed typologies. It is hoped that the materials mined in later chapters from clinical, developmental, social, and community psychology hold potential for remediating this deficiency.

CURRENT GANG DEMOGRAPHICS

Data on the number, nature, structure, and functioning of delinquent gangs, especially accurate data, are hard to come by. No national level agency has assumed responsibility for the systematic collection and reporting of gang-related information. Each city or region is free to, and does, formulate its own definition of *gang* and decides what gang-related data to collect. Police (the major source of gang information in most cities), public service agencies, schools, media representatives, and others regularly exposed to gang youths frequently exaggerate or minimize their numbers and illegal behaviors to serve political, financial, or other needs related to the management of perceptions. Compounding the difficulty in obtaining adequate, accurate, objective, and relevant information are gang youths themselves. Hagedorn and Macon (1988) warn:

> Be wary of your information. Gang members are quite
> adept at telling social workers and policemen self-serving
> lies. Glib misinformation is, in fact, a survival tool for
> many gang members. It is easy for outside people (and
> that is practically everybody) to believe social workers
> and policemen because they have direct contact with
> gang members. Yet this direct contact is often managed
> by the gang members themselves, sometimes for survival,
> sometimes even for self-glorifying exaggeration, and
> police and gang workers also have some self-interest in
> the images they purvey. (p. 4)

Thus, the available data must be accepted cautiously and used conservatively.

Given these caveats, what is currently known about the structure and demographics of the contemporary delinquent gang? As noted earlier, in 1974 Miller conducted a major national survey seeking gang-related information from a wide spectrum of public

Table 1.1 Gang Typologies

AUTHOR	CLASSIFICATION BASIS	CATEGORIES
W. H. Sheldon (1898; cited in Furfey, 1926)	Activity	Secret clubs, predatory organizations, social clubs, industrial associations, philanthropic organizations, athletic clubs
Thrasher (1927/1963)	Organization Social adaptation	Diffuse, solidified, conventionalized, criminal, secret society
Cohen and Short (1958)	Activity	Theft, conflict, addict
New York City Youth Board (1960)	Activity	Corner group, social club, conflict group, pathological group
Cloward and Ohlin (1960)	Activity	Criminal, conflict, retreatist
Yablonsky (1967)	Activity	Social, delinquent, violent
Spergel (1964)	Purpose	Racket, conflict, theft, drug
Gannon (1967)	Purpose	Fighting, defensive
Kobrin, Puntil, and Peluso (1968)	Criminality	Sophisticated, versatile, occupational, unconventional, respectable
Mulvihill, Tumin, and Curtis (1969)	Organization	Spontaneous versus self-contained, traditional versus cluster
B. Cohen (1969)	Criminality	Active, sporadic, dominant, defensive, criminal

20

Collins (1979)	Organization	Vertical, horizontal
Collins (1979)	Purpose	Defensive, aggressive, passive-aggressive, active
Collins (1979)	Stage of development	Early, marginal, well established
Savitz, Rosen, and Lalli (1980)	Activity	Structural, functional
Miller (1982)	Purpose	Turf, gain-oriented/extended network, fighting
Campbell (1984)	Activity	Tomboys, sex objects
Philadelphia Police Department Preventive Patrol Unit (1987)	Criminality	Active, sporadic, inactive
Klein and Maxson (1989)	Organization/activity	Traditional, spontaneous, specialty clique, violent
Bobrowski (1988)	Purpose	Turf, retaliation, prestige, representing
E.C. Pleines (1988; cited in Spergel, Ross, Curry, and Chance, 1989)	Criminality	Serious, minor, mixed
Baca (1988)	Thematic	Heavy metal, punk rock, satanic, skinhead
Spergel et al. (1989)	Demographic setting/activity	Race, ethnicity, age, gender, street, motorcycle, drug, prison
Huff (1989)	Purpose	Informal, instrumental, predatory
Taylor (1990)	Purpose	Scavengers, territorial, corporate

and private service agencies, police departments, probation offices, courts, juvenile bureaus, and similar sources. Particular attention was paid to the six United States cities reporting the most gang activity. Philadelphia and Los Angeles reported the highest proportion of gang members within their male adolescent populations (6 per 100). For the other survey cities, the proportions were as follows: New York, 4 per 100; Chicago, 2 per 100; Detroit and San Francisco, fewer than 1 per 100. The combined rate for all six cities was 37 per 1,000, or approximately 4 percent.

Miller's (1974) survey produced overall numerical estimates for the group of six cities ranging from a low of 760 gangs with 28,500 members to a high of 2,700 gangs with 81,500 members! New York City, according to its police department, at that time estimated 315 gangs with between 8,000 "verified" and 21,000 "alleged" members. These figures, the highest for the six cities, contrast with San Francisco's estimate of 250 gang members, the lowest. The New York figures also contrast dramatically with comparable police department information reported in 1990 (see chapter 10), showing but 37 active youth gangs with an estimated membership of 1,036. Although this marked reduction probably reflects an actual reduction in numbers, it is also surely due in large part to changing definitions of what constitutes a delinquent gang, as well as to political, funding, and related considerations. The survey's demographic findings were consistent with those from earlier decades: Gang members in the surveyed cities were predominantly male; were aged 12 to 21; resided in the poorer, usually central city areas; and came from families at the lower occupational and educational levels. Gang youths were Afro-American (1/2), Hispanic (1/6), Asian (1/10), and non-Hispanic White (1/10); they strongly tended to group themselves into ethnically homogeneous gangs. In some of the surveyed cities, the slums that produced gang youths had migrated from their traditional center city location to ring-city or suburban areas. Still poor ghettos but in new locations, these disproportionate sources of gang youths were often large-scale housing projects.

Needle and Stapleton (1982) surveyed police departments in 60 United States cities of various sizes. Half the cities with populations between a quarter and a half million, and more than a third of those with populations between 100,000 and a quarter million, reported gang problems. Delinquent youth gangs were no longer a big-city problem. Though the popular mythology holds that most gangs in smaller cities are branches intentionally exported to such locations by particular big-city gangs or megagangs (especially Los Angeles's

Crips and Bloods), the reality appears a bit more complex. Although a modest amount of such "franchising," "branching," or "hiving off" may occur, most gangs in midsize or smaller cities either originate locally or are started by nonresident gang members via kinship, alliance, expansion of turf boundaries, or movement of gang members' families into new areas (Moore, Vigil, & Garcia, 1983).

By 1989, according to yet another particularly extensive survey, conducted by Spergel et al., delinquent gangs were located in almost all 50 states, with the possible exception of a few north central mountain states and perhaps some northeastern states. Collectively, 35 surveyed cities reported 1,439 gangs. California, Illinois, and Florida have substantial gang concentrations. Spergel et al. report especially high numbers of youth gangs in Los Angeles County (600), the city of Los Angeles (280), and Chicago (128). Of the total of 120,636 gang members reported for all the surveyed cities combined, 70,000 were estimated to be in Los Angeles County (including 26,000 in Los Angeles) and 12,000 in Chicago.[1] But these three jurisdictions are clearly not alone in expressing concern. Spergel et al. report that just 14 percent of their survey's law enforcement respondents and 8 percent of other respondents saw improvement in the gang situation in their jurisdictions since 1980. At the same time, 56 percent of the police and 68 percent of the non–law enforcement respondents claimed their situations had worsened.

Males continue to outnumber female gang members at a ratio of approximately 20 to 1. Gang size varies with a number of determinants, including density of the youth population in a given geographical or psychological area (i.e., the pool to draw on), the nature of the gang's activities, police pressures, the season of the year, gang recruitment efforts, relevant agency activity, and additional factors (Spergel, 1965). Females are responsible for 5 percent or less of gang crime; they join gangs later than do males, and they leave earlier. As gang involvement in drug dealing has increased, the age range of gang membership appears to have expanded, now encompassing ages from 9 to 30. Gangs often use younger members as runners, lookouts, and so on, with the knowledge that

---

[1] This numerical litany of gang participation should, however, be tempered with the reminder that most youths, even those living where gangs are common, do not join gangs. Vigil (1983), for example, estimates that only 4 to 10 percent of Chicano youths are affiliated with gangs.

younger perpetrators, if caught, are likely to receive more lenient treatment from the judicial system. Older members tend to remain in the gang as a result of both the profitability of drug dealing and the paucity of employment opportunities for disadvantaged populations in the legitimate economy. Blacks, Hispanics, Asians, and Whites are gang members in the United States.[2] Spergel et al. (1989) report some specialization in the kinds of criminal behavior predominantly practiced by these ethnically different gangs: "Black gangs are more involved in drug trafficking, Hispanic groups in turf-related battling, Asians in a variety of property crimes, and Whites in both organized property crimes and vandalism" (p. 239). Such semispecialization, Spergel and colleagues assert, may result more from acculturation patterns, access to criminal opportunities, and community stability than from ethnicity per se. White gangs appear particularly diverse in their organizing foci, encompassing, for example, motorcycle gangs or bikers, stoners, heavy metal groups, satanic worshippers, neo-Nazi groups, and fighting gangs.

Huff (1989) conducted a comprehensive survey of Ohio police chiefs to learn about gang activity in that state. Cleveland (50 gangs) and Columbus (20 gangs) were the leading gang centers. These gangs appeared to have originated mostly from either existing break-dancing/rap groups or street corner groups that evolved into gangs via increasing conflictual competition with similar groups. Analogous information on the origins, demographics, and delinquent activity of gangs in California and New York appears in chapter 10 in the form of reports recently issued by task forces in those two states.

What do gangs do? Mostly they just "hang out," engaging, as this book will show, in the diverse interpersonal behaviors characteristic of almost all adolescents. They also commit delinquent acts and engage in various forms and levels of aggression, activities that will be examined in depth later in the book. In order to claim and topographically define their turf or territory, they may use graffiti, sometimes extensively and often in the form of a wall painting of

---

[2] There is a strong tendency for membership to continue, and often further solidify, when gang youths are incarcerated (Camp & Camp, 1985; Jacobs, 1974; Lane, 1989). Gott (1989), for example, reports that in 1989 approximately 5,000 of the 9,000 youths incarcerated in California Department of the Youth Authority facilities were gang members and that, as others have also observed, gang cohesiveness and activity appear to be substantially accelerated by and during incarceration.

the gang's name, a member's name, or the gang's symbol. Graffiti may also be used to challenge or show contempt for a rival gang, by crossing out the latter's graffiti or by drawing it backwards or upside down. In an effort to create both cohesiveness (within the gang) and difference (from other gangs), gang members often incorporate distinctive colors or color combinations within their dress, use special hand signs to communicate, and engage in "representing" —that is, wearing clothing to emphasize either the left or right side of the body. A report by the Illinois State Police (1989) describes these often highly elaborate efforts at creating distinctiveness:

> The Discipline Nation and their affiliates . . . refer to themselves as the Folks, their major insignia is the Six Pointed Star, and their dress is "right." Their basic color is black and if they wear an earring it will be in the right ear. They wear their hat tilted to the right and one of their favorite hats is the blue Civil War cap, they will wear one glove on the right hand, they may have one pocket on the right side turned inside out and it will be dyed in the gang's color or colors, they will roll up the right pants leg, they may have two of the fingernails on the right hand colored with the gang's colors, the hood of their sweatshirt will be dyed with the gang's colors, their shoes will either be colored or the laces of the right shoe will be in the gang's color, their belt buckle will be loose on the right side, and they may wear a bandanna in the gang's colors anywhere on the right side of their body. (pp. 9–10)

What else do gangs do? On occasion they fight, act aggressively, behave violently. Although the absolute amount of such behavior is small, its effect on the chain of media response, public perception of gang youth behavior, and police and public agency countermeasures is substantial. The next chapter will examine more fully the sources, scope, and impact of such gang behavior.

CHAPTER 2

Gangs as Aggressors

This chapter will offer a broad examination of violence as perpetrated by gang youths in the United States. It will trace the history of such behavior, describe its diverse manifestations, and share professionals' speculations regarding the causes and motivations underlying gang aggression. But first, it is important to situate the behaviors of concern within the proper context. The levels, forms, and distal (if not proximate) causes of aggression by gang youths appear largely to parallel and reflect the levels, forms, and causes of aggression in general in the United States. Skogan (1989) summarizes the picture accurately:

> Those [diverse national] data portray steadily increasing rates of violence in the United States since the mid-1950s. The rate of violent crime [murder, rape, robbery, aggravated assault] rose slowly between then and near the middle of the 1960s, but it rose without interruption every year. Between 1955 and 1975, levels of violent crime increased by a factor of more than four; the property crime rate followed almost exactly the same pattern. Then, there was a three-year respite in this trend, a brief period during which both violent and property crime rates leveled off at nearly their 1975 high; this was followed by a climb to a new high in 1982, and again in 1986. Between 1953 and 1986, the violent crime rate rose almost exactly 600 percent and the property crime rate 400 percent. (p. 236)

These trends continue. The most recent compilations, comparing crime statistics for 1988 and 1989, reveal an overall increase of 5 percent for violent crimes in the United States (Federal Bureau of Investigation, 1989). The murder rate was 8.4 per 100,000 in 1988, compared to 5.6 per 100,000 in 1966. Not only has the frequency of violent crime in the United States risen in recent decades, so too has the degree of violence in the crimes that are perpetrated (Goldstein & Segall, 1983). Thus, for example, in 1967, one robbery

27

victim in five was physically injured during the robbery; by 1977, the comparable statistic was one in three.

The American home is no stranger to physical aggression. A nationwide survey conducted in 1968 for the National Commission on the Causes and Prevention of Violence (Mulvihill, Tumin, & Curtis, 1969) revealed that 93 percent of survey respondents reported having been spanked in childhood; 55 percent had been slapped or kicked, 31 percent punched or beaten, 14 percent threatened or cut with a knife, and 12 percent threatened with a gun or actually shot at. Domestic violence is visited not only upon children; spouses—particularly wives—are also frequent targets of physical abuse. Strauss (1977–1978) estimates that approximately 25 percent of wives have been targets of physical aggression by their husbands, an estimate generally accepted as accurate (Rosenbaum, 1979). An equally grim picture emerges for elderly citizens. In 1990, the United States House of Representatives Subcommittee on Health and Long-Term Care reported that 1.5 million elderly Americans, or 5 percent of all elderly United States citizens, are physically abused each year, most by their own children. In 1980, the comparable estimate was 1 million ("Elderly Abuse," 1990).

The recent history of child abuse in the United States has followed a parallel path. As recently as the mid-1960s, the terms *child abuse* and *battered child syndrome* were not part of either public or professional awareness. Largely through the efforts of such persons as Gil (1970); Helfer and Kempe (1976); and Kempe, Silverman, Steele, Droegemueller, and Silver (1962), significant consciousness raising has occurred. The nation is now keenly aware of child abuse. The number of child abuse incidents is quite substantial, reported in 1984 to be 1.7 million, an increase of 17 percent from 1983 and 158 percent from 1976, the first year such data were systematically collected (American Humane Association, 1986). Subsequent years continue to show a steady rise in the number of children reportedly abused—1.9 million in 1985, 2.0 million in 1986, 2.1 million in 1987, 2.2 million in 1988, and 2.4 million in 1989 (Federation on Child Abuse and Neglect, 1990).

A similar pattern of increasing violence is seen in American schools. A United States Congressional report (Bayh, 1975) indicated that between 1970 and 1973, in junior and senior high schools in the United States, homicides increased by 18.5 percent, rapes by 40.1 percent, assaults on students by 85.3 percent, assaults on teachers by 77.4 percent, and weapons confiscated by school authorities by 54.4 percent. In 1975, secondary school youngsters, especially in urban areas, committed 63,000 attacks on teachers, perpetrated 270,000 school burglaries, and destroyed by vandalism 200 million dollars worth of school property. In 1978, the New York City schools saw 1,856 assaults, 1,097 robberies, 310 suspicious fires, and 317 incidents involving weapons. In 1979, schools in the United States reported 20 million thefts, 400,000 acts of vandalism, and 110,000 assaults on teachers (Goldstein, Apter, & Harootunian, 1984). The situation has not improved. In the 1988–1989 school year, compared to the preceding year, school crime increased 5 percent and in-school weapons possession rose 21 percent in California's public schools ("School Violence," 1990). In a similar comparison, the New York City public school system has reported a 35 percent increase in assaults on students and school staff, a 16 percent increase in harassment, a 24 percent increase in larceny, and an overall crime rate increase of 25 percent. Noteworthy is the fact that the greatest increase in crime rate occurred at the elementary school level ("School Crime Rates," 1990).

In addition to street, home, and school, the United States' fourth major setting for the expression of unremittingly frequent and varied aggression is its mass media—newspapers, books, comics, radio, movies, and especially television. The impact of contemporary mass media on behavior is immense. One manifestation of this impact has been an increase in violence. This assertion is still disputed in some quarters, but a reading of the combined evidence about the influence of television viewing (in particular, on overt aggression) leaves little room for doubt or equivocation (Comstock, 1983). The very heavy diet of violence offered by television appears to contribute substantially to both the acquisition of aggressive behavior and the instigation of its actual enactment.

Prime time television in the United States during 1989 showed an average of 9.5 acts of violence per hour. The comparable figure for 1982 was 7 such acts per hour. Saturday morning cartoons now portray 25 violent acts per hour. By age 16, the average adolescent —who views approximately 35 hours of television programming per week—will have seen 200,000 acts of violence, 33,000 of which are murders or attempted murders (National Coalition on Television Violence, 1990). No wonder a substantial minority of viewers will engage in actual, copycat violence.

The pernicious effects of television violence go further, extending to the substantial decrease in sensitivity, concern, and revulsion toward violence among the general viewing audience. Higher and higher levels of violence become more and more tolerable. These and other aggression-enhancing and aggression-tolerating effects of television have been documented in many sources (Baker & Ball, 1969; R. Brown, 1976; Comstock, 1983; Feshbach & Singer, 1971; Howitt & Cumberbatch, 1975; Lefkowitz, Eron, Walder, & Huessman, 1977; Liebert, Neale, & Davidson, 1973).

The levels and forms of aggression evident in the street, home, school, and mass media provide a relevant context for the central topic of this chapter, aggression by gang youths. Acts of violence perpetrated by such youths are best viewed not as a phenomenon apart, but merely as another manifestation of behavior trends that characterize so much of contemporary life in the United States.

TRENDS IN GANG VIOLENCE

The delinquent gang of yesteryear (Thrasher, 1927/1963) committed acts of theft, burglary, and perhaps vandalism. Although there occurred very occasional within- or between-gang fighting, such behaviors were markedly uncommon (Puffer, 1912; Thrasher, 1927/1963).

The 1950s were the years of the gang rumble and its variants. Gardner (1983) observes:

> The gangs of the 1950s engaged in big fights called rumbles, which had definite arrangements and rules to be followed. Times, places, and uses of weapons were agreed upon in advance by the war council or leadership of the two warring gangs. Usually, the location chosen would be a deserted area of the city, where the police were not likely to discover them. In those days, gangs fought each other with bats, bricks, clubs, and chains. Occasionally, someone flashed a switchblade or used a homemade zip gun. (p. 23)

These rumbles had diverse purposes: "to inflict humiliation and insult on the opposing group . . . to increase the victor's reputation and status . . . to regain territory [and] sometimes to gain new territories . . . to re-establish discipline . . . [in response to] boredom and apathy" (New York City Youth Board, 1960, p. 83).

Such fighting between gang members or entire gangs did occur, though the frequency and the resultant damage were often exaggerated by the mass media and sometimes by the participants themselves. Gang members often anticipated such experiences with considerable ambivalence but, under considerable peer pressure as well as an overriding need to maintain "rep"—reputation—proceeded to fight nevertheless. Sometimes, under rep-maintaining circumstances, the rumble was avoided. Spergel (1964) notes:

> Youngsters may literally pray silently that something will occur to prevent them from reaching their destination. Consequently, almost any excuse to avoid contact with the opposing group may be utilized. The appearance of the worker, the arrival of the police, or a sudden flat tire on a car which was to take the group into enemy territory may be sufficient to prevent the spontaneous or planned attack. (p. 115)

Klein and Maxson (1989) similarly note that "in the 1950s and 1960s, gang members talked much about their fighting episodes, but [homicide] data from several projects revealed their bark to be worse than their bite" (p. 218).

Intergang member fighting took a variety of forms. The New York City Youth Board (1960) classified such fighting as follows:

- Fighting without weapons between two members of opposing groups
- Fighting with weapons between two members of opposing groups
- Fighting between a small group from one gang and a single member from another gang
- Fighting between two small groups
- Fighting between two large groups

Miller, in his 1975 national survey report "Violence by Youth Gangs and Youth Groups as a Crime Problem in Major American Cities," offers the following subtyping of assaultive gang member behaviors:

- Planned rumble, a prearranged encounter between sizable rival groups
- Rumble, an encounter between sizable rival groups
- Warfare, a continuing series of retaliatory engagements between members of rival groups
- Foray, in which smaller bands of youths engage rival bands

- Hit, in which smaller bands of youths engage one or
  two rivals

- Fair fight, in which a single gang member engages
  a single rival

Sometimes fighting between two gangs extended over long periods and several separate altercations. Horowitz (1983) comments:

> In seeking to protect and promote their reputations,
> gangs often engage in prolonged "wars," which are kept
> alive between larger fights by many small incidents and
> threats of violence. Following each incident one gang
> claims precedence, which means that the other group
> must challenge them if they want to retain their honor
> and reassert their reputation. (p. 94)

Into and through the 1970s and 1980s, the levels and forms of gang violence in the United States gradually changed for the worse, reflecting, as noted earlier, developments elsewhere on the national scene. Whereas some gang intervention programs of the 1950s and 1960s (the Roxbury Project, Miller, 1980; the Group Guidance Project, Klein, 1968b; and the Ladino Hills Project, Klein, 1968b) collectively revealed almost no homicides and only modest amounts of other types of gang violence, there were 81 gang-related homicides in Chicago in 1981, 351 such deaths in Los Angeles in 1980, and over 1,500 in Los Angeles during the 1985–1989 period (Gott, 1989). Spergel et al. (1989) report that only about 1 percent of all the violent crime committed in Chicago was perpetrated by gang members. The seriousness of such crime figures, however, resides not only in their relative increase from past years, but also, and especially, in the nature of the crimes—primarily homicide and aggravated assault. Such violent offenses, Spergel and colleagues observe, are three times more likely to be committed by gang members than by nongang delinquents, a finding also reported by Friedman, Mann, and Friedman (1975) and Tracy (1979).

In the next section we will examine both fact and speculation regarding the reasons for this contemporary increase in gang violence. In addition to the substantial levels of violent behavior directed by gang members toward persons or groups (i.e., gangs) outside of their own gang, considerable amounts of aggression occur on an intragang basis. Miller, Geertz, and Cutter (1968) examined this phenomenon and set its occurrence at 70 percent of all gang member aggression. Of the 1,395 aggressive acts recorded during their observational period, 7 percent were physical attacks, and 65 percent were derogations, devaluations, or other directly hostile statements.[1]

BASES FOR INCREASED VIOLENCE

Elsewhere we have argued for a complex conceptualization of aggression as a multicausal, multiply determined, primarily learned set of behaviors (Goldstein, 1988a). This view of aggression, we believe, more accurately captures its diverse origins. In the present section, which seeks to identify bases for the increased levels of contemporary gang violence, we will seek to take a similarly complex, multicausal position. Thus, the factors enumerated and discussed in this section are to be seen as an additive combination of likely causes, not as alternative explanations. It will also be apparent that the causes proposed are, as a group, consistent with contemporary psychology's increasingly popular interactionist philosophy, which holds that human behavior springs both from characteristics of the individual actor and qualities of the environment.

Environmental Enhancers of Violence

The major environmental enhancers of contemporary gang violence, in addition to the heightened general levels of aggression in society described earlier, appear to be drugs, territory, and guns.

---

[1] Combined evidence suggests that delinquent gangs in the United States are indeed behaving more violently in recent years (Miller, 1990; Short, 1990). However, it is important to note that this apparent increase may derive, at least in part, from artifactual sources. Media interest in youth gangs ebbs and flows, and it tends to be accentuated in direct proportion to increases in youth violence. The current perceived increase in violent behavior may be partially just such a media-interest effect. This possibility is enhanced by a second potential artifact, the shortage of reliable sources of information about gangs. As Klein and Maxson (1989) note, "The 1960s gang programs, which permitted detailed description of gang structure and activity patterns, are now largely absent. . . . [T]he current picture is based on evidence that is largely hearsay rather than empirical" (p. 209). Finally, given the fact that most current available gang-related information comes from police sources, it is possible that information regarding increased gang violence is in part also an artifact of more, and more intensive, activity on the part of police gang intelligence units.

Drugs

Increasingly, gang fighting is more about selling and economic territory and less about turf ownership and physical territory, though the latter considerations still fuel their share of violent incidents. Competition for drug markets, at least in some regions of the United States, appears in fact to be an especially important source of gang aggression. This seems to be more the case in West Coast cities, where horizontal gangs may control the drug business (Spergel et al., 1989), than in East Coast cities, where the drug trade is more likely to be controlled by organized adult crime and gang youths have more ancillary roles, such as runner, lookout, and the like (New York State Division for Youth, 1990).

Territory

The traditional major source of gang violence—territoriality—continues to be a relevant concern. Though the scene has been altered by enhanced mobility away from one's turf via automobile use, dispersal of many school-age youths to distant schools through desegregation efforts, and enhanced focus on economic rather than physical territory, many gangs continue to mark, define, claim, protect, and fight over their turf. Vigil (1988) quotes one gang youth who powerfully makes this point:

> The only thing we can do is build our own little nation.
> We know that we have complete control in our
> community. It's like we're making our stand. . . . We're
> all brothers and nobody fucks with us. . . . We take pride
> in our little nation and if any intruders enter, we get
> panicked because we feel our community is being
> threatened. The only way is with violence. (p. 131)

With whom do they fight? Spergel (1965), cited in Ley (1976), observes:

> Propinquity emerges as a critical factor in motivations
> for gang conflict. Of 188 gang incidents between 32 gangs
> in Philadelphia . . . (homicides, stabbings, shootings and
> gang fights), 60 percent occurred between gangs who
> shared a common boundary and another 23 percent
> between gangs whose territories were two blocks or
> less apart. Only two incidents occurred between groups
> whose turfs were separated by more than 10 blocks.
> (pp. 262–263)

Miller (1982) suggests that such territorial defense seeks to protect both identification and control and can be manifested in three types of rights claimed by the defending (or attacking) gang members:

1. Ownership rights, in which gang members claim, and are willing to fight for, ownership of the entire property and all activity within it, including control of who may enter and leave

2. Occupancy rights, in which gangs engage in shared use of a given territory under conditions specifying, for example, time, duration, and purpose

3. Enterprise monopoly rights, in which gangs claim exclusive rights to conduct certain criminal activities (theft, drug selling, etc.) within a specified territory

Guns

There are 200 million privately owned guns in the United States (Goldstein, 1983). Since 1900, over 750,000 civilians in this country have been killed with privately owned guns. Each year, there are 200,000 gun-related injuries and approximately 20,000 gun-related deaths: 3,000 by accident, 7,000 by homicide, and 9,000 by suicide. Guns are involved in two out of every three murders in the United States, one third of all robberies, and one fifth of all aggravated assaults. Such a remarkable level of possession and use of weaponry has major implications for both the level and lethality of gang violence. The gang rumbles of decades ago, whatever their group or individual expressions, typically involved fists, sticks, bricks, bats, pipes, knives, and an occasional home-made zip gun. The geometric proliferation of often sophisticated automatic and semiautomatic guns and their ready availability have changed matters considerably (Fisher, 1976; Zimring, 1977). Klein and Maxson (1989) put it well:

Does the ready access to guns explain much of the increase in violence? The notion here is that more weapons yield more shootings; these, in turn, lead to more "hits"; and these, in turn, lead to more retaliations in a series of reciprocal actions defending honor and territory. . . . The theory is that firearms have been the teeth that transform bark into bite. (p. 219)

In his commentary, aptly titled "When the Trigger Pulls the Finger," Berkowitz (n.d.) summarizes a series of investigations (Berkowitz & LePage, 1967; Leyens & Parke, 1975; Turner, Simons, Berkowitz, & Frodi, 1977) pointing to a second means beyond sheer number by which guns may provoke, not merely express, overt aggression. These studies appear to demonstrate that

> weapons stimulate people to act aggressively because of their aggressive meaning. In other words, many of us associate guns with the idea of killing and hurting. Because of these associations, the mere sight of a weapon can elicit thoughts, feelings and perhaps even muscular reactions in us that we have previously learned to connect with aggressive behavior. If we do not have any strong inhibitions against aggression at that moment, these elicited thoughts, feelings and motor reactions can heighten the chances that we will show open aggression toward others who happen to be available. (Berkowitz, n.d., pp. 2–3)

Qualities of Gang Members

Contemporary gang members in this country appear to have certain characteristics that, when catalyzed by the environmental enhancers just described, contribute importantly to the currently observed increases in gang violence.

Numbers and Age

Two salient gang characteristics are straightforwardly demographic—more gangs and older gang members. Both Klein and Maxson (1989) and Spergel et al. (1989) have speculated that these qualities may themselves help account for the apparently heightened levels of gang violence. There may also be a relevant interaction between weaponry and gang member age:

> The older age of gang members may also be responsible for greater use of sophisticated weaponry and consequent violence. More and better weaponry may be [more] available to older teenagers and young adults than to juveniles. The median age of the gang homicide offender has been 19 years . . . in Chicago for the past ten years (Spergel, 1985). Los Angeles data (Maxson, Gordon, & Klein, 1983) and San Diego police statistics (San Diego

Association of State Governments, 1982) also indicate that older adolescents and young adults are mainly involved in gang homicide. Younger gang members are engaged in a pattern of gang assault which leads to less lethal consequences. (Spergel et al., 1989)

Notions of Honor

Honor and several related qualities—machismo, self-esteem, status, power, heart, "rep"—gang youth characteristics long purported to contribute importantly to overt aggression, may do so even more today.[2] Miller (1982) wonders if honor has become a less important factor in the etiology of gang member aggression. In his opinion, as such aggression has changed in form and frequency from intergang rumbles in defense of local turf to individual or small group acts of mugging, robbery, or other "gain" or "control" behaviors, the protection and enhancement of "rep" perhaps has become less focal. We would posit the opposite. Gardner (1983) has noted in this context, "With few resources available to poor urban young people, a reputation for being tough and a good fighter is one of the only ways to attain status" (p. 27). It is a sad commentary on priorities in the United States, but such resources appear to have become even scarcer in the years since Gardner's observation, the potential status-enhancing avenues available to low-income youths even fewer, and thus their need to enhance status by means designated by the larger society as illegal or inappropriate— including overt aggression—even greater.

Sociopathy

One further gang member characteristic that may be relevant to an understanding of increased gang violence is sociopathy. Although sociopathy is no longer used as an official DSM-III-R diagnostic category (American Psychiatric Association, 1987), it remains both a term extant in the criminology literature and a label communicating considerable information about traits and behaviors. The sociopath has been variously described as an individual who possesses the following qualities:

---

[2] Vigil (1988) suggests that fighting with rival gangs is most common among gang members still in their early adolescence—that is, still in the reputation-building stage. Older adolescents, he proposes, are more likely to be initiators of gain-associated criminal activities.

- Is aggressive, reckless, cruel to others, impulsive, superficial, callous, irresponsible, cunning, and self-assured (Magdid & McKelvey, 1987)

- Fails to learn by experience; is unable to form meaningful relationships; is chronically antisocial, unresponsive to punishment, and unable to experience guilt; is self-centered; and lacks a moral sense (Gray & Hutchison, 1964)

- Is unreliable, untruthful, and shameless; shows poor judgment; and is highly egocentric (Cleckley, 1964)

- Is unable to show empathy or genuine concern for others, manipulates others to satisfy personal needs, and shows a glib sophistication and superficial sincerity (Hare, 1970)

- Is loveless and guiltless (McCord & McCord, 1964) and shows particular deficiency either in perspective taking or in taking on the role of another person (Gough, 1948)

Yablonsky (1967) asserts that "the violent gang structure recruits its participants from the more sociopathic youths living in the disorganized slum community" (p. 189). He adds that

the selection of violence by the sociopathic youth in his adjustment process is not difficult to understand. Violent behavior requires limited training, personal ability, or even physical strength. Because violence is a demon-stration of easily achieved power, it becomes the paramount value of the gang. (p. 199)

Reuterman (1975) has similarly observed that "adolescent residents of slum areas who exhibit these traits tend to constitute the membership of violent gangs" (p. 41). If Fahlberg (1979), Magdid and McKelvey (1987), and Rutter (1980) are correct in their contention that early childhood failures of bonding and attachment are important roots of such sociopathy, and that societal conditions of the 1980s and 1990s are conducive to such failure, the current climate may foster increased development of sociopathic individuals. Particularly relevant here are the several manifestations of dysfunctional family life currently apparent. Problems in infant attachment are especially pertinent:

Because of necessity or desire, more and more mothers are returning to work, many just weeks after the birth of their babies. Parents need to know that this may be putting their children at risk for unattachment. Other factors can contribute to faulty infant attachment: high divorce rates, day care problems, lack of a national parent leave policy, epidemic teenage pregnancies, too-late adoptions, the foster care system. (Magdid & McKelvey, 1987, p. 4)

It is important to avoid circularity here. The tendency of sociopathic individuals to behave aggressively, coupled with increased aggression by gang youths, does not constitute evidence that sociopathy has itself increased. However, given the apparently increased presence of the conditions thought to produce sociopathic youths, this is not an improbable speculation. Yablonsky (1967) has often been criticized in the academic literature on gangs for purportedly holding that most gang youths and most gang violence have sociopathic roots. We are less declarative and more speculative here. It may be that Yablonsky's observations fit the contemporary gang in the United States even better than the gang youths he observed earlier (and, some hold, misdescribed).

Immediate Provocations

Environmental features (drugs, territory, weapons) and gang member characteristics (number, age, notions of honor, sociopathy) may function collectively as the distal causes of heightened gang violence in the United States. What of its proximal or immediate causes? What are the common provocations or triggers that spark the fuse? No doubt triggers change with culture, time, and place, but the following list from the New York City Youth Board (1960) appears remarkably current. The board identifies separately "exterior" and "interior" provocations, recalling the dichotomy of individual and contextual causes discussed in this chapter.

Exterior provocations
Bad looks
Rumors
Territorial boundary disputes
Disputes over girls
Out of neighborhood parties
Drinking
Narcotics
Ethnic tensions

Interior provocations
Leader power needs
Compensation for inadequate self-esteem
Acting out to convince self of potency
Acting out to obtain group affection
Acting out to retaliate against fantasized aggression (p. 63)

These are, of course, but a sampling of possible provocations to aggression. Moore, Garcia, Garcia, Cerda, and Valencia (1978) have demonstrated that gang youths are frequently hypervigilant in their attention to possible slights, and Dodge and Murphy (1984) have shown that such attention often leads to misperceptions of hostile intent and related misinterpretations of neutral events. As the New York City Youth Board (1960) observes:

The possibilities [for provocation] are almost limitless since the act itself in many cases is relatively unimportant, but rather is seen in a total context of the past, the present, and the future. Further, the act is seen in a total context of its stated, implied, and imagined meanings, all of which are subject to distortion by the groups, individuals, and the gangs. (p. 69)

GANGS AS ENEMY

As gangs in the United States have become more violent; as drug involvement and availability of weapons have increasingly characterized gang life; as social work with its rehabilitation philosophy has faded from the gang scene and the police with their orientation to deterrence and control have become the primary concerned profession; and, especially, as the United States has moved rightward and become more conservative in its attitudes toward delinquency and delinquents, the youth gang increasingly has come to be viewed as enemy: "The basic strategy for coping with gangs remains the iron fist, a strategy that moves the problem from visibility in the community to the invisibility of the prison" (Hagedorn & Macon, 1988, p. 150). Three law enforcement officers, in personal communication, have stated this view even more explicitly: "Don't half-step them. Hit the ground hard, put them down, all the way"; "These people are more than gangs, they're terrorists"; "As a cop, my problem is what they do, not why they do it. I'm not a sociologist." McKinney (1988) also issues this call for deterrence: "Jurisdictions must develop visible and vigorous arrest and prosecution programs against gang violence. Law enforcement must make gang membership very uncomfortable . . . so we can create a deterrent effect in gang activity" (p. 3). And Needle and Stapleton (1982) observe:

> It has become increasingly clear that the level of gang activities involving violent crime and drug-related offenses is enormous, the similarity between gangs and organized crime is undeniable, and much gang activity can and should itself be characterized as organized crime. (p. 71)

This section will examine the police gang management strategies and tactics that follow from this prevailing "get tough," deterrence-oriented, gangbusting attitude.[3] The general strategy underpinning police gang intervention tactics is captured well in the following statements:

> Successful investigation, followed by an aggressive and successful prosecution, will greatly reduce the level of gang activity in a community. Knowing that they will be aggressively pursued through the court system will destroy the idea among the street gang members and the community that they have a special sanctuary in which, because of their youth, they can hide. (Illinois State Police, 1989, p. 29)

> The police stress two points. First, they feel that juvenile gangs coalesce around delinquent activities and that they form, at least partly, specifically to commit illegal acts. Second, police see the structure of the gang as revolving around a few central leaders, usually older boys, who "call the shots" on what will and will not be done. This latter premise in turn leads to one of the primary police tactics in dealing with gangs—to "get the leaders." (Klein & Maxson, 1989, p. 18)

---

[3] We do not wish to overdraw the singularity of this stance. As we will describe in chapter 10, there exist a substantial number of police-originated and police-implemented gang programs aimed at prevention and rehabilitation, rather than gangbusting, strategies. Nonetheless, the latter do prevail in most police jurisdictions.

Spergel et al. (1989) have suggested that two broad police strategies vis-à-vis delinquent gangs have emerged, the first being clearly more common, the second being probably more effective. The so-called Model A strategy is singularly suppressive and urges such tactics as surveillance, stakeout, aggressive patrol, intelligence gathering, infiltration, and follow-up investigation. The Model B strategy incorporates the foregoing but also gives serious attention to preventive and rehabilitative police programming. This strategy is exemplified in the recent Illinois State Police report (1989) calling for police departments to establish both gang control units (for "high visibility patrols, surveillance, and aggressive pursuit and apprehension") and prevention units (to "concentrate on available social services, educational programs, employment or employment training, counseling services, [and] recreational facilities") (p. 31).

Several police and criminological sources have provided detailed statements of gangbusting tactical recommendations. Much of this procedural material is reflected in a national survey of 60 police departments, titled *Police Handling of Youth Gangs*, by Needle and Stapleton (1982). Of the police departments surveyed, 27 reported one of the following organizational arrangements as their response to gang problems in their city:

1. Youth service programming, in which one or more police officers, usually from the department's juvenile section, are assigned gang-related duties as an added responsibility

2. The gang detail, in which one or more police officers, again typically from the existing youth unit, are assigned exclusively to gang control work

3. The gang unit (more typical of police departments in larger cities with substantial gang problems), similar to the gang detail but typically involving more personnel, more specialized personnel, and a fuller range of police functions

What do these units do? Any and all of the following:

1. *Intelligence gathering and processing.* This activity involves the collection, maintenance, and analysis of information regarding gangs and their members. Such information may include names, addresses, automobiles owned or driven, weapons owned or used, and items that constitute the individuals' criminal histories.

2. *Prevention.* Police involvement is quite diverse and ranges from primary prevention efforts targeting youths at risk for gang involvement to tertiary prevention efforts aimed at forestalling further crime by youths already deeply involved in gang activity. An example of the former cited by Needle and Stapleton (1982) is school information programs; an example of the latter is police mediation between rival gangs.

3. *Enforcement.* These activities are often the core of police gang work. Enforcement activities include diverse proactive and reactive attempts to suppress criminal activity by gang members and apprehend youths who are believed to have committed crimes. Patrol, surveillance, apprehension, and arrest are examples of enforcement procedures.

4. *Follow-up investigation.* These are an array of also fairly standard police procedures, in this instance used in conjunction with and in response to the enforcement activities just described. Included are such dispositions of apprehended youths as counsel and release, and referral to juvenile court.

The chapters constituting Part II of this book will examine the diverse ways in which several fields of contemporary psychology may provide insights of value in better comprehending, reorienting, and assisting the typical youth gang member. For both gang members and victims, past and future, it is hoped that the present examination of the scope and sources of gang violence will encourage the meaningful use of these psychological contributions.

PART II

Psychological Foundations

CHAPTER 3

Gangs as Delinquents

Chapter 1 surveyed the history of delinquent gangs in the United States and noted that the theories of delinquency and delinquent gang formation receiving most attention throughout this history were primarily sociological. These theories' core concepts, target variables, and very language were almost exclusively the concepts, variables, and language of sociology. The individual and collective contribution of these perspectives both to an understanding of delinquent gang youths and to the alteration of their behavior has been substantial. But any one discipline can provide only a partial understanding of such complex human behavior. This chapter will present the theoretical contributions to the study of gangs and delinquency that have been made by psychology, alone or in combination with sister disciplines.

CONSTITUTIONAL THEORIES

The tenor and substance of each psychological theory of delinquency causation to be examined reflect the temper of each theory's scientific, moral, and political times. The mid-1800s was an era of biological determinism, greatly influenced by Darwin's theory of evolution, which by 1870 had begun to leave its imprint not only on the biological sciences but on the social sciences as well. In 1911, Cesare Lombroso, an Italian physician, proposed that criminals were morally (by dint of their criminal behavior) and physically (by dint of the qualities to be enumerated) a more primitive form of human being. The specific anthropometric indices of criminality suggested by Lombroso included cranial asymmetries, large ears, sloping shoulders, short legs, flat feet, and numerous other facial and bodily physical characteristics. *Homo delinquens,* in psychological makeup, was held to be insensitive to pain, lazy, shameless, and tending toward cruel and impulsive behavior more adapted to earlier prehistoric eras. Such physical and psychological qualities, Lombroso held, could aid not only in differentiating criminals from noncriminals but also in differentiating among types of criminals (e.g., sexual offenders purportedly had full lips; murderers, very sloping foreheads). Lombroso was also cognizant of the important contribution of social forces to the occurrence of crime, but his clear emphasis was on the physical atavism just exemplified. Lombrosian thinking eventually posited less a criminal-noncriminal dichotomy and more a criminaloid continuum, with

> people who were less atavistic than Mr. Hyde but more so than Dr. Jekyll. Criminaloids, unlike born criminals, were not doomed to commit crime; they had a criminal tendency that might or might not be triggered by their experiences. The biological disposition to commit crime could, in other words, range from irresistible to non-existent, according to Lombroso. (Wilson & Hernnstein, 1985, pp. 73–74)

Though some evidence later emerged in support of the existence of criminal-noncriminal physiognomic differentiations (Kozeny, 1962; Thornton, 1939), and considerable historical and contemporary evidence has appeared for the criminaloid continuum notion of a biological predisposition toward criminality (Christiansen, 1977; Dalgaard & Kringlen, 1976; Rosenthal, 1970; Trasler, 1987), the social Darwinist core of Lombrosian thinking has received little philosophical or empirical support and considerable methodological criticism (Ellis, 1914; Goring, 1913; Wilson & Hernnstein, 1985). Much the same negative result (Hoskins, 1941; Montagu, 1941) has emerged for early etiological notions of crime and delinquency resulting from endocrine gland disorders (Schlapp & Smith, 1928).

But if the notion that specific facial or bodily features or glandular dysfunction could distinguish criminals from noncriminals fell into early disrepute, this was not the case for somatotyping, the idea that general physique (rather than localized measurements) was a significant cause and/or correlate of criminality. In a series of investigations conducted in the 1940s, William Sheldon put forth and evaluated the proposition that body build correlates with temperament as well as with overt behavioral tendencies. His somatotyping procedure yielded three categories of bodily physique: endomorphic, a build tending toward roundness; mesomorphic, a build tending toward muscularity; and ectomorphic, a build tending toward linearity. Sheldon's (1949) study of nude photographs of 200 incarcerated delinquent youths showed them to be strikingly mesomorphic—muscular, broad chested, large boned, low waisted. Several investigators, working in diverse settings and comparing matched delinquent and nondelinquent samples, have confirmed this finding, whether through photographs or direct bodily measurements (Cortes & Gatti, 1972; Epps & Parnell, 1952; Gibbens, 1963; Glueck & Glueck, 1950). Why should there be a relationship between physique and delinquency? Sheldon (1942) observed that mesomorphy was characteristic not only of delinquents but also of salesmen, politicians, and certain other occupational groups. A number of studies have shown mesomorphy to be associated with what Sheldon called a *Dionysian temperament*— extroverted, expressive, domineering, highly active, and, in its more extreme form, impulsive and uninhibited in its seeking of self-gratification. As comparative personality trait studies discussed later in this chapter support, temperamental disposition appears to provide the "correlational glue" joining mesomorphic physique and delinquent behavior.

PSYCHOANALYTIC THEORIES

Freud (1961) spoke of criminal behavior as growing from a compulsive need for punishment, stemming from unconscious, incestuous oedipal wishes. Crimes were committed, in his view, in an effort by the perpetrator to be caught, punished, and thus cleansed of guilt. Alexander and Healy (1935) have stressed the criminal's inability to postpone gratification. Bowlby (1949) points to the role of maternal separation and parental rejection. Johnson and Szurek (1952) have sought to explain criminal behavior as a substitute means of obtaining love, nurturance, and attention, or as a result of permissive parents' seeking vicarious gratification of their own id impulses via their offsprings' illegal transgressions. A number of other psychoanalytic theorists have sought to distinguish delinquent subtypes as a function of their hypothesized etiology—for example, latent versus behavioral delinquency (Aichhorn, 1949), neurotic versus characterological delinquency (Glover, 1960), neurotic versus milieu delinquency (Levy, 1932), sociologic delinquency (A.M. Johnson, 1949), and Redl's (1945) fourfold categorization of (a) essentially healthy youths who commit delinquent acts in response to environmental stresses; (b) youths who commit delinquent acts in response to acute adolescent growth crises; (c) neurotic delinquents; and (d) "genius" delinquents, who suffer from disturbances of impulse control/superego functioning. The latter category also emerges in Binder's (1987) description of the delinquent who operates, like the infant, under the pleasure principle and can neither endure frustration nor postpone gratification. A poorly formed and ineffective superego, stemming from inadequate handling in infancy, cannot overcome the pleasure-seeking forces of the moment, and the result is truancy, sexual offenses, theft, and other delinquent acts. (p. 20)

A.M. Johnson's (1949, 1959) subsequent explorations of a "superego lacuna" in delinquent adolescents provide a similar etiological focus. A.K. Cohen (1955), Nietzel (1979), and others are correct in critically pointing to the tautology inherent in this psychoanalytic position: "Aggressive or acquisitive acts are often explained by underlying aggressive or acquisitive impulses. The evidence for these impulses . . . turns out to be the aggressive or acquisitive act to be explained" (Nietzel, 1979, p. 78). Nevertheless, the explicit and implicit emphasis in each of these psychoanalytic positions on the major role of early childhood and familial contributors to subsequent delinquency has proven quite accurate (e.g., Patterson, 1982).

PERSONALITY THEORY

As did the diverse psychoanalytic perspectives on criminal and delinquent behavior, those promoting one or another explanation of crime and delinquency based on the personality of the perpetrator essentially place the etiological source of such behavior exclusively within the delinquent youth. In comparison to nondelinquents, the delinquent youth is purportedly more assertive, resentful, suspicious, narcissistic, ambivalent toward authority, impulsive, and extroverted (Glueck & Glueck, 1950); less submissive, anxious, cooperative, dependent, conventional, or compulsive (Glueck & Glueck, 1950); more egocentric, interpersonally disruptive, and unfriendly (Conger & Miller, 1966); less shy, worried, or timid (Taylor & Watt, 1977); more deficient in attachment to social norms, alienated, and unproductively hyperactive (Megargee & Bohn, 1979); more sensation seeking and externally controlled (Quay, 1965); and poorer in sociomoral reasoning, interpersonal problem solving, role taking, and empathy (Arbuthnot & Gordon, 1987).

Early interpretations of such purported personality differentiation data were strongly negative:

Several reviews have found little or no support for an association between personality and criminal behavior. Metfessel and Lovell (1942) concluded that sex and age were the only constants and that no clear-cut picture of a criminal personality could be drawn. Similarly, Schuessler & Cressey (1950) reviewed twenty-five years of research on thirty different personality tests. They concluded "the evidence favors the view that personality traits are distributed in the criminal population in about the same proportion as in the general population." (Feldman, 1977, p. 140)

Part of this critique sought to explain the several personality differentiators previously noted as differences not between criminals and noncriminals per se but, instead, as artifactual differences associated with socioeconomic status, intelligence, cultural background, and—because most such research was conducted on incarcerated prisoners—institutionalization itself (Hindelang, 1972; Wilson & Hernnstein, 1985). When appropriate matching procedures were used to control for such influences, over 80 percent of the studies showed significant personality differences between groups of criminals and noncriminals (Tennenbaum, 1977; Waldo & Dinitz, 1967). In part on the basis of these data, a number of delinquency causation theories emphasizing one or another personality dimension or cluster of dimensions have emerged. These theories concern extroversion, neuroticism, and psychoticism (Eysenck, 1977); psychopathy (Cleckley, 1964; McCord & McCord, 1964; Quay, 1977); moral reasoning (Arbuthnot & Gordon, 1987; Jennings, Kilkenny, & Kohlberg, 1983; Laufer & Day, 1983); conceptual level (Hunt, 1972); irresponsible thinking (Yochelson & Samenow, 1976); and rational choicefulness (Cook, 1980). Although it clearly provides less than the total etiological picture, such personality causation thinking—as a later examination of integrative, multicomponent theories will show—is an important contribution to a comprehensive understanding of the roots of juvenile delinquency.

BIOGENETIC AND NEUROHORMONAL THEORIES

The suggestion of a substantial genetic contribution to criminal and delinquent behavior dates back to at least 1916, in Goddard's "pedigree analysis" study of the so-called Kallikak family. Goddard proposed that feeblemindedness was inheritable and was associated 50 percent of the time with eventual criminality. Dugdale's (1942) subsequent examination of the genealogy of the Jukes family yielded rather similar conclusions. As Nietzel (1979) correctly observes, however, the genealogical method suffers from a number of limitations, especially the frequently poor reliability of birth and court records and the great difficulty of achieving "an unambiguous untangling of what it is exactly that the family transmits: genetic predisposition, psychosocial characteristics, or both" (p. 71).

A second approach to examining the possibility that criminal behavior grows in part from a genetic base, the comparative study of identical versus fraternal twins, has proven more adequate. Rather than relying on often inadequate records, conjecture, and deductive reasoning, twin studies compare the concordance rate for criminality (the percentage of twins sharing the characteristic) for monozygotic twins, who are genetically identical, and for dizygotic twins, who are only as genetically similar as siblings of either sex born at different times. If the monozygotic concordance rate is significantly higher, one may appropriately conclude that the given behavior is indeed genetically influenced. This is precisely the conclusion that has, in fact, been drawn in response to an extended series of such twin comparisons over the past 60 years. In the first such study, Lange (1928) found 30 prisoners in a Bavarian prison who were twins—13 apparently monozygotic and 17 dizygotic. Of the 13 monozygotic prisoners, 10 had twins who had also been in prison, as opposed to only 2 of the twins of the 17 dizygotic prisoners. Legras (1932; cited by Rosenthal, 1970), Krantz (1936), Christiansen (1977), and Dalgaard and Kringlen (1976) report similar findings, "presenting apparently impressive evidence of genetic transmission of the propensity to break the law" (Trasler, 1987, p. 187). It must also be noted, however, that over the decades when these comparative studies were conducted, as tests for zygosity became more reliable and recorded evidence of criminality more accurate, the criminality rate differences for the two types of twins became less pronounced. Furthermore, some investigators have speculated that pairs of monozygotic twins may be reared in social and even physical environments that are more similar than are the analogous environments of dizygotic twins. In keeping with the multiple causation perspective toward which this chapter is leading, Trasler (1987) has responded to these concordance studies by noting the likely interface of genetic transmission effects with companion social influences on criminality:

The basic lesson to be drawn from twin studies seems
to be that the intergenerational mechanism which
predisposes some [monozygotic] twin pairs to high
concordance for officially recorded delinquency is
probably mediated by both genetic transmission and by
social processes of bonding and interdependence. There
is no known way in which the respective influences of
inherited characteristics and learned social patterns can
be disentangled. (p. 189)

A second biogenetic research strategy is the adoption or cross-
fostering study. In Denmark, where most such research has been
conducted, adoptions and foster family arrangements are commonly made within a few days or weeks of birth, resulting in the child's
having minimal contact with the biological parents. In these
investigations, comparison is made of the criminality and delinquency rates for (a) adopted or foster family offspring of biological
parents having and lacking criminal records and (b) offspring of
analogously criminal and noncriminal adoptive parents (Bohman,
Cloniger, Sigvardsson, & vonKnorring, 1982; Crowe, 1975;
Mednick, 1977; Pollock, Mednick, & Gabrielli, 1983). These investigations, even more convincingly than the twin studies, provide
evidence that the potential for criminality, especially persistent or
recidivistic criminality, is influenced by biological inheritance. The
degree of such influence—"major" according to Trasler (1987,
p. 190), "very small" in the view of Nietzel (1979, p. 75)—and the
specific physiological and/or psychological means by which the
influence occurs (Rosenthal, 1970) largely remain to be clarified.[1]
A final physiological perspective on the roots of juvenile
delinquency—neurohormonal theory—though apparently not yet
widely incorporated into current etiological theorizing, seems quite
promising and is thus included here. L. Ellis (1987) notes that three
seemingly disparate neurological views of delinquency have been
put forth recently. The first, *arousal theory,* asserts that people most
likely to engage in criminal behavior appear to have nervous

---

[1] A third biogenetic avenue of research into the etiology of delinquency
and criminality, cytogenetic studies, has proven much less fruitful. After
a flurry of considerable interest, it now appears likely that chromosomal
abnormality in the form of supernumerary chromosomes, perhaps
associated with certain intellectually subnormal populations, is not to
be found disproportionately among incarcerated delinquent youths
(Wegmann & Smith, 1963; Witkin et al., 1976).

systems that are, in a sense, well insulated from the environment. They are more difficult to condition, more likely to endure pain, and more prone to seek high levels of stimulation. Further, Ellis notes, evidence suggests that such people, when threatened, are unusually slow to shift from low or average arousal levels to a state of high arousal and slow to return to low or average levels when the threat has passed. *Seizuring theory* notes that epilepsy is disproportionately present in the criminal, versus the general, population and that brain seizures may often be provoked by stress or alcohol consumption. On the basis of such findings, Mark and Erwin (1970) and Monroe (1970) have each speculated about seizuring as a possible cause of criminal behavior, especially regarding so-called crimes of passion. *Hemispheric functioning theory* suggests that the manner in which the two cortical hemispheres functionally relate may dispose certain people toward criminality. This view is responsive to evidence of right hemispheric involvement in the processing of emotional information (especially such so-called negative emotions as jealousy, hate, and cynicism), to the fact that the same hemisphere tends to control movement on the left side of the body, and to the several studies reporting that left-handed males are disproportionately represented in delinquent and criminal groups as compared to the general population.

In his neurohormonal theory of delinquency, L. Ellis (1987) proposes that each of these three neurological perspectives appears to describe effects of exposing the nervous system to high levels of androgens, especially testosterone. He marshals evidence suggesting that androgens affect brain function by lowering overall responsiveness to arousal, by increasing the probability of seizures, and by causing cortical functioning to shift to the right hemisphere. The relevance of these findings to the etiology of delinquency lies in the association of the pubertal surge in testosterone with the rise in the incidence of delinquency linked with chronological age. Ellis thus asserts that "androgen infiltration of the nervous system . . . after puberty is likely to alter brain function in ways that increase the probability of delinquency and criminal behavior" (p. 509).

MULTICOMPONENT THEORIES

If this chapter were a competition for the "etiological truth" vis-à-vis juvenile delinquency, each of the theories examined here, as well as the sociological perspectives presented in chapter 1, would score a partial victory, yet none would be the winner. Juvenile delinquency is many behaviors, diversely motivated and expressed, apparently reflective of a broad array of physiological, hormonal, personality, socioeconomic, familial, societal, and other roots. Any monocausal theory of its (their!) origin is destined to be incomplete. With very few (mostly historical) exceptions, however, each provides a partial truth, contributing at least to some extent toward a better understanding of the etiology of juvenile delinquency. This understanding, and the resultant ability to better predict and control delinquent behaviors, will be further advanced if a monocausal, one-true-light, theory-A-versus-theory-B way of thinking is abandoned for a more comprehensive theoretical posture in which the more potent monocausal theories are combined, in a rational and multimodal manner, to yield heuristic multicomponent theories. Several such theories have been proposed; they are the focus of this section.

Social Learning Theory

Social learning theory (Bandura, 1969, 1986) is a combined situational, cognitive, and physiological orientation to the acquisition of behavior. Although it has appropriately been used to examine the learning of many types of behavior, one of its major applications has been to the acquisition, instigation, and maintenance of antisocial behavior, especially overt aggression (Bandura, 1973; Feldman, 1977).

Table 3.1 summarizes the processes that, according to social learning theory, are responsible for the individual's acquisition or original learning of aggressive behaviors, the instigation of overt acts of aggression at any given moment, and the maintenance of such behavior (Bandura, 1973).

Acquisition

Social learning theory, reflecting its aspiration to comprehensiveness, acknowledges that an unknown and perhaps substantial contribution to a person's potential to behave aggressively stems from neurophysiological characteristics. Genetics, hormones, the central nervous system, and the individual's resultant physical characteristics, it is held, influence the person's capacity or potential for aggression. Given the neurophysiological capacity to acquire and retain aggression in the behavioral repertoire, Bandura (1969, 1973) suggests that such acquisition proceeds by means of either direct or vicarious experiences. In both instances, the role of

Table 3.1 Social Learning Theory: Processes Underlying Aggressive Behavior

ACQUISITION	INSTIGATION	MAINTENANCE
Neurophysiological characteristics Genetics Hormones Central nervous system involvement (e.g., hypothalamus, limbic system) Physical factors	**Aversive events** Frustration Adverse reductions in reinforcement Relative deprivation Unjustified hardships Verbal threats and insults Physical assaults	**Direct external reinforcement** Tangible (e.g., money, tokens) Social (e.g., status, approval) Alleviation of aversiveness Expressions of injury

Observational learning
Family influences (e.g., abuse)
Subcultural influences (e.g., delinquency)
Symbolic modeling (e.g., television)
	Modeling influences
	Disinhibitory-reduced restraints
	Response facilitation effects
	Emotional arousal
	Stimulus-enhancing effects (attentional)
		Vicarious reinforcement
		Observed reward
		  (receipt-facilitation effect)
		Observed punishment
		  (escape-disinhibitory effect)

Direct experience Combat Reinforced practice	**Incentive inducements** Instrumental aggression Anticipated consequences	**Self-reinforcement**
	Instructional control	**Neutralization of self-punishment** Moral justification Palliative comparison Euphemistic labeling Displacement of responsibility Diffusion of responsibility Dehumanization of victims Attribution of blame to victims Misrepresentation of consequences Graduated desensitization
	Environmental control Crowding Ambient temperature Noise Pollution Traffic congestion Other characteristics of the physical, sensory, psychological environment	

Note. This table originally appeared in *Delinquents on Delinquency* (p. 28) by A.P. Goldstein, 1990, Champaign, IL: Research Press.

reinforcement looms large. Reinforcement of overtly aggressive acts, occurring in the context of trial-and-error behavior or under instructional control of others, is likely to increase the probability that the individual will learn or acquire aggression. Bandura speaks of reinforced practice as a particularly consequential event in the learning of aggression via direct experiences—be it childhood pushing and shoving, adolescent fighting, or adult military combat.

But social learning theory places heaviest emphasis on vicarious processes for the acquisition of aggression. Such observational learning is held to emanate from three types of modeling influences: familial, subcultural, and symbolic. The physically abused person who, as a child, strikes out at peers and who, as an adult, batters his or her own child may be seen as having acquired such behaviors in part by observing the abusive examples enacted by his or her own parents. Subcultural modeling influences on the acquisition of aggression are often exemplified by adolescents' behavior in response to their observation of peer aggression or the behavior of new soldiers successfully indoctrinated into combative behaviors. And vicarious symbolic modeling on television, in the movies, and in comic books is also apparently a major source for the learning of aggression in the United States. Crucial here is the fact that such aggression usually "works." The aggressive model, be it parent, peer, or television character, is very often reinforced for behaving aggressively. Central to the observational learning process is the fact that individuals tend to acquire those behaviors that they see others enacting and being rewarded for.

Instigation

Once the individual has learned how to aggress (and learned when, where, with whom, etc.), what determines whether he or she will in fact do so? According to social learning theory, the actual performance of aggressive behaviors is determined by the following factors.

Aversive events. Aversive events may occur and serve to evoke aggression. Frustration is one such aversive instigator. Adverse reductions in reinforcement are a second purported type of aversive instigation to aggression. Many commentators on collective aggression have pointed to this differential-opportunity type of instigation—especially in the form of a perceived sense of deprivation relative to others or hardship perceived as unjustified, rather than deprivation or hardship in an absolute sense—as a major source of mob violence, riots, and the like. Verbal insults and physical assaults are additional, particularly potent aversive instigators to aggression. Toch (1969) has shown that, at least among chronically assaultive persons, the types of insults most likely to evoke physically assaultive behavior include threats to reputation and manly status and public humiliation. Physical assault is most likely to instigate reciprocal behavior when avoidance is difficult and the instigating assaultiveness is both intense and frequent.

Modeling influences. Just as modeling influences serve as a major means by which new patterns of aggression are acquired, so too can they function as significant instigators to overt aggressive behavior. If one observes another person (the model) behaving aggressively and not being punished for it, the observation can have a disinhibitory effect. If the model not only goes unpunished but is rewarded by approval or by tangible means for the displayed aggression, a response facilitation effect may occur. The model's behavior, in this instance, functions as an external inducement to engage in matching or similar behavior. The sheer sight of others behaving aggressively may instigate similar behavior in yet another way: Viewing such behavior often engenders emotional arousal in the observer, and considerable empirical evidence exists that arousal facilitates aggressive behavior, especially in persons for whom such a response is well practiced and readily available in the behavioral repertoire. Finally, Bandura (1978) also notes that modeling may influence the likelihood of aggression through its stimulus-enhancing effects. The observer's attention, for example, may be directed by the model's behavior to particular implements and ways to use them aggressively.

Incentive inducements. Feshbach (1970) and others have drawn the distinction between angry aggression and instrumental aggression. The goal of the former is to hurt another individual; the latter is an aggressive effort to obtain tangible or other rewards possessed by or otherwise at the disposal of the other. Incentive inducements to aggression relate to this second definition. As Bandura (1978) comments, "A great deal of human aggression . . . is prompted by anticipated positive consequences. Here the instigator is the pull of expected reward rather than the push of painful treatment" (p. 46).

Instructional control. Individuals may aggress against others because they are told to do so; such subcultural instigation to aggression is common in a gang delinquency context. Furthermore, obedience is taught and differentially rewarded by family and school during childhood and adolescence, and by many social institutions during adulthood (e.g., at work, in military service, etc.). Again, Bandura (1973) comments:

> Given that people will obey orders, legitimate authorities can successfully command aggression from others, especially if the actions are presented as justified and necessary and the enforcing agents possess strong coercive power. Indeed, as Snow (1961) has perceptively observed, "When you think of the long and gloomy history of man, you will find more hideous crimes committed in the name of obedience than have been committed in the name of rebellion." (p. 175)

Environmental control. The empirical examination of an array of external events as instigators to aggression has become a substantial investigative focus. Crowding, ambient temperature, noise, pollution, traffic congestion, and several other characteristics of the physical, sensory, and psychological environment have been studied for their possible instigative potency. Evidence reveals that each may (but does not necessarily) instigate aggression. Whether aggressive behavior does, in fact, grow from crowded conditions, hot days and nights, high noise levels, and the like appears to be a somewhat complicated function of the physical intensity of these environmental qualities, their perception and interpretation, the level of emotional arousal they engender, their interaction, external constraints, and several other factors.

Maintenance

Whether aggressive behavior persists, disappears, or reappears is largely a matter of reinforcement. When aggression pays, it will tend to persist; when it goes unrewarded, it will tend to extinguish. This simple and traditional stimulus-response notion as applied to aggression becomes a bit more complex in social learning theory, as the number and types of reinforcements held to influence the maintenance of aggression become elaborated.

Direct external reinforcement. The persistence of aggressive behavior is directly influenced by the extrinsic rewards it elicits. Such rewards may be tangible (e.g., objects, money, tokens) or social (e.g., status, approval, recognition). They may take the form of the alleviation of aversive treatment (e.g., reduction of pain or other negative reinforcement) or, possibly, expressions of pain by the victim of the aggression. These kinds of external reinforcement have been shown to have a maximal effect on the maintenance of aggression as a function of the principles of reinforcement influencing any other behavior: latency, magnitude, quality, intermittency, and so forth.

Vicarious reinforcement. Vicarious processes, central to the acquisition and instigation of aggression, are no less important in its maintenance. Observed consequences influence behavior much as do the effects of direct external reinforcement. The aggression-maintaining effects of seeing others rewarded for aggression come about, Bandura (1978) suggests, via (a) the informational function —that is, the event tells the observer what aggressive acts are likely to be rewarded under what circumstances; (b) the motivational function—that is, the observer is encouraged by the observation to believe that similar aggressiveness will yield similar rewards; and (c) the disinhibitory effect—that is, the observer sees others escaping punishment for their aggressive behavior.

Self-reinforcement. Social learning theory proposes that there are also self-produced consequences by which individuals reward or punish, and hence regulate, their own behaviors. With regard to aggression, most people in the course of socialization learn by example or rules that aggressive behavior should be negatively sanctioned, and they impose sanctions on themselves by what they say, do, or feel about themselves following their own aggressive behavior. In contrast, there are also people whose own criteria for dispensing self-reinforcement make overt aggression highly rewardable and a source of pride. They are prone to combativeness and derive an enhanced feeling of self-worth from indulging successfully in aggression.

Neutralization of self-punishment. A number of other self-originated processes are suggested in social learning theory as factors that often function to maintain aggressive behavior. These primarily involve neutralization of self-punishment. They may take the several forms listed in Table 3.1, each of which is a cognitive effort on the part of the aggressor to justify, excuse, ignore, or otherwise avoid self-condemnation for aggression and its consequences.

Social learning theory has been the target of extensive empirical evaluation and, as reflected in the attention devoted to it here, has received considerable investigative support. Its centrality in current psychological theorizing is clearly justified. Stumphauzer and colleagues (Stumphauzer, Veloz, & Aiken 1981; Stumphauzer, Aiken, & Veloz, 1977) have creatively suggested applications of the social learning perspective to a better understanding of youth gangs. Their proposals well deserve empirical test and elaboration. In all, social learning theory is a multicomponent perspective immensely useful both in its own right and, as will be seen, as a component in other multicomponent theories of juvenile delinquency.

Differential Association–Differential Reinforcement Theory

Burgess and Akers (1966) and Akers (1985) have creatively combined and integrated major aspects of Sutherland's (1937, 1947) differential association perspective and social learning theory's (Bandura, 1969) focal concern with the role of reinforcement. Differential association–differential reinforcement theory is operationalized in the following principles:

1. Deviant behavior is learned according to the principles of operant conditioning.

2. Deviant behavior is learned both in nonsocial situations that are reinforcing or discriminating and through social interaction in which others' behavior is reinforcing or discriminating for such behavior.

3. Most learning of deviant behavior occurs in the groups that constitute or control the individual's major source of reinforcement.

4. The learning of deviant behavior, including specific techniques, attitudes, and avoidance procedures, is a function of the effective and available reinforcers and the existing reinforcement contingencies.

5. The specific class of behavior learned and the frequency of its occurrence are a function of the effective and available reinforcers and the deviant or nondeviant direction of the norms, rules, and definitions that in the past have accompanied the reinforcement.

6. The probability that a person will commit deviant behavior is increased by normative statements, definitions, and verbalizations that, in the process of differential reinforcement of such behavior over conforming behavior, have acquired discriminative value.

7. The strength of deviant behavior is a direct function of the amount, frequency, and probability of its reinforcement. The modalities of association with deviant patterns are important insofar as they affect the source, amount, and scheduling of reinforcement.

Akers (1985) summarizes the theory as follows:

Social behavior is learned by conditioning . . . in which behavior is shaped by the stimuli that follow or are consequences of the behavior and by imitation . . . of others' behavior. Behavior is strengthened by reward . . . and avoidance of punishment . . . or weakened . . . by aversive stimuli . . . and lack of reward. . . . Whether deviant or conforming behavior persists depends on the past and present rewards and punishments and on the rewards and punishments attached to alternative behavior—differential reinforcement. (p. 57)

The principal behavioral effects come from interaction in or under the influence of those groups with which one is in differential association and which control sources and patterns of reinforcement, provide normative definitions, and expose one to behavioral models. The most important of these are primary groups such as peers and friendship groups and the family. (p. 58)

Social Developmental Theory

Control and social learning approaches are the components of social developmental theory. Hawkins and Weis (1985) observe:

Delinquent behavior is likely to be a . . . result of experiences from birth through adolescence. . . . [E]arly experiences in the family are likely to influence social bonding to the family . . . as well as the likelihood that social bonds of attachment to school and commitment to education will develop. . . . The social influence of peers becomes salient during adolescence itself. If the process of developing a social bond to prosocial others and prosocial activities has been interrupted by unconcerned or inconsistent parents, by poor school performance, or by inconsistent teachers, youths are more likely to come

under the influence of peers who are in the same
situation and are also more likely to be influenced by
such peers to engage in delinquent activities. (p. 242)

The central variables of social developmental theory are opportunity for involvement (in the bonding process), skills (those necessary
to perform competently in family, school, and prosocial peer
settings), and reinforcements (rewards consequent to skill use in the
involved settings). To the degree that such involvements, skills,
and/or reinforcements are inadequate, the probability of delinquent behavior is purportedly enhanced.

Integrated Learning Theory

Feldman's (1977) comprehensive attempt to explore the
sources of criminal and delinquent behavior is both multicomponent and multilevel in structure. Criminal behavior, he
asserts, grows jointly from individual predisposition, social learning, and social labeling. Borrowing from Eysenck's (1977) views on
inherited aspects of personality—especially temperament, condi-
tionability, and the potential for conscience development—
Feldman notes that both extroverted neurotics and persons high on
psychoticism measures may have high crime potential. The former,
Eysenck holds, have poor potential for adequate socialization; the
latter may be insufficiently responsive to the distress of others. As
Nietzel (1979) observes, "The potential criminal is someone whose
genetically influenced personality predispositions make it difficult
to acquire the classically conditioned avoidance responses which
Eysenck held were the elemental components of human conscience
and the ability to resist temptations to antisocial conduct" (p. 88).

Such individual predisposing factors set the stage, in effect, for
the acquisition of delinquent behaviors. Learning processes further
the acquisition—as well as the likelihood of both subsequent
performance and maintenance—of the behaviors and include, in
Feldman's view, both learning to offend and learning not to offend.
Although integrated learning theory draws on diverse approaches to
learning and behavior change, social learning theory is its primary
feature. Criminal behaviors (especially in genetically predisposed
persons) are acquired, performed, and maintained largely as a
function of the social learning processes identified in Table 3.1. Of
additional consequence to the actual performance of criminal
behaviors are such situational determinants as risk of detection,
level of punishment if detection occurs, level of incentives, presence

or absence of transgressive models, low self-esteem, nature of the victim, and alternative legitimate means to obtain gains:

> Thus, probability is greatest when detection is unlikely, punishment minimal, incentive high, alternatives are absent, transgressing models are present, the transgression requires little skill, the victim is both a stranger and unlikely to report the offense, and self-esteem is temporarily low. (Feldman, 1977, p. 103)

Once delinquent behavior is performed, its continuation is in part, according to Feldman, a function of social labeling. The labeling process and its purported consequences are conceptualized in integrated learning theory as described in the earlier consideration of social labeling theory.

Other Multicomponent Theories

Complementing the integrative efforts presented thus far, a number of additional investigators have sought to describe the etiology of juvenile delinquency in a manner more fully reflecting the apparent complexity of its roots. These efforts include Cohen and Land's (1987) criminal opportunity theory, which synthesizes control and differential opportunity theories; Kornhauser's (1978) social disorganization theory, which similarly blends control and strain propositions; Aultman and Wellford's (1978) combined model of control, strain, and labeling theories; Wilson and Hernnstein's (1985) incorporation of genetic predispositional and social learning influences; Elliott, Huizenga, and Ageton's (1985) "fully integrated model," consisting of control, strain, and social learning perspectives; Hogan and Jones's (1983) socioanalytic theory, seeking to blend structural sociological, social learning, psychoanalytic, symbolic interactionist, and biological conceptualizations; M.Q. Warren's (1983) interpersonal maturity theory, combining strain, cultural deviance, control, and psychodynamic proposals; and the diversely composed, partial theory construction calls of Bahr (1979), Corning and Corning (1972), W. Glaser (1969), Goldstein (1983), Himelhoch (1965), R.E. Johnson (1979), Rutter and Giller (1983), and West (1967). This multicomponent perspective merits support for its likely superior explanatory power and for its positive utilitarian implications for the design and implementation of effective delinquency interventions.

The purpose of this chapter has been twofold. First, it has presented psychology's theoretical contribution to an understanding of the etiology of delinquent behavior as expressed by both individuals and groups or gangs. Diverse psychological theories have been described both alone and in combination with other (usually sociological) theories in a combined, multicomponent perspective. Second, the chapter has made an explicit case for the desirability of such multicomponent thinking, with its enhanced clarifying and predictive potency. Such a perspective on diverse causality will be reviewed later in this book for its gang intervention implications.

CHAPTER 4

Gangs as Hyperadolescents

As Muuss (1975) writes:

> The word "adolescence" is derived from the Latin verb
> *adolescere,* meaning "to grow up" or "to grow into
> maturity." Sociologically, adolescence is the transition
> period from dependent childhood to self-sufficient
> adulthood. Psychologically, it is a marginal situation
> in which new adjustments have to be made, namely
> those that distinguish child behavior from adult
> behavior. . . . Chronologically, it is the time span from
> approximately twelve or thirteen to the early twenties,
> with wide individual and cultural variations. (p. 4)

Recent theory and research in developmental psychology have focused on the adolescent life period in considerable depth. In the present chapter, we wish to draw upon this literature to help clarify the nature of, and the bases for, gang formation and gang life. To set the stage for this clarification effort, we first sketch a picture of the more typical, non-gang-involved American adolescent, emphasizing what might be termed the hallmark characteristics of such a youngster.

It appears that, in terms of both their prepotent needs and characteristic overt behaviors, adolescent members of delinquent gangs are what we would term *hyperadolescents:* They exhibit needs and behaviors typical of most adolescents but to a substantially intensified degree. Building on this notion of the hyperadolescent gang member, the chapter will indicate how such exaggerated qualities readily lead to gang formation, gang involvement, and the diverse behaviors held to characterize the daily lives of gang youths.

THE AMERICAN ADOLESCENT

The American adolescent has been described as a "marginal man" (Lewin, 1951) whose behavior vacillates from the childish to the adult and whose major preoccupations in life are a striving to define a stable identity (Erikson, 1975; Marcia, 1980) and a continuing struggle to attain and maintain a secure status in the peer group. Self-esteem and its enhancement are major and continuing sources of concern (Beck, 1987). Overtly, such striving for peer group status and security is manifested in dress, language, ideology, and diverse group-centered behaviors (Gross & Levin, 1987). Alienation from parents is purportedly common (Rutter, 1980), as are other manifestations of a striving for independence and autonomy (New York City Youth Board, 1960). Adolescents frequently can be moody and ruminative, yet they probably experience less of the "storm and stress" than is typically attributed to them in the lay literature (Kelly & Hansen, 1987). Especially in the earlier adolescent years, young people can be ingenuous and naively moralistic, evolving toward greater cynicism and pragmatism as adolescence proceeds (Rutter, 1980).

These characteristic adolescent emotional, cognitive, and behavioral qualities have been the focus of numerous explanatory theories of adolescent development: philosophical (Muuss, 1975), biological (Richards & Peterson, 1987), psychodynamic (Lerner, 1987), developmental (Havighurst, 1987), social psychological (Lewin, 1951), social learning (Gross & Levin, 1987), and sociological (Davis, 1944). The diversity of these several theoretical perspectives notwithstanding, it is clear that "typical" adolescent behavior is culture bound to a substantial degree. Although the major goals of adolescent striving are similar across cultures, the means of reaching such goals can be quite different (Bloch & Niederhoffer, 1958). We strongly concur with Rutter's (1980) view that adolescence, especially "psychosocial adolescence," is a social creation. The incarnation of this social creation is characterized well in Rutter's observation that

> adolescence is recognized and treated as a distinct stage of development because the coincidence of extended education and early sexual maturation have meant a prolonged phase of physical maturity associated with economic and psychosocial dependence; because many of the widely held psychological theories specify that adolescence should be different; because commercial interests demand a youth culture; and because schools and colleges have ensured that large numbers of young people are kept together in an age-segregated social group. To that extent, psychosocial adolescence is created by society and has no necessary connection with the developmental process. (p. 7)

Establishing a stable sense of identity and striving for peer acceptance are two central—and interrelated—features of adolescent development. Their forms of expression in that social creation called American adolescence are central to this chapter's speculations about gang youths as hyperadolescents. Erik Erikson's (1975) theory of identity development provided many of the core constructs, since built upon by others, for better understanding of identity striving and its central role in adolescent development. The essential task of adolescence, in this view, is to establish one's own identity, which means putting aside childhood identifications; struggling with the development of a system of values, beliefs, and aspirations; and moving toward a more mature, autonomous, adult personality configuration. It is, as Muuss (1975) notes, a search for answers to the questions, Who am I? Where am I going? and, What do I believe? Marcia (1980) describes this search as typically unfolding gradually, nonconsciously, in bits and pieces, and as comprising all of the trivial and major decisions the youth is called upon to make as daily life unfolds:

> whom to date, whether or not to break up, having intercourse, taking drugs, going to college or working, which college, what major, studying or playing, being politically active, and so on. Each of these decisions has identity-forming implications. The decisions and the bases on which one decides begin to form themselves into a more or less consistent core or structure. (p. 160)

In the contemporary United States, especially for many youths from backgrounds marked by dysfunctional family life, economic disadvantage, and social disorganization, the search may be fraught with difficulty:

> The search for an identity involves the production of a meaningful self-concept in which past, present, and future are linked together. Consequently the task is more difficult in a historical period in which the past has lost the anchorage of family and community tradition, the present is characterized by social change, and the future has become less predictable. (Muuss, 1975, p. 63)

Often the outcome of the search is positive, integrative, and developmental. The youth grows and matures, developing an increasingly broad, deep, and cohesive sense of self. Other times the outcome is less positive, less enhancing, and poorly integrated.

Erikson (1975) speaks of "that malignant turn toward a negative group identity which prevails where conditions of economic, ethnic, and religious marginality provide poor bases for positive identities, here negative identities are sought" (p. 345). But the purported negativity of such group-based identity is itself a social construction. From the gang youth's perspective, the picture looks very different. Bynner, O'Malley, and Bachman (1981), for example, have provided evidence that engaging in delinquent behavior may in fact enhance identity and self-esteem, perhaps because of affirmation of such behavior by similarly engaged peers.

Identity—answers to the questions, Who am I? Where am I going? and, What do I believe?—is found partly through reflection but primarily via interpersonal encounters. Muuss (1975) comments on this:

> Since an identity can be found only through interaction
> with other people, the adolescent goes through a period
> of compulsive peer group conformity as a means of
> testing roles to see whether and how they fit him. The
> peer group, the clique, and the gang do help the
> individual in finding his own identity in a social context,
> since they provide the individual with both a role model
> and direct feedback about himself. (p. 64)

Further, as Marcia (1980) states, "The less developed this structure is, the more confused individuals seem about their own distinctiveness from others . . . [and] the more they have to rely on external sources to evaluate themselves" (p. 159).

Indeed, there appears to be general agreement, both empirical and impressionistic, that for many—probably most—adolescents, the peer group is an exceedingly powerful formative influence. The peer group, it is held, becomes the youth's primary source of status, self-esteem, anchorage, and security (Ausbel, 1974); ego satisfaction and emancipation (New York City Youth Board, 1960); mutual support (Adams & Gullotta, 1989); and affection (Bell, 1981). The peer group shapes values, ideals, attitudes, and interests (Muuss, 1975) and provides the major arena for trying out new roles (Thornburg, 1972). Bloch and Niederhoffer (1958) have demonstrated the broad cross-cultural validity of such assertions about the power of peer group attachments and influence for adolescents from diverse societies. Why are peer groups so potent? Coleman (1980) asserts:

In the first place, during the teenage years the young
person faces a marked upheaval in physical development
as well as considerable reorganization in the social and
emotional spheres of life. Such fundamental changes
force on the individual the necessity of coping with new
and unknown experiences as well as create a major
challenge to identity and self-esteem. Circumstances of
this sort usually result in greatly increased dependence
on support from others, especially those who are facing
or have recently faced similar events in their own lives.
In the second place . . . at some level all adolescents are
involved in a process whereby adult standards are
questioned, adult authority is challenged, and the
emotional dependence on the parents . . . is gradually
weakened. Thus, paradoxically at a time when
uncertainty and self-doubt is greatest and when support
is more needed, many adolescents find themselves in an
emotional position where it is difficult, if not impossible,
to turn to their parents. Under such circumstances it is
hardly surprising that peers play an unusually important
role. Third and last, it is in the nature of transitions that
they involve experimentation . . . .Teenagers have
to . . . discover what sorts of behavior are acceptable and
what are not, which facets of their personality are liked
and which are rejected. Above all, they have to find out
how their needs and motives interact best with the social
environment and which roles are compatible with their
own developing identities. This process of discovery . . .
is dependent on the involvement of a peer group. (p. 409)

These three hallmark qualities of adolescence (physical and
psychosocial development, movement away from adults as sources
of support, and interpersonal experimentation), each of which
heightens the desirability of peer involvement, fluctuate over the 8
to 10 years typically held to constitute adolescence (Bigelow &
LaGaipa, 1975; Coleman, 1980; Powell, 1955). In early adolescence
(ages 11 to 13), peer relationships are typically more activity
oriented than interaction oriented. Youngsters do things together
but with little focus on mutuality or depth of friendship. In middle
adolescence—that is, between ages 14 and 16—loyalty, trustwor-
thiness, and security appear to be the primary interpersonal peer
concerns. By late adolescence, studies suggest, peer relationships

are more relaxed. Perhaps, it is held, older adolescents need friendships less intensely and are thus less concerned with fears of abandonment.

The potency of the peer group across these adolescent stages can be seen in the attraction it holds (Brown, Eicher, & Petrie, 1986), the sheer amount of time youths spend among peers (Csikszentmihalyi & Larsen, 1984), and, especially, in the pressure toward conformity the peer group successfully wields (Ausbel, 1974). Conformity to peer group pressures and demands, asserts Ausbel, is compelling for at least three reasons. The first he describes as structural:

> In its effort to establish a new and distinctive subculture
> and to evolve a unique set of criteria for the determi-
> nation of status and prestige, the peer society must do
> everything in its power to set itself off as recognizable,
> distinct and separate from the adult society which refuses
> its membership. . . . If this distinctiveness is to be
> actually attained in fact, it cannot admit the possibility
> of widespread non-conformity; since obviously if every
> adolescent were permitted to exercise his newly acquired
> craving for individuality, an unrecognizable medley of
> behavior patterns would ensue. Under such conditions,
> there would be no peer culture, and hence no compen-
> satory source of status. (p. 354)

The second basis for the intense pressure to conform follows largely from fear of rejection. Ausbel observes:

> Any person with marginal status is excessively sensitive
> to the threat of forfeiting what little status he enjoys as a
> result of incurring the disapproval of those on whom he
> is dependent. To allay the anxiety from the threat of
> disapproval he conforms more than is objectively
> necessary to retain group acceptance or to avoid censure
> and reprisal. (p. 354)

Finally, high levels of conformity to the peer group may enhance the value of in-group status:

> The larger the number of persons who can be perceived
> as outside the charmed circle, the more individuals they
> can perceive as inferior to themselves, the greater their
> own self-esteem becomes by comparison, and the more

status value their in-group membership acquires. These ends can be most expeditiously effected by (a) elevating by fiat certain esoteric practices or characteristics into unique virtues, values, and symbols of status, (b) imposing these standards upon others by having them accept them at face value and (c) acquiring a very low threshold for the perception of deviancy from these standards so that very few individuals can qualify for admission to the select circle of the originators and only "true" exemplifiers of the hallowed norms. (p. 355)

THE GANG ADOLESCENT

The first part of this chapter described an array of characteristics typical of the American adolescent: marginality, a chronic challenging of those in authority, a need to experiment with diverse adult-like roles, a search for status (especially vis-à-vis peers), a concern with enhancement of self-esteem, and a striving for independence. An especially important adolescent characteristic is a deep involvement in the task of identity formation; related to this and many other needs is a preoccupation with developing and maintaining peer relationships. For reasons of structure, compensation, and enhancement of self-esteem, conformity pressure in adolescent peer groups is intense and very often effective.

All of these qualities that mark the typical American adolescent are equally characteristic of youths involved in delinquent gangs—in fact, even more so. Those youngsters are not only adolescents in all the senses described earlier, they are, more accurately, hyperadolescents.

Our recent interview investigation seeking the perspectives of delinquent youths regarding both the etiology and remediation of juvenile delinquency is germane (Goldstein, 1990). Their responses were infused with the several prototypical adolescent themes identified in this chapter: the search for identity, oppositionalness, hyperindependence, the seeking of limits, externalization of responsibility, role experimentation, peer pressure, and more. We concluded:

> Our ability to understand the roots of juvenile
> delinquency and effect its prevention and reduction will
> also be advanced, we believe, if we more fully remember
> and respond to the fact that delinquents are also
> adolescents. In fact, with no implication intended that

this developmental stance mitigates the seriousness of adolescent crime, or that we are assuming a "boys will be boys" attitude, it ought to be said that delinquents often are *hyperadolescents,* and this status must, in ways yet to be determined, be factored into our causal thinking and intervention selection. (p. 156)

Others share this view regarding delinquent gang youths. Klein (1968a), for example, speaks of such youngsters' behavior as "a caricature of adolescence" and "adolescence overplayed." Their use of humor, boasting, insecurity, reliance on the peer group, and similar behaviors leads Klein to suggest that "all those behavioral manifestations which allow one to say of a person's behavior that it is adolescent can be seen in the gang members—usually in excess" (p. 81). Bloch and Niederhoffer (1958), Gold and Petronio (1980), and Miller (1958) hold similar views.

IMPLICATIONS FOR GANG BEHAVIOR

If, as seems amply demonstrated here, gang youths are indeed often hyperadolescents, what are the implications of this view for a better understanding of gangs and their functioning? One such implication concerns delinquent behavior itself. Cartwright, Schwartz, and Tomson (1975) propose that delinquent acts by gang members are committed less for profit, spite, or similar motives than for status, reputation, and the like. Klein (1968a) takes a similar view and notes that gang youths seek the status-enhancing value of violent delinquent acts in particular. Bloch and Niederhoffer (1958) agree:

Most gang boys are driven by a need for what they call "rep." Reputation, standing, is the most important thing in their lives. They're denied it in their homes. The schools, overcrowded and understaffed, can't give it to them. So they look for it in their gangs. That explains why they fight such ferocious wars over the right to softball fields or a stolen girlfriend or a casual shove or some imaginary insult. (p. 166)

Erikson (1975) and Mulvihill, Tumin, and Curtis (1969) similarly note the centrality of delinquent behavior—especially violent behavior—for status-enhancing purposes.

If adolescents in general are narrowly peer oriented, gang member hyperadolescents are all the more so. They appear to be more susceptible to peer pressure and more willing to incorporate peer-initiated evaluations into a developing sense of self (Cartwright et al., 1975; Spergel et al., 1989; F. Wright, 1985). Miller (1980) captures this level of peer potency well:

> Peer-group membership is important for all adolescents;
> and for gang members, many of whom are products of
> unusually stressful and unstable home or family
> environments, the gang represents a precious island of
> security in the dangerous and turbulent sea of life. Gang
> members . . . stress the support, the sense of identity,
> and the sense of belonging provided by gang member-
> ship, frequently likening the gang to a family, often a
> more satisfactory family than their own. (p. 301)

Three of many possible additional examples of gang-relevant behavior deriving from hyperadolescence may be described. One is the intense need for approval:

> Gang boys emerge from their family and community
> experiences with a great need for positive regard that has
> been unfulfilled so far. In the gang they can obtain . . .
> positive regard, mainly respect, deference, and admira-
> tion; even mere acceptance as a member of the gang
> constitutes some positive regard satisfaction. (Cartwright
> et al., 1975, p. 73)

A second minor but highly illustrative example is offered by Klein (1968a):

> The boys do a great deal of boasting about their
> individual exploits. . . . [B]oasting serves the purpose
> of ego-building where few objective qualities or accom-
> plishments are available for the task. More than their
> non-gang age peers, these boys feel little confidence in
> themselves. (p. 82)

Finally, we would assert that, compared to nongang adolescents, the gang member hyperadolescent is substantially more active in the search for adult status. In a sort of continuing pseudoadult declaration, the youth engages in "adolescent drinking, sexual escapades, wild automobile rides, immature assertiveness, violent reactions to parental restraints, protests against authority, and other forms of intransigence which, to the youth at any rate, appear to be the prerogatives of the mature adult" (Bloch & Niederhoffer, 1958, p. 30).

We will provide further examples in support of this theme of hyperadolescence. Particularly important are intensity of group affiliation (examined in chapter 5), exaggerated need for social support (discussed in chapter 6), and heavy reliance on cultural sources of identity formation (explored in the book's coda).

We have in this chapter sought to describe the diverse qualities that capture the American adolescent, the manner in which these same qualities in accentuated form also accurately describe members of delinquent gangs, and the ways in which the concept of gang members as hyperadolescents begins to illuminate the processes of gang formation and gang behavior. In sum, we view this chapter as an initial demonstration of both the relevance and fertility of developmental psychology as a source of insights into the gang phenomenon.

CHAPTER 5

Gangs as Groups

Both the process by which this book has proceeded and its essential goal are extrapolation. We seek to describe and draw upon those major domains of contemporary psychology that may be useful in furthering an understanding of delinquent gangs. Some of this theoretical and research literature has already been applied to such youths. Much, however, remains a potentially highly relevant but as yet largely untapped source of useful extrapolation. Such was the case with regard to developmental psychology's literature on adolescence, discussed in chapter 4. The present chapter will examine social psychology's perspectives on group dynamics: formation, conflict, norm development, cohesiveness, leadership, and much more. Some of these findings and speculations have already been fruitfully drawn upon by gang researchers, and these offerings will be presented. Much of what follows, however, is offered for the first time in this context. These perspectives appear highly relevant to matters of gang formation, gang structure, and gang behavior. We strongly urge that the requisite extrapolatory effort be made. Ultimately, of course, the theoretical and applied value of such an effort will be a function of formal and informal empirical tests.[1]

---

[1] There has been, and to a lesser degree still is, debate in the sociological literature regarding the appropriateness of viewing gangs as merely one type of group (Sherif & Sherif, 1967) or as something quite distinct from groups as usually defined (B. Cohen, 1969). In addition to these polar views, Yablonsky (1959) delineates a continuum anchored by *group* and *mob,* placing *gang* at an intermediate position, calling it a *near-group.* Rafferty and Bertcher (1963) assume a similar perspective. Miller's (1980) distinction between gangs and law-violating youth groups is also relevant in this context, as is Horowitz's (1983) discussion of gangs, groups, and pseudogroups. Although there is much to be learned about gangs, the group dynamics literature appears most relevant to this task. Which aspects of this literature in fact prove relevant, which aspects help professionals better understand and work with gangs, and which aspects eventually lack such value is, in our view, an empirical matter. We would urge open-minded, creative extrapolation—that is, efforts to view (understand, predict, control) the gang phenomenon through the perspective of group dynamics.

DEFINITIONS

What constitutes a group? How has *group* been defined? As Mullen (1987) observes, the major alternative definitions are based on diverse criteria:

1. Social categorization (Reicher, 1982): Two or more people who share a common social identification of themselves, who see themselves as belonging to the same social category

2. Social reward (Bass, 1960): A collection of people who experience their collective existence as reinforcing

3. Interdependence (Fiedler, 1967): Two or more individuals sharing a common fate—that is, experiences that affect one of them have impact on all of them

4. Interaction and influence (M.E. Shaw, 1981): A set of persons who interact with one another in such a way that each influences and is influenced by every other person

Each of these definitional criteria—categorization, reward, interdependence, and interaction and influence—seems fully relevant to the contemporary delinquent gang in the United States.

GROUP PROCESSES

An understanding of the diverse events and processes that constitute the birth and development of many types of groups is enhanced by a framework or schema that meaningfully organizes those events and processes. Tuckman (Tuckman, 1965; Tuckman & Jensen, 1977) has offered just such a framework. His stage formulation seems quite relevant to gangs of all types, though different stages may be more significant for different types of gangs. For example, a report on juvenile gangs from the California Council on Criminal Justice (1989) reveals that delinquent gangs in that state are typically well structured and of long standing. A comparable report by the New York State Division for Youth (1990) shows that gangs in that state tend to be much more loosely organized and of short duration. (See chapter 10 for more on these two reports.) Nevertheless, each type of gang passes through the stages of forming, storming, norming, performing, and sometimes adjourning, though in different ways, in different sequences, and over differing time spans. The general model fits well; its application varies in form, sequence, and duration.

Table 5.1, which depicts Tuckman's model, captures the approximate developmental sequence that characterizes many different types of groups at various age levels, organized for diverse purposes, in several types of settings. In this sequence, a group first organizes and establishes itself. It then begins dealing with potential obstacles to meeting its group goals and solidifies its structure, its "groupness," and the roles and norms that will facilitate goal-related performance. Next it performs its task. Finally, it adjourns.

Table 5.1   Five Stages of Group Development

STAGE	MAJOR PROCESSES	CHARACTERISTICS
Forming	Development of attraction bonds; exchange of information; orientation towards others and situation	Tentative interactions; polite discourse; concern over ambiguity; silences
Storming	Dissatisfaction with others; competition among members; disagreement over procedures; conflict	Ideas are criticized; speakers are interrupted; attendance is poor; hostility
Norming	Development of group structure; increased cohesiveness and harmony; establishment of roles and relationships	Agreement on rules; consensus-seeking; increased supportiveness; we-feeling
Performing	Focus on achievement; high task orientation; emphasis on performance and productivity	Decision making; problem solving; increased cooperation; decreased emotionality
Adjourning	Termination of duties; reduction of dependency; task completion	Regret; increased emotionality, disintegration

Sources. Tuckman (1965); Tuckman and Jensen (1977). From *Group Dynamics,* 2nd Edition by D.R. Forsyth. Copyright ©1990, 1983 by Wadsworth, Inc. Reprinted by permission of Brooks/Cole Publishing Company, Pacific Grove, CA 93950.

Forming

Why do groups form? Why do people need, seek, and appear to benefit from the company of others? An early answer (Edman, 1919; McDougall, 1908) spoke of the "herd instinct," an answer that has more recently reappeared in sociobiological writings about a biologically rooted urge to affiliate (E.O. Wilson, 1975). Like instinctual explanations of other behaviors, however, such specula-tions—however elaborate they may be—are essentially circular and untestable. An explanation of group behavior based on need satisfaction is rather more tenable, especially when the formulation is sufficiently complex to include both need similarity and need complementarity among group members, as well as particular needs and need patterns demonstrated empirically to relate to the quality of the group experience and the quantity of the group product. Schutz's (1967) perspective on interpersonal need as a prime influence on group process fits this description well. His work points to group formation and process as resulting from the members' need to express or receive inclusion (associate, belong, join), control (power, dominance, authority), and affection (cohe-siveness, love, friendship). A related position on group formation as a function of interpersonal need emphasizes the need for affiliation as the central determinant of member behavior (Murray, 1938; Smart, 1965). The social comparisons theory of group formation takes a somewhat more cognitive direction. According to Festinger (1954) and Schachter (1959), people affiliate into dyads or groups when to do so provides useful information derived from comparing oneself, one's attitudes, or one's beliefs with those of others. This basis for group formation is especially attractive, these writers hold, when attitudes or beliefs are shaken and the act of communicating with and comparing oneself to others has potential to restore equanimity and clarity or at least to provide a sense of safety in numbers.

The social exchange view of group formation is rather more "economic-like" in its specifics. According to its main proponents (Thibaut & Kelley, 1959; Kelley & Thibaut, 1978), individuals base their decisions about group affiliation on their estimates of the interpersonal value of group participation. *Value* is defined in terms of both estimated rewards and potential costs. What are the primary rewards and costs of belonging to groups? Rewards may include social support, the group's process, or the group's activities; the benefits of experiencing certain group member characteristics suggestive of likely success at group goals (e.g., authenticity, competence, sociability); and, especially, the group goals themselves. Costs of affiliation may be discomfort with the ambiguous or unfamiliar; the possible required investment of time, energy, self-disclosure, or other resources; possible social rejection; inefficiency or ineffectiveness in progress toward the group's goals; and reactance (i.e., the loss of a sense of freedom, autonomy, or choicefulness as the group exerts pressure on its members to conform, reach consensus, or behave in a synchronous manner).

Starting early in its formation and continuing throughout its life, the group develops a sense of cohesiveness. This central quality of groups has been defined in terms of (a) the attraction members feel toward one another and the group as a unit, (b) member motivation to participate in the group's activities and contribute to its goals, and (c) the coordination of group members' efforts. Cohesiveness has sometimes been measured by questionnaire (e.g., Schachter, Ellertson, McBride, & Gregory, 1951). Among the questions often included in such measures are the following:

1. Do you want to remain a member of this group?

2. How often do you think this group should meet?

3. If it seems this group might discontinue, would you like the chance to persuade members to stay?

More typically, intermember attraction (which emerged as the prime definition of cohesiveness) has been measured by sociometrics, a technique for estimating the social relationships among group members (Moreno, 1960). Members are asked to indicate whom they like most and least, with whom they would most like to work, and so forth. Responses are plotted on a sociogram, which not only reflects the level, spread, and content of intermember attraction but also reveals such cohesiveness-related selections as the group's stars, isolates, pairs, chains, rejections, integration, and so forth.

Cohesiveness has been singled out as primary among the processes characteristic of group development because cohesiveness has been shown to be an especially powerful influence on the character and quality of group interaction as well as a major determinant of the group's longevity and success at reaching its goals. The more cohesive the group, the more likely its members will behave as follows:

1. Be more open to influence by other group members

2. Place greater value on the group's goals

3. Be active participants in group discussion

4. Be more equal participants in group discussion

5. Be less susceptible to disruption as a group when a member terminates membership

6. Be absent less often

7. Remain in the group longer

Cohesiveness is indeed a crucial foundation of group formation and development. It will tend to diminish the more there is disagreement within the group, the more the group makes unreasonable or excessive demands on its members, the more the group leader or other members are overly domineering, the higher the degree of self-oriented behaviors, the more membership limits the satisfactions members can receive outside the group, the more negatively membership is perceived by outsiders, and the more conflict exists within the group.

Cohesiveness in Gangs

There is already a considerable literature on group cohesiveness as it relates to both gang formation and gang behavior. In an effort to understand this literature, it is helpful to remember that gangs (like any other group) can and do differ significantly from one another, both over time and across locations at the same time. Thus, as will be apparent, Thrasher's gangs of 1927 typically differ in several ways—including cohesiveness—from the gangs of today. And, as chapter 10 will show, California gangs clearly tend to be more fully cohesive than are those in New York State. These caveats in place, what is known about gang cohesiveness? Two major issues have been addressed. The first concerns how cohesive gangs are; the second concerns the relationship between gang cohesiveness and delinquent behavior. Klein (1968b) comments with regard to the first issue: "Earlier writers stressed the esprit de corps, face-to-face relations, and general camaraderie to be found in juvenile gangs. More recently, however, gangs . . . are found to be rather loosely structured with varying but generally low cohesiveness" (p. 103).

Klein (1968b) offers several bases for this decline in intermember attraction.[2] They include the very size of many contemporary gangs and their vertical (age-graded) structure—both of which decrease interaction opportunities—and the fact, emphasized in the next paragraph, that many youths are drawn to gang membership less by the positive pull of the gang than by the negative push of their own communities, combined with their individual social disabilities.

Klein and Crawford (1968) draw the valuable distinction between internal and external sources of cohesiveness, providing further explanations for possible diminution in gang cohesiveness. Cohesiveness for many groups, they observe, rests on a within-group foundation of attraction and positive interaction, groupwide goals, membership stability, group norms, and role differentiation. For gangs, however, they assert that such internal sources of cohesiveness are nonexistent or substantially weaker today than are external sources of influence, such as poverty, educational deficits, poor job opportunities, dysfunctional family relations, and the antipathy of adults in the community. These external realities, according to Klein (1968b), help drive youths together via a sense of deprivation and dissatisfaction, and an effort to make the most of an unhappy life situation:

> When a number of boys in a neighborhood withdraw
> from similar sets of environmental frustrations and
> interact with one another enough to recognize, and
> perhaps generate, common attitudes, the group has begun
> to form. Added to threats of rival groups are the many
> ways in which society reinforces this tendency—police
> behavior, teacher reactions, lack of acceptance by adults
> on playgrounds and in local business establishments, and
> so on. (p. 106)

In addition to such external sources of cohesiveness, intermember attraction may be enhanced in gangs, according to Cartwright, Howard, and Reuterman (1970), via selective recruitment, shared neighborhood residence, and diverse pressures for conformity within the group.

The position that cohesiveness in delinquent gangs is often modest or low, perhaps a surprise given the popular writings about gang youths' acting in concert and with esprit, also has implications

---

[2] Cartwright (1975) also correctly observes that, although gangwide cohesiveness may be lower than is popularly believed, there often exist highly cohesive within-gang cliques, especially among core members.

for intervention. These implications will be treated in detail later in the book, but it seems valuable briefly to anticipate part of that discussion with the note that

> because gang cohesiveness is not generally high, by and large gangs do not act as gangs; rather, temporary groups and cliques are normally the functional units of activity beyond the individual level. For control and prevention efforts, this means that "the" gang presents a shifting, elusive target, permeable and elastic, and thus inherently resistant to outside intervention. It presents not a cohesive force but, rather, a spongelike resilience. (Klein & Maxson, 1989, p. 211)

Cohesiveness and Delinquent Behavior

After the issue of the degree of cohesiveness within gangs, the second concern is the relationship between gang cohesiveness and delinquent behavior. Quicker (1983b) asserts that gangs do not need to be cohesive to be delinquent. In fact, he proposes that the more cohesive the gang, the less property and conflict offenses it perpetrates. Tognacci's (1975) understanding of the relevant data is similar. Thrasher (1927/1963) early on suggested otherwise, and Klein (1968b), Lucore (1975), and Spergel et al. (1989) have more recently concurred. Gang cohesiveness and gang delinquency do appear to be positively related, though it must quickly be added that the causal directions of this association are unclear. Does cohesiveness cause delinquency, does delinquency enhance cohesiveness, do both phenomena occur, or is a third variable responsible? There is good reason to suspect that cohesiveness and delinquency reciprocally influence one another. Lucore (1975) agrees but wonders if the relationship may be more complicated, perhaps curvilinear:

> In this discussion about which comes first, the cohesive behavior or the delinquent behavior, it is at least clear that delinquent behavior and cohesive behavior increase and decrease together, whether in response to each other or in response to an outside force. A circular, dependent relationship seems to exist: delinquent behavior increases with more contact among gang members, and gang solidarity also increases with common involvement in delinquent activity. There may be some optimal level of attitudinal gang cohesiveness at which most delinquent

activity occurs. Certainly some minimum level of mutual trust and loyalty is needed to enable the gang to act together. On the other hand, very high levels of attitudinal cohesiveness seem to preclude delinquent action. (p. 96)

Attempts to discern the nature of possible cohesiveness/delinquency relationships will be furthered by efforts to understand how these phenomena might directionally or reciprocally influence each other. In a manner consistent with Tannenbaum's (1938) social labeling theory of delinquency, examined in chapter 3, Klein and Crawford (1968) provide helpful direction for such efforts:

Most gang theorists presently concur that, if offenses are affected by mutual gang membership, it is because the antecedent deviant values, the requisite skills, and the opportunities for misbehavior are learned and reinforced through association with other members. . . . These processes can occur and persist because the external sources of cohesion continually throw the gang members together, forcing the kinds of interactions which are preliminary to increased gang-related offenses. These interactions become secondary sources of cohesion in conjunction with offense behavior, each reinforcing the other as the members mingle and verbalize the deviance which labels them as different. (p. 264)

Cohesiveness appears to be an especially important group dynamic for better understanding why gangs form, why they persist, and what they do while they exist. Further empirical effort is needed to follow the previously discussed leads regarding its sources, levels, and consequences.

Storming

Conflict Within the Group

Groups may experience conflict at any stage in their development. Forsyth (1983) proposes that group conflict characteristically moves through five phases. The first is *disagreement,* in which members discover that two or more of them are in conflict regarding a group task, an interpersonal matter, or some other group-related concern. *Confrontation* is the second phase of a typical group conflict. Here the opposing factions openly debate the issues in contention. This phase is often characterized by attempts to convert or discredit one's opponent; increased or intensified commitment to one's own position; heightened tension among the disputants and within the group at large; and the formation of coalitions as previously neutral group members elect, or are pressured, to choose sides. Flowing from such positional commitment, heightened tension, and polarization within the group, the third conflict phase, *escalation,* may ensue. Forsyth (1983) graphically describes this process:

> Many groups are caught up in a conflict spiral. . . .
> The final remnants of group unity are shattered as the
> combatants' exchanges become increasingly hostile;
> persuasive influence is dropped in favor of coercion,
> promises are replaced by threats, and in extreme cases
> verbal attacks become physically violent assaults. (p. 84)

If the group holds together and weathers the storm of disagreement, confrontation, and escalation, the fourth phase of group conflict, *de-escalation,* may occur. Group members tire of fighting, feel their efforts and energy are being wasted, become increasingly more rational, begin to accept a bit of the other side's perspective, and decide to reinvest their efforts in movement toward the group's original, or now modified, purposes and goals. Finally, the last phase, *resolution,* occurs when the conflict is terminated. Conflict may end via compromise, in which both sides gain some and yield some until an agreement is reached; via withdrawal, in which one side essentially yields for the sake of peace and unity; via imposition, in which by sheer power of numbers or authority one viewpoint is made to prevail; or by conversion, in which the discussion, persuasion, and promises of one side cause the other side to be won over and change its position.

Conflict Between Groups

A second broad class of group-related conflict—conflict between groups—should be considered here as germane to the intergang rumbles of the 1940s and 1950s, as well as to their more lethal modern counterparts. A considerable amount of research and theorizing has been done in this domain, especially concerning conflict associated with intergroup competition. The work of Sherif and his group (Sherif, Harvey, White, Hood, & Sherif, 1961) on conflict between camp groups of adolescents is the classic, initiating research on this topic. It inspired a great deal of subsequent research, focused mainly on the effects of such conflict and on means to reduce it. Intergroup competition increases the level of cohesiveness within groups (Coser, 1956; Sherif & Sherif, 1953), an effect that is particularly pronounced within the group that wins the competition (Dion, 1973; Ryan & Kahn, 1970; Wilson & Miller, 1961). Intergroup competition tends to increase the rejection of the other group's members. Such mutual rejection is heightened or moderated by the degree of similarity between the groups, by whether they anticipate future interaction, and by features of the competitive task itself (Brewer, 1979; Coser, 1956). Intergroup competition serves to establish and maintain boundaries between groups, as reflected in member tendencies to emphasize between-group differences and minimize between-group similarities (Cooper & Fazio, 1979; Coser, 1956). Intergroup competition often leads to significant misperception of the other group's behavior and intentions. The other group may be stereotyped, dehumanized, or seen as immoral or malevolent; one's own group may be overidealized as being moral, overly powerful, or totally right in its views (Linville & Jones, 1980; Oskamp & Hartry, 1968; White, 1970, 1977).

Recently, Tajfel (1981) has offered social categorization theory as an alternative to intergroup competition to explain such intergroup conflict, stereotyping, and overidealization of one's own group. It is not, Tajfel holds, the rivalrous competition per se that produces these outcomes but, instead, the mere fact of feeling oneself part of a group and others part of a different group—that is, social categorization. Tajfel demonstrated systematic in-group preference and out-group bias even when the out-group was a "minimal group" whom members of the in-group never met, with whom they never interacted, and about whom they knew little.

The various negative effects of conflict between groups can be reduced. Contact between the competing groups helps considerably in this regard, especially if (a) the contact is between persons of equal status from each group, (b) the contact is in depth and not superficial, (c) the social climate in which the contact takes place is friendly, (d) the behavior during the contact contradicts previously formed stereotypes, and (e) the contact occurs within a reward structure that reinforces cooperation but not competition (Amir, 1969; Cook, 1972; Foley, 1976; Wilder, 1986). A creative attempt to reduce the level of conflict between gang youths and their "most hated" police officers in Philadelphia incorporated a number of these methods to reduce contact-engendered conflict (H.G. Fox,

1970). Impressionistic evidence, at least, indicates that the project's gang youth–police "live-in" substantially reduced the groups' reciprocal hostility. Between-group hostility and the accompanying negative effects of intergroup competition and/or social categorization are reduced even more reliably when members of the two groups are brought together to deal with tasks or challenges at which each is motivated to succeed but that can't be accomplished by one group alone. The conflict-reducing effect of superordinate goals or common enemies is a finding that psychologists have proposed as useful not only at the level of small-group conflict (Sherif & Sherif, 1953), but also as it might apply to nations in conflict (Lindskold, 1978, 1979; Osgood, 1979).

Norming

As the group deals effectively with potential and emergent instances of intermember conflict, and as intermember attraction and groupwide cohesiveness build, the way becomes clearer for the group to establish its explicit and implicit norms or guidelines, to solidify its choice of leaders and leadership styles, to carve out and begin enacting individual roles for its members, and to settle on patterns of communication that members find comfortable and effective. These group dynamics (norms, leadership, roles, and communication patterns) form the primary concerns of the present section.

Norms

Norms are the overtly stated or covertly assumed rules of action specifying which behaviors are appropriate (prescriptive norms) or are not appropriate (proscriptive norms) for group members. Thus, norms are evaluative standards implying or even directing that some group member behaviors are better or more desirable than others. Norms often come into being less through discussion and overt choice than through gradual use and implicit adoption. They may come to be assumed and taken for granted by group members and may become evident only when they are violated. Normative behavior may be adopted initially from positive feelings of group cohesion; because continuation of membership is desired; or in order to avoid pressure, rejection, or other group sanctions. Eventually, such behavior comes to be internalized or "owned" by group members. Norms are the organizers, shapers, and broad guidelines determining much of what occurs or does not occur in any given group, what the group expects and aspires to achieve, how it allocates its resources, how it will be led, and much more.

An important contributor to norm setting and compliance is the individual's reference group (Hyman & Singer, 1959; Kelley, 1959). This may be a *membership reference group,* composed of persons with whom the individual actually interacts. On the other hand, it may be a group that is not in interaction with the individual but that he or she uses in making judgments and evaluations (a *comparison reference group*). Shibutani (1959) observes:

> A reference group, then, is that group whose outlook is used by the actor as the frame of reference in the organization of his perceptual field. All kinds of groupings, with great variations in size, composition, and structure, may become reference groups. Of greatest importance for most people are those groups in which they participate directly. (p. 107)

The delinquent gang clearly functions as a norm-setting, compliance-demanding, membership reference group. M.E. Shaw (1981) has suggested that both personality and situational factors influence the substance of the norms. Short and Strodtbeck (1965) actually found this duality to underlie the common (Chicago) gang norms of toughness, sharpness, being cool, being a good fighter, being sexually active, and having superior athletic ability. It appears that such norms still largely characterize the standards set and aspired to in the contemporary delinquent gang.

Leadership

The topic of effective leaders and leadership has been a central concern of group dynamics researchers. For decades, through the 1940s, the "Great Man" theory of leadership prevailed. This view essentially held that effective leaders are persons who are born with or have come to possess certain personality traits and who, by dint of those characteristics, can and do lead in a variety of settings and situations. The research task thus became one of leadership-associated trait identification, and, in fact, leaders have been shown to be somewhat more achievement oriented, adaptable, alert, ascendant, energetic, responsible, self-confident, and sociable than other group members (Bass, 1981; Forsyth, 1983; C.A. Gibb, 1969). Over time, however, the correlations between these traits and effective leadership behavior proved modest. Although such traits certainly contribute to the success of leadership attempts, their importance is eclipsed by the potency of the group situation itself. Carron (1980) comments with regard to this more modern, situational view of leader effectiveness:

> It is now generally accepted that there are no inherent traits or dispositions within an individual which contribute to ascendancy and maintenance of leadership [across diverse situations]. Instead, it is believed that the specific requirements of different situations dictate the particular leadership qualities which will be most effective. (pp. 126–127)

Such situational thinking about leadership led to two research tasks. The first was the identification of specific behaviors, not traits, characteristic of acts of leadership. The second was the prescriptive determination of which leader behaviors were optimal for which group members in which situations. Successful leadership, in this perspective, becomes a matter of matching leader behaviors with situations appropriate (members, tasks, goals, settings) for their use. The Ohio State Leadership Studies (Hemphill & Coons, 1957) identified the following behaviors as constituting what leaders actually do: initiation, membership, representation, integration, organization, domination, communication, recognition, and production. As is consistent with the situational view of effective leadership, Chelladurai and Saleh (1978) applied the Ohio State results to coaching behavior in athletic contexts. Table 5.2 indicates how optimal leader behavior is held to vary by task demand.

Though their categories of leadership behavior vary somewhat, both studies yield two broad classes of effective leadership behavior—those that are task oriented and focus on performance and group goals, and those that are relationship oriented and hence more concerned with enhancing group cohesiveness and reducing group conflict. This view of group leadership behavior as consisting of two broad dimensions—task orientation and relationship orientation—has become quite popular in group dynamics theory and research, taking the diverse expressions reflected in Table 5.3.

As the situational view of effective leadership proposes, research demonstrates that neither a task nor a relationship orientation is uniformly optimal. With some groups, under some circumstances, and when working toward certain goals, a task focus

Table 5.2   Leader Behavior Dimensions in Sport

DIMENSION	DESCRIPTION
Training behavior	Behavior aimed at improving the performance level of the athletes by emphasizing and facilitating hard and strenuous training, clarifying the relationships among the members
Autocratic behavior	Tendency of the coach to set himself (herself) apart from the athletes, and to make all decisions by himself (herself)
Democratic behavior	Behavior of the coach that allows greater participation by the athletes in deciding on group goals, practice methods, and game tactics and strategies
Social support behavior	Behavior of the coach indicating his (her) concern for individual athletes and their welfare and for positive group atmosphere
Rewarding behavior	Behavior of the coach that provides reinforcement for an athlete by recognizing and rewarding good performance

Note. From "Preferred Leadership in Sport" by P. Chelladurai and S.D. Saleh, 1978, *Canadian Journal of Applied Sport Sciences, 3,* p. 91. Copyright 1978 by the *Canadian Journal of Applied Sport Sciences.* Reprinted by permission.

on work, production, performance, and solutions is appropriate. For other situations, support, relationships, conflict reduction, and similar emphases are appropriate. Not surprisingly, there appear to be many group situations in which the most effective leadership behaviors reflect a balanced combination of task and relationship orientations.

Other systems for categorizing leadership behavior exist. Lewin's research team (Lewin, Lippitt, & White, 1939; White & Lippitt, 1968) early on offered the dimensions of authoritarian, democratic, and laissez-faire leadership. Vroom and Yetton (1973) more recently suggested autocratic, consultative, and group leadership behavioral patterns. What is noteworthy about these and other leadership category systems is their uniformity in agreeing that, whatever the system, one must first take account of the "attributes of the group situation to consider in judging which type of leadership to use" (Forsyth, 1983, p. 235).

Table 5.3 The Two Basic Dimensions of Leadership Behavior

LEADERSHIP DIMENSIONS	ALTERNATIVE LABELS	CONCEPTUAL MEANING	SAMPLE BEHAVIORS
Consideration	**Relationship orientation** Socioemotional Supportive Employee centered Relations skilled Group maintenance	Degree to which the leader responds to group members in a warm and friendly fashion; involves mutual trust, openness, and willingness to explain decisions.	Listens to group members Easy to understand Is friendly and approachable Treats group members as equals Is willing to make changes
Initiating structure	**Task orientation** Goal oriented Work facilitative Production centered Administratively skilled Goal achiever	Extent to which leader organizes, directs, and defines the group's structure and goals; regulates group behavior, monitors communication, and reduces goal ambiguity.	Assigns tasks to members Makes attitudes clear to the group Is critical of poor work Sees to it that the group is working to capacity Coordinates activity

Sources. Halpin and Winer (1952); Lord (1977). From *Group Dynamics,* 2nd Edition by D.R. Forsyth. Copyright © 1990,1983 by Wadsworth, Inc. Reprinted by permission of Brooks/Cole Publishing Company, Pacific Grove, CA 93950.

Before sharing a sense of what the gang literature indicates regarding gang leadership, in a manner consistent with the extrapolatory spirit and intent of this book, we offer the following description by Ausbel (1974) regarding characteristics of adolescent leaders in general.

> Although the characteristics of effective leaders vary depending on the requirements of the specific subculture, peer group, and situation, certain traits obviously have more leadership value than others in the majority of adolescent peer group situations within the general framework of the American culture. Research findings agree that the adolescent leader surpasses the nonleader in five broad areas of personality that are self-evidently related to leadership functions: (a) physical appearance: height, weight, strength, athletic prowess; (b) intelligence; (c) decision-making ability: discriminating judgment, firmness of decision, low suggestibility, self-confidence, and imagination; (d) interests: maturity and breadth of interests; (e) socially relevant aspects of temperament: extroversion, dominance, liveliness, and good sportsmanship. (p. 372)

The confluence of Ausbel's observations regarding nongang youth leadership with observations of gang leadership to be discussed shortly underscores the unity of the phenomena we are considering here. Thrasher (1927/1963) echoes Ausbel as he lists the qualities of the gang leader of yesteryear: gameness, quickness, clear thinking, firmness of decision. The modern gang may still have a formal leadership position (variously known as leader, president, king, prince, prime minister, general, ambassador, don, chief; Spergel et al., 1989) or a leadership clique (Reuterman, 1975). However, in keeping with the contemporary situational view of group leadership, it is more likely to have a cluster of leadership functions fulfilled at different times by different gang members. Klein (1971) asserts:

> One cannot come to grips with a gang by dealing with the leader but only by dealing with leadership as a distributed and often shifting phenomenon. Leadership cannot be considered merely as a personal quality of an individual because it is also a product of group interaction and a response to the context in which the group finds itself. (p. 77)

Perhaps this shifting leadership explains why there is often failure of police gangbusting efforts to apprehend, arrest, and incarcerate a gang's apparent leadership.

What else is known about gang leadership, besides its joint roots in personality and situation and its shifting occupancy? It is often hesitant leadership (Klein, 1971) or cautious leadership (Quicker, 1983b), as it requires that status be put on the line and tested. It is often tenuous leadership (Tognacci, 1975) resting "on the leader's ability to [continually] provide interesting activities, and his ability to [continually] demonstrate his superiority in the gang's status hierarchy" (p. 108). And, closely related to this last quality, Quicker (1983b) reports that gang leaders who persist over time clearly tend toward aggressiveness and the selective use of such behavior.

Roles

The role of leader is but one of many that are assumed by group members. As is the case for the leader, the way in which an individual in the group behaves at a given time is partly a matter of that individual's dispositions or traits, but it is even more a result of the situational demands and opportunities within the group. Such situational determinants of members' roles include the leader's behavior, the behavior of other group members, the group's cohesiveness level, group tasks, group communication patterns, group goals, and other salient group characteristics. As it has for the role of leader, group dynamics thinking has gravitated toward categorizing member behavior in terms of task-oriented roles and relationship-oriented (socioemotional) roles (see Table 5.4). Kelling (1975) suggests that this task-versus-relationship role pattern may also characterize member behavior in juvenile gangs. Other gang member roles—varying with gang size, structure, goals, and the like— include warlord, war counselor, armorer, spokesman, peacemaker, jester, leader, lieutenant, checker, and runner (B. Cohen, 1969; Illinois State Police, 1989; Kelling, 1975).

Communication Patterns

A final aspect of the norm-setting process occurring in groups is the establishment and maintenance of viable communication patterns or networks through which the group will conduct its task- and relationship-oriented business. The communication network(s) reflect many qualities of the group but especially its preferred leadership style and the nature of its goals.

Table 5.4 Task Roles and Socioemotional Roles in Groups

ROLE	FUNCTION
Task roles	
1. Initiator-contributor	Recommends novel ideas about the problem at hand, new ways to approach the problem, or possible solutions not yet considered.
2. Information seeker	Emphasizes "getting the facts" by calling for background information from others.
3. Opinion seeker	Asks for more qualitative types of data, such as attitudes, values, and feelings.
4. Information giver	Provides data for forming decisions, including facts that derive from expertise.
5. Opinion giver	Provides opinions, values, and feelings.
6. Elaborator	Gives additional information—examples, rephrasing, implications—about points made by others.
7. Coordinator	Shows the relevance of each idea and its relationship to the overall problem.
8. Orienter	Refocuses discussion on the topic whenever necessary.
9. Evaluator-critic	Appraises the quality of the group's efforts in terms of logic, practicality, or method.
10. Energizer	Stimulates the group to continue working when discussion flags.
11. Procedural technician	Cares for operational details, such as the materials, machinery, and so on.
12. Recorder	Provides a secretarial function.

Table 5.4 (cont'd)

ROLE	FUNCTION
Socioemotional roles	
1. Encourager	Rewards others through agreement, warmth, and praise.
2. Harmonizer	Mediates conflicts among group members.
3. Compromiser	Shifts his or her own position on an issue in order to reduce conflict in the group.
4. Gatekeeper and expediter	Smooths communication by setting up procedures and ensuring equal participation from members.
5. Standard setter	Expresses, or calls for discussion of, standards for evaluating the quality of the group process.
6. Group observer and commentator	Informally points out the positive and negative aspects of the group's dynamics and calls for change if necessary.
7. Follower	Accepts the ideas offered by others and serves as an audience for the group.

Note. From "Functional Roles of Group Members" by K.D. Benne and P. Sheats, 1948, *Journal of Social Issues, 4,* p. 46. Copyright 1948 by the Society for the Psychological Study of Social Issues. Reprinted by permission.

Figure 5.1 depicts three of the more common group communication patterns. Each letter in these networks represents a different group member, and each line represents a two-person communication linkage. Marked variability exists among these networks in the degree to which members are free to communicate with one another. Group member B, for example, is free to communicate with all other group members in the Comcon (or All-Channel) network, with two other members (A and C) in the Circle network, and with only one member (C) in the Wheel network. Differences also exist in member centrality—that is, the number of linkages tied to members and the number of linkages (distance) from a member to each other member. In the Wheel network, member C is most central. Within the other two networks, all members are equally central or peripheral. Studies demonstrate that, in centralized networks like the Wheel, central position members (leader, teacher, boss) are more satisfied than are peripheral members. Most people, in fact, tend to prefer one or another decentralized network because it permits, and may even encourage, independence of action, autonomy, and self-direction (M.E. Shaw, 1964). Centralized networks organize more rapidly, are more stable in performance, and are most efficient for the performance of simple tasks. However, as task complexity grows, the decentralized networks prove superior (M.E. Shaw, 1964). This finding is one more example of the need to vary a group characteristic depending on the situation—in this instance, the group's task.

**Figure 5.1   Communication Networks Relevant to Group
Therapy Leadership**

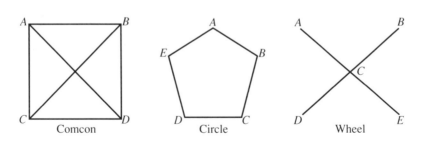

Note. From *Psychotherapy and the Psychology of Behavior Change* (p. 383) by A.P. Goldstein, K. Heller, and L.B. Sechrest, 1966, New York: Wiley.

Performing

The tasks facing youngsters in their peer, family, school, and other groups are numerous and varied. As such groups develop, deal with conflict, and establish participation norms and roles, they concomitantly seek to perform the tasks that motivated the group's formation in the first place. This section will present the approaches group dynamicists have taken to categorize group tasks, examine means that have been identified for improving group performance on such tasks, and consider the implications for member performance of the use of power to wield influence. Concluding the section, a discussion of such collective behaviors as deindividuation and groupthink will enhance understanding of the performance behavior of individuals in groups characterized by high pressure to conform.

Group Tasks

Forsyth (1983) points out that a group's specific tasks depend, in the first place, on the group's ultimate goals. Is the group organized to make decisions, solve problems, generate ideas, learn facts, create products? Tasks to be performed, according to M.E. Shaw (1981), are also determined by (a) the difficulty of the group's overall problem, (b) the number of acceptable solutions, (c) the intrinsic interest level of the task, (d) the amount of cooperation required of group members for successful task performance, (e) the intellectual and related demands presented, and (f) the members' familiarity with task components. Steiner (1972, 1976) has proposed a system for classifying tasks (see Table 5.5) based on task divisibility, the type of performance desired, and the manner in which group member inputs contribute to group goals.

How well will the group perform its designated tasks? In part, the answer depends on task characteristics. On additive tasks, for example, it has been shown that the larger the group, the lower the quantity or quality of each individual's contribution to task performance. This so-called *Ringelmann effect* (Forsyth, 1983) has been attributed by Latane, Williams, and Harkins (1979) to "coordination losses" (e.g., pulling on a tug-of-war rope at different times) and "social loafing" (i.e., working less hard when one's own contribution to task performance will remain unknown by other group members). Conjunctive group tasks, as a second example, pose a different performance problem. Here, because all group members must contribute to task performance, the group as a whole performs at the level of its weakest member. As Forsyth (1983) notes, the speed of a group of mountain climbers, a truck convoy, or a funeral procession is determined by its slowest member. However, conjunctive task performance can be improved if the task is divided and the weakest members assigned the least difficult subtasks.

Task performance is affected substantially by the group's task-relevant communication patterns. Deutsch and Krauss (1960), Harper and Askling (1980), Katz and Tushman (1979), and numerous other investigators have shown that, in comparison to unsuccessful groups, successful groups have a significantly higher rate and accuracy of communication. Task performance, by contrast, may be impeded when the group's climate and associated communication patterns become defensive. Forsyth (1983) comments:

> Whenever members of a group feel personally threatened, they begin to behave defensively. Effort is shifted from the group tasks to defensive tactics, and individual efficiency drops as concern over evaluations, worry about others' intentions, counterattack planning, and defensive listening escalate. (p. 163)

J.R. Gibb (1961, 1973) proposes a number of ways in which groups engender such defensive, task-impeding communication and also highlights the features of a more supportive, communication-encouraging group climate (see Table 5.6).

Power

Thus far, it has been shown that performance in groups is significantly influenced by the nature of the group's tasks, as well as by the rate and accuracy of members' task-related communication. However, task performance in group contexts is also a function of the relative power bases, levels, and tactics utilized by group leaders and group members. *Power* has been diversely defined as "control or influence over the actions of others to promote one's goals without their consent, against their will, or without their knowledge or understanding" (Buckley, 1967, p. 186); "the capacity to produce intended and foreseen effects on others" (Wrong, 1979, p. 21); and "the interaction between two parties, the powerholder and the target person, in which the target person's behavior is given new direction by the powerholder" (Kipnis, 1974, p. 9). French and Raven (1959) have proposed that an individual's power in a group may derive from one or more of several sources (see Table 5.7). As is consistent with the situational view of group leadership presented

Table 5.5 A Summary of Steiner's Typology of Tasks

QUESTION	ANSWER	TASK TYPE	EXAMPLES
Can the task be broken down into subcomponents or is division of the task inappropriate?	Subtasks can be identified	Divisible	Playing a football game, building a house, preparing a six-course meal
	No subtasks exist	Unitary	Pulling on a rope, reading a book, solving a math problem
Which is more important: quantity produced or quality of performance?	Quantity	Maximizing	Generating many ideas, lifting the greatest weight, scoring the most runs
	Quality	Optimizing	Generating the best idea, getting the right answer, solving a math problem
How are individual inputs related to the group's product?	Individual inputs are added together	Additive	Pulling a rope, stuffing shoveling snow
	Group product is average of individual judgments	Compensatory	Averaging individuals' estimates of the number of beans in a jar, weight of an object, room temperature

Group selects the product from pool of individual members' judgments	Disjunctive	Questions involving "yes-no, either-or" answers such as math problems, puzzles, and choices between options
All group members must contribute to the product	Conjunctive	Climbing a mountain, eating a meal, relay races, soldiers marching in file
Group can decide how individual inputs relate to group	Discretionary	Deciding to shovel snow together, opting to vote on the best answer to a math problem, letting leader answer question

Sources. Steiner (1972, 1976). From *Group Dynamics*, 2nd Edition by D.R. Forsyth. Copyright © 1990, 1983 by Wadsworth, Inc. Reprinted by permission of Brooks/Cole Publishing Company, Pacific Grove, CA 93950.

Table 5.6 Characteristics of Defensive and Supportive Group Climates

CHARACTERISTIC	DEFENSIVE CLIMATE	SUPPORTIVE CLIMATE
1. Evaluation versus description	1. People in the group seem to be judging your actions.	1. People in the group are seen as trying to describe outcomes and information.
2. Control versus problem oriented	2. Others are seen as manipulative, attempting influence.	2. Others seem to be focused on the problem at hand.
3. Strategy versus spontaneity	3. Members seem to plan out their "moves," interactions, and comments.	3. Interaction seems to flow smoothly with little strategic control.
4. Neutrality versus empathy	4. People in the group seem to react to you with aloofness and disinterest.	4. People in the group seem to identify with your ideas and interests.
5. Superiority versus equality	5. Others seem condescending, acting as if they are better than you are.	5. Group members treat one another as equals.
6. Certainty versus provisionalism	6. Some people in the group seem to feel that their own ideas are undoubtedly correct.	6. People in the group are not committed to any one viewpoint, for they are keeping an open mind.

Sources: J.R. Gibb (1961, 1973). From *Group Dynamics*, 2nd Edition by D.R. Forsyth. Copyright © 1990, 1983 by Wadsworth, Inc. Reprinted by permission of Brooks/Cole Publishing Company, Pacific Grove, CA 93950.

Table 5.7   **Five Bases of Power**

LABEL	DEFINITION
1. Reward power	The powerholder's control over the positive and negative reinforcements desired by the target person.
2. Coercive power	The powerholder's ability to threaten and punish the target person.
3. Legitimate power	Power that stems from the target person's belief that the powerholder has a justifiable right to require and demand the performance of certain behaviors.
4. Referent power	Power that derives from the target person's identification with, attraction to, or respect for the powerholder.
5. Expert power	Power that exists when the target person believes that the powerholder possesses superior skills and abilities.

Note. From "The Five Bases of Power" by J.R.P. French, Jr., and B. Raven. In *Studies in Social Power* (p. 160) edited by D. Cartwright, 1959, Ann Arbor, MI: The University of Michigan, Institute for Social Research. Copyright 1959 by the Institute for Social Research. Reprinted by permission.

earlier in this chapter, the effects and effectiveness of the five alternative bases for leader or member power or influence, as well as the effectiveness of the tactic(s) employed to express it (see Table 5.8), are very much a function of characteristics of the particular group. Group cohesiveness; the manner in which the group's leader has been selected, elected, or imposed; the group's size; and the group's task and any associated deadlines are among the group qualities determining the impact of diversely based expressed power.

Falbo (1977) has shown that the power tactics described in Table 5.8 vary on two dimensions: rationality and directness. Bargaining, compromise, and persuasion are rational means for exerting influence on task performance; evasion, threat, and deceit are nonrational means. Threat, persistence, and fait accompli are direct power tactics; hinting and thought manipulation are more indirect. Research has shown that group leaders and members who

Table 5.8 Examples and Definitions of Sixteen Power Tactics

STRATEGY	DEFINITION	EXAMPLE
Reason	Any statement about using reason or rational argument to influence others.	I argue logically. I tell all the reasons why my plan is best.
Expertise	Claiming to have superior knowledge or skills.	I tell them I have a lot of experience with such matters.
Compromise	Both agent and target give up part of their desired goals in order to obtain some of them.	More often than not we come to some sort of compromise, if there is a disagreement.
Bargaining	Explicit statement about reciprocating favors and making other two-way exchanges.	I tell her that I'll do something for her if she'll do something for me.
Persuasion	Simple statements about using persuasion, convincing, or coaxing.	I get my way by convincing others that my way is best.
Simple statement	Without supporting evidence or threats, a matter-of-fact statement of one's desires.	I simply tell him what I want.
Persistence	Continuing in one's influence attempts or repeating one's point.	I reiterate my point. I keep going despite all obstacles.
Assertion	Forcefully asserting one's way.	I voice my wishes loudly.

Thought manipulation	Making the target think that the agent's way is the target's own idea.	I usually try to get my way by making the other person feel that it is his idea.
Fait accompli	Openly doing what one wants without avoiding the target.	I do what I want anyway.
Hinting	Not openly stating what one wants; indirect attempts at influencing others.	I drop hints. I subtly bring up a point.
Emotion-target	Agent attempts to alter emotions of target.	I try to put him in a good mood.
Threat	Stating that negative consequences will occur if the agent's plan is not accepted.	I'll tell him I will never speak to him again if he doesn't do what I want.
Deceit	Attempts to fool the target into agreeing by the use of flattering or lies.	I get my way by doing a good amount of fast talking and sometimes by telling some white lies.
Emotion-agent	Agent alters own facial expression.	I put on a sweet face. I try to look sincere.
Evasion	Doing what one wants by avoiding the person who would disapprove.	I got to read novels at work as long as the boss never saw me doing it.

Note. From "The Multidimensional Scaling of Power Strategies" by T. Falbo, 1977, *Journal of Personality and Social Psychology, 35,* p. 540. Copyright 1977 by the *Journal of Personality and Social Psychology.* Reprinted by permission.

are especially concerned with being accepted and liked by their fellow members rely more on rational and indirect influence tactics than on nonrational and direct means. In contrast, nonrational and indirect tactics are the power methods of choice for manipulative group leaders and members.

The foregoing discussion suggests how power holders in groups seek to influence other group members. But what are the effects of holding power on the power holders themselves? First of all, researchers have found that, in experimental groups, people with power clearly tend to use it (Deutsch, 1973; Kipnis & Consentino, 1969). If successful in its use, they often feel self-satisfaction, overestimate their interpersonal influence, and assign themselves unrealistically positive self-evaluations (Kipnis, 1974; Raven & Kruglanski, 1970). They may assume that they themselves are the major determinant of other people's behavior (Kipnis, Castell, Gergen, & Mauch, 1976), devalue those toward whom the influence attempt was directed (Zander, Cohen, & Stotland, 1959), and in other ways distance from and derogate the targets of their power tactics (Sampson, 1965; Strickland, 1958). Powerful members of groups, in addition, tend to protect the sources of their influence (Lawler & Thompson, 1979) and seek to expand upon it (McClelland, 1975).

Deindividuation and Groupthink

Deindividuation is the process of losing one's sense of individuality or separateness from others and becoming submerged in a group. A mob in a riot situation, an aroused audience at an athletic event or a rock concert, a congregation at an emotional religious meeting, those listening to an impassioned speaker at a political rally, and the crowd assembled at a hostage event or watching a potential suicide unfold are all examples of large groups in which one can psychologically lose oneself and one's sense of self in the collective experience. Some have tried to explain this phenomenon in terms of "the convergence of people with compatible needs, desires, motivations, and emotions" (Forsyth, 1983, p. 311). In the last century, LeBon (1895) held otherwise and asserted that deindividuated behavior in crowds and mobs was due to a process of contagion. He observed that riotous behavior, not unlike the spread of a physical disease, began at one point in the larger group and then involuntarily spread throughout it. Yet a third perspective seeking to explain deindividuation is the emergent-norm theory (Turner & Killian, 1972), in which a variety of group phenomena combine to foster the emergence of an array of arousal-associated and often antisocial behaviors. Forsyth (1983) correctly points out that all three explanations may fit a given instance of deindividuated collective behavior:

> The three perspectives on collective behavior—
> convergence, contagion, and emergent-norm theory—are
> in no sense incompatible with one another. . . . For
> example, consider the behavior of baiting crowds—
> groups of people who urge on a person threatening to
> jump from a building, bridge, or tower. . . . Applying the
> three theories, the convergence approach suggests that
> only a certain "type" of person would be likely to bait
> the victim to leap to his or her death. Those shouts
> could then spread to other bystanders through a process
> of contagion until the onlookers were infected by a norm
> of callousness and cynicism. (p. 315)

What is known about the deindividuation process? Zimbardo (1969) has described the conditions that promote it, the cognitive states that reflect it, and the overt behaviors that characterize it (see Table 5.9). Substantial research evidence supports Zimbardo's observations regarding the causes, concomitants, and behavioral consequences of deindividuation (Diener, 1976; Prentice-Dunn & Rogers, 1980; Singer, Brush, & Lublin, 1965; Zillman, Bryant, Cantor, & Day, 1975; Zimbardo, 1969).

A different, if related, influence of the group on individual member behavior has been termed *groupthink*. Forsyth (1983) defines this influence as

> a strong concurrence-seeking tendency that interferes
> with effective decision making. . . . At the core of the
> process is the tendency for group members to strive for
> solidarity and cohesiveness to such an extent that they
> carefully avoid any questions or topics that could lead to
> disputes. If members anticipate arguments over an issue,
> they never raise it. If they are unable to answer a
> question, they never ask it. If they can find shortcuts and
> reach simplistic solutions, they take them. Thus, as a
> result of an irrational emphasis on maintaining
> unanimity and cohesiveness, the group's decisions are
> ill-considered, impractical, and unrealistic. (p. 341)

Table 5.9   The Process of Deindividuation

CONDITIONS OF DEINDIVIDUATION	THE STATE OF DEINDIVIDUATION	DEINDIVIDUATED BEHAVIORS
1. Anonymity	Loss of self-awareness ↓ Loss of self-regulation	Behavior is emotional, impulsive, irrational, regressive, with high intensity
2. Responsibility		
3. Group membership	1. Low self-monitoring	1. Not under stimulus control
4. Arousal	2. Failure to consider relevant norms	
5. Others (sensory overload, novel situations, drug usage, altered states of consciousness, and so on)	3. Little use of self-generated reinforcements	2. Counternormative 3. Pleasurable
	4. Failure to formulate long-range plans	

Note. From "The Human Choice" by P.G. Zimbardo. In 1969 *Nebraska Symposium on Motivation* (p. 293) edited by W.J. Arnold and D. Levine. Copyright © 1970 by the University of Nebraska Press. Adapted by permission.

Groupthink is not an uncommon phenomenon. It surfaces to varying degrees in groups that are highly cohesive, insulated, headed by powerful leaders, and under pressure to make important decisions (Janis, 1972, 1979). Gangs, certain committees, policy-making groups, industrial planning teams, and adolescent peer groups are concrete examples of potential groupthink settings.

Groupthink is more likely to occur when two sets of conditions are operating. The first is premature concurrence seeking or excessive in-group pressure early in the group's decision-making deliberations. Premature concurrence seeking occurs if certain factors exist: (a) high pressure to conform with norms that support compliance and rule out disagreement; (b) self-censorship of dissenting ideas; (c) "mindguards" that divert controversial information away from group consideration by "losing it, forgetting to mention it, or deeming it irrelevant and thus unworthy of the group's attentions" (Forsyth, 1983, p. 345); and (d) apparent unanimity, in which group members focus on their areas of agreement and deemphasize divergencies. The second set of conditions promoting groupthink involves illusions and misperceptions. These include illusions of invulnerability and morality, biased perceptions of the out-group, and collective rationalizing (Forsyth, 1983; Janis, 1972).

Correspondingly, groupthink can be reduced or eliminated by steps that limit premature concurrence seeking and that correct illusions and misperceptions. A leader can thwart premature concurrence seeking by promoting open inquiry and welcoming new ideas and perspectives; by moderating the directiveness of his or her behavior; and by (a) not stating his or her own beliefs until late in the group's discussion, (b) requesting that all pros and cons of an issue be presented and explored, (c) rewarding criticism and dissent, and (d) arranging for the group to meet without its leader on a number of occasions. Errors in perception can be corrected if (a) members acknowledge their own lack of knowledge on given topics and seek expert consultation, (b) an effort is made to understand the out-group's views and feelings, and (c) "second chance" meetings are held after the group reaches a tentative decision so that residual doubts and questions can be raised and considered. Janis (1972) provides an interesting case study of the causes, development, and reduction of groupthink as it occurred with President Kennedy and his panel of advisors at the time of the Cuban Bay of Pigs invasion.

Groupthink, deindividuation, contagion, and related phenomena have long been observed to characterize the collective behavior of delinquent gangs. As early as 1927, Thrasher wrote of the gang's "mental unity":

> The gang, as an intimate primary group, develops an excellent basis for control through rapport. Life together over a more or less extended period results in a common social heritage shared by every member of the group. Common experience of an intimate and often intense nature prepares the way for close sympathy—for mutual interpretation of subtle signs indicating changes in sentiment or attitude. Collective representation embodied in signs, symbols, secret grips and words, and the argot of the group, all promote mutual responsiveness in the more subtle forms of communication. The consensus of habits, sentiments, and attitudes becomes so thoroughly unified in some of these cases that individual differences seem swallowed up. (Thrasher, 1927/1963, pp. 209–210)

One important implication of groupthink, demonstrated in research and likely of considerable relevance to gang functioning, is the *risky shift phenomenon.* This is the tendency for groups to make decisions that are riskier than is compatible with the average of the individual members' preferences (Pruitt, 1971; Wallach, Kogan, & Bem, 1962). It is not a substantial leap to wonder if some of the aggressive, dangerous, and flamboyant behaviors characterizing much of what delinquent gangs do are examples of the risky shift. Mulvihill et al. (1969) concur in this speculation:

> The gang inadvertently leads to violence because of a "shared misunderstanding" that leads each member to assume that peer norms call for greater involvement than he himself would undertake. Combined with status anxiety that prevents members from testing the limits of the presumed group norms for fear of seeming "chicken," this may result in commitment to mutually undesired activities. As Spergel has described it, a dozen youngsters suddenly find themselves walking down the street to a fight, and eight or ten or even all of them, individually, may be wondering why he is there. (p. 1443)

Adjourning

The short-term, task-oriented, problem-solving groups that are the subject of most of the theory and research discussed here have established themselves, dealt with areas of conflict, developed norms governing leader behavior and member roles, performed their tasks, and therefore reached their goals. Longer term groups, such as delinquent gangs, follow a parallel but extended sequence. They form, storm, norm, perform, and, in the end, also adjourn. Some gangs—the loosely structured, pick-up types—adjourn in days. With the multigenerational, multilayered, vertical gang, adjournment may not occur for decades. A gang may adjourn via police gangbusting activity (not infrequently followed by re-formation in prison); via voluntary dissolution in order to re-form in another grouping or merge into a "nation," "ring," or "supergang"; or as individual members gradually drift away, move away, marry out, or age out. In the contemporary United States, the adjournment process, it should be noted, is frequently delayed considerably by the attractiveness of opportunities in the illegal economy vis-à-vis the relative paucity of job opportunities for many gang youths in the legitimate economy. Thus, today, it is not uncommon to find members of juvenile gangs (veteranos, seniors) who are in their 20s and 30s, an unusual situation in the relatively recent past.

This chapter has offered a broad picture of the group dynamics theory and research literature and, where appropriate, has drawn on this literature for its apparent gang-related implications. There is more—for example, social comparison theory (Goethals & Darley, 1987), group syntality theory (Cattell, 1948), self-presentation theory (Baumeister & Hutton, 1987), self-categorization theory (Turner, 1987), social identity theory (Tajfel & Turner, 1986), and the path-goal (R.J. House, 1971) and normative decision (Vroom & Yetton, 1973) theories of leadership behavior. These and other contributions in the areas of group dynamics are sources yet to be mined for valuable information and perspectives that can aid in the difficult and continuing task of understanding delinquent gang behavior, reducing its occurrence, and ameliorating its consequences.

CHAPTER 6

Gangs as Communities

Q. What does being in a gang mean to you?

A. Being in a gang to me means if I didn't have no family, I'd think that's where I'll be. If I didn't have no job, that's where I'd be. To me it's like community help without all the community. They understand better than my mother and father. It's just like a community group, but it's together you know. You don't see it but it's there. (Hagedorn & Macon, 1988, p. 126)

Gangs are adolescents, gangs are groups, and gangs are communities also. The two preceding chapters have drawn on developmental psychology and social psychology; this chapter will make extrapolations from a hierarchy of constructs central to community psychology—namely, community, neighborhood, social network, and social support.

A community consists of one or more psychological and physical neighborhoods; it may function as a social network and serve as the locus for both the giving and receiving of social support. It will be helpful to examine these four constructs—their definitions, concretizations, antecedents, and consequences—and to share findings and speculations bearing on their utility for better understanding the contemporary delinquent gang. It appears that many gangs, in a psychological sense, *are* communities, derive from neighborhood influences, function as social networks, and do active commerce in the provision and receipt of social support.

COMMUNITY

Definitions

First by sociology, and more recently community psychology, the construct of *community* has received an array of diverse, if overlapping, definitions. Early offerings were especially varied. Hillery (1955) was able to locate 94 such definitions. Although most

113

agreed that "community consists of persons in social interaction within a geographic area and having one or more additional common ties" (Hillery, 1955, p. 111), some emphasized self-sufficiency, some common life, others a population's conscious awareness of its own homogeneity, and still others the possession of common norms, means, and ends. Following is a small sampling of these early sociological definitions of community. According to Hill and Whiting (1950), it is "an organization of interconnected culture bearers" (p. 17). MacIver and Page (1949) wrote, "Wherever the members of any group, small or large, live together in such a way that they share, not this or that particular interest, but the basic conditions of a common life, we call that group a community" (p. 6). Nelson (1948) defined community as "a group of people inhabiting a limited area, who have a sense of belonging together and who through their organized relationships share and carry on activities in pursuit of their common interests" (p. 113).

R.L. Warren (1963) helped frame community in a more explicitly psychological manner:

> The term "community" implies something both psychological and geographical. Psychologically, it implies shared interests, characteristics, or association, as in the expression "community of interest". . . . Geographically, it denotes a specific area where people are clustered. (p. 6)

> Its reality exists only in its constituting a social entity, only in the behaviors and attitudes which its members share, only in the patterns of their interaction. (p. 8)

Warren asserted that communities, in addition to their possible economic roles, served a number of psychological functions:

1. Socialization: the transmission of prevailing knowledge, social values, and behavior patterns to the individual members of the community

2. Social control: the process through which a group influences the behavior of its members toward conformity to its norms

3. Social participation: the provision of opportunity for often diverse arenas of social interaction

4. Mutual support: the provision of psychological assistance, exchange of labor, tangible aid, or other means of support

By 1972, the psychological thrust appeared even more central to the definition of community. In a book perhaps paradoxically titled *The Sociology of Community,* Bernard (1972) suggests that community "is characterized not so much by locale as by a high degree of personal intimacy, emotional depth, moral commitment, social cohesion, and continuity in time" (p. 37). This psychological thrust has continued in parallel with the birth and development of community psychology as an organized discipline. For example, there is Sarason's (1974) specific notion of a psychological sense of community,

> the sense that one was part of a readily available, mutually supportive network of relationships upon which one could depend and as a result of which one did not experience sustained feelings of loneliness. . . . It is not merely a matter of how many people one knows, or how many close friends one has, or even the number of loved ones. . . . [I]f they are not part of the structure of one's everyday living, if they are not available to one in a "give and get" way, they can have little effect on one's immediate or daily sense of community. (p. 1)

Stronger yet is Bender's (1978) assertion:

> Community is best defined as a network of social relations marked by mutuality and emotional bonds. . . . Relationships are close, often intimate, and usually face to face. Individuals are bound together by affection or emotional ties rather than by a perception of individual self-interest. There is a "we-ness" in a community; one is a member. Sense of self and of community may be difficult to distinguish. In its deepest sense, a community is a communion. (p. 7)

Elements of a Sense of Community

McMillan and Chavis (1986), in a manner that seems particularly relevant to the internal processes characteristic of many contemporary gangs, elaborated on the notion of psychological sense of community and sought to define the elements constituting it. Psychological sense of community, defined as "a feeling that members have of belonging and being important to each other, and a shared faith that members' needs will be met by their commitment to be together" (p. 7), reflects four processes: membership, influence, reinforcement, and emotional connection. *Membership,* the writers note, is a feeling of belonging, of being a part, of sharing a sense of personal relatedness—a feeling that one has invested part of oneself to become a member. Membership in a community is simultaneously a process of inclusion and of exclusion. A community has boundaries, and thus some people belong and others do not. Such boundaries purportedly "provide members with the emotional safety necessary for needs and feelings to be exposed and for intimacy to develop" (p. 9). In many communities, and most certainly in many gangs, the creation of in-group/out-group membership boundaries is facilitated by specialized language, dress, decoration, and ritual. The individual's level of personal investment, expressed in the effort necessary to obtain and maintain membership in the community, contributes importantly to a psychological sense of community. Gang initiation rituals and membership-qualifying hurdles are clearly examples here.

Influence, according to McMillan and Chavis (1986), is a second key ingredient underlying a psychological sense of community. They see influence as a sense of mattering, of making a difference to the larger group; reciprocally, there is a sense that the group has impact on the individual. The group dynamics constructs of cohesiveness, norms, and conformity examined in chapter 5 are highly relevant in this context. Also important is reciprocity: The community or group influences its members, the members influence the larger community or group, and both help build the psychological sense of community.

Reinforcement is the third key element of a psychological sense of community. Emphasis here is on community-mediated need fulfillment. McMillan and Chavis (1986) suggest that "for any group to maintain a positive sense of togetherness, the individual-group association must be rewarding for its members" (p. 12), an assertion especially well documented in the group dynamics literature on interpersonal attraction, cohesiveness, and related variables. The array of group-provided rewards for gang youths, noted earlier, includes status, self-esteem, shared values, material goods, social support, protection against perceived threats, and so on.

Finally, a sense of community rests on shared *emotional connection.* McMillan and Chavis (1986) describe such connection as "the commitment and belief that members have shared and will share history, common place, time together, and similar experiences" (p. 9). The concepts of *soul* in the Black community and *carnalismo* and *camarada* in the Hispanic community are strong examples of the spiritual bond that may be central to such shared emotional connection. Both the duration of contact and the degree to which it is rewarding contribute importantly to this fourth element.

McMillan and Chavis (1986) share the view proposed in this book that all of the foregoing describes not only communities in general, but also the community of focus here, the delinquent gang:

> The youth gang is a community generally considered to be composed of alienated individuals. Its formation and maintenance are based on its members' hard experience of estrangement from traditional social systems and on the security that membership provides. Gangs develop both territorial and symbolic boundaries. Gang colors (dress and symbols) and initiation rites serve as the basis for the integration and bonding of members and as important mechanisms for differentiating gang members from others. The gang exerts tremendous pressure on members to conform, and the gang's status and victories enhance the bonding even more so. The rules to which members conform are based largely on the shared values and needs met by the gang. (p. 17)

NEIGHBORHOOD

Definitions

Just as a community can be both physical and psychological, a neighborhood is likewise both a place and a state of mind. Traditionally, it is first of all a physical location. Typically, its area falls somewhere between the *microneighborhood,* defined by Altman and Zube (1987) as "the next-door neighborhood, the person in the next apartment, or the most immediate set of adjacent households" (p. xviii) and the *walking distance neighborhood,* usually specified as the elementary school district. The residential block, or a small cluster of such blocks, in most instances is the physical definition of neighborhood (S.I. Keller, 1968; Rivlin, 1987). Sheer proximity is its physically defining characteristic. Its interpersonal implications, as J. Cohen (1983) notes, exist even before members of its population meet, as characteristics of setting help to segregate people with similar personal characteristics—especially by social class, ethnicity, and life-style. Cohen adds that

the type of setting affects the type of friend selected by
(a) preselecting a pool of peers available in that setting,
(b) establishing patterns of proximity and contact, and
(c) prescribing task and reward structures that condition
opportunities and preferences for friendship choice.
(p. 166)

Neighboring: Antecedents and Consequences

The sense of belonging to a neighborhood may be intense. Proshansky, Fabian, and Kaminoff (1983) speak of place identity, Rivlin (1987) of place attachment, and Seaman (1979) of one's phenomenological sense of connection to a place. Though on average Americans move once every 5 years (Rivlin, 1987), local social ties, physical amenities and familiarity, individual household characteristics, and the perceived rewards of remaining in rather than leaving the neighborhood may lead to a positive emotional bond between individuals and their residential environment. The strength of such person-environment bonding may be influenced not only by the perceived positive features of the neighborhood but also by the perception of shared threat directed at the neighborhood's population. Suttles' (1972) notion of the defended neighborhood is relevant here. He proposes that an area's physical characteristics and its residents' beliefs, expectations, fears, and, more generally, their cognitive map combine under certain circumstances (e.g., poverty, ethnic differences, high levels of anonymity, or high levels of criminality) to create a defended neighborhood.

Neighborhood and Gang Formation

Such intense place attachment may contribute importantly to gang formation, as observed by Altman and Zube (1987):

Although the defended neighborhood does not always
seem to arise from preexisting cohesive groupings, it may
itself create cohesive groupings. The defensive measures
of these neighborhoods . . . generally call for some level
of concerted action. (p. 34)

Because they are so restricted to their neighborhood or
its immediate vicinity, children may be the major
producers and carriers of neighborhood life: its local
stereotype, its named boundaries, its known hangouts, its

assumed dangers, and its informal groupings. . . . In many inner city areas, the adults may remain rather atomized while their children quickly coalesce into local street-corner gangs. (p. 38)

Evidence supporting this perspective appeared as early as Thrasher's (1927/1963) work, in which both physical neighborhood qualities—as general as "slums" and as specific as the "layout of buildings, streets, alleys, public works, and the general topography of their environments" (p. 106)—and perceived need for neighborhood defense were seen as gang-generating phenomena. Thrasher concluded in this context:

It is not true that the habitat makes gangs, but what is of more practical importance, it is the habitat which determines whether or not their activities shall assume those perverse forms in which they become a menace to the community. The gangs studied here are not a product of the city merely, but . . . of a clearly defined area. . . . It is the slum, the city wilderness . . . which provides the city gang its natural habitat. (p. ix)

Delinquent gangs still appear to spring disproportionately from low-income neighborhoods, though gang origination appears to be more geographically dispersed than was earlier the case. As Bloch and Niederhoffer (1958) correctly note, the concentric circle or gradient theory of neighborhood-determined gangs is no longer accurate. That theory, put forth decades ago by the University of Chicago sociologists oriented toward notions of ecological/social disorganization, held that delinquent gangs were most concentrated at city center and progressively decreased as one moved toward city periphery. Widespread use of and demand for drugs, dispersed housing projects, mass media communication, mass availability of automobiles, ganging by middle-class youths, and related phenomena have substantially loosened and diversified the connection between physical neighborhood and gang formation. Let us, then, turn to a more central concern, the psychological neighborhood.

Taxonomies of Neighborhoods

Rivlin (1987) has provided a taxonomy of neighborhoods, employing interaction, identity, and connections as his organizing criteria. Six patterns constitute his schema:

1. *The integral neighborhood.* This area has high levels of face-to-face contact and norms and values supportive of the larger community. This is a highly cohesive neighborhood, with such features as block associations and wide participation in both within-neighborhood and outside organizations.

2. *The parochial neighborhood.* This neighborhood is high in within-neighborhood interaction but low in outside-neighborhood connection. It is protective of its own values and tends to filter out values in conflict with its own.

3. *The diffuse neighborhood.* This neighborhood has little informal social participation. Though local organizations may exist, its leadership, which is indigenous, does not represent the local residents' values.

4. *The stepping-stone neighborhood.* This neighborhood is made up of residents with little commitment to the area and strong connections outside it. Within-neighborhood interaction tends to be formal.

5. *The transitory neighborhood.* This area is low in interaction, participation, and identity. It is a neighborhood of urban anonymity, characterized by high population turnover.

6. *The anomic neighborhood.* This type of neighborhood lacks participation or identification with either the local or larger community. Rivlin (1987) describes it as "a completely disorganized and atomized residential area" (p. 212).

A different but overlapping taxonomy, in this instance not of neighborhoods but of neighboring behavior, is suggested by S.I. Keller (1968):

There is the *tribal pattern,* where neighbors are enmeshed in a diversified round of exchanges and contacts; the *intimate pattern,* where families are involved with only a few of their neighbors; the *casual pattern,* where a series of overlapping contacts link many families to one another indirectly; the *clique pattern,* where there is a dominant group and many isolated families; the *ring-around-the-rosie pattern,* in which every family has one or two contacts but there is no direct network linkage among them; and finally the *anomie pattern,* in which isolation of families from neighbors and neighborhoods is the rule. (p. 40)

The pattern that emerges, according to Keller, is a complex function of such physical and psychological factors as the density of residences, the distance between dwelling units, the economic well-being of the inhabitants, the degree of cooperation demanded or permitted among residents, and the general trust placed by individuals in nonrelatives.

Unger and Wandersman (1985) have also sought to determine what constitutes neighboring. First, they suggest a social component comprising personal and emotional support, instrumental assistance, informational support, and social network linkages. Second, they propose a cognitive component. This consists of (a) cognitive mapping, which helps individuals identify safe people and safe places within the neighborhood, and (b) symbolic communication, embodied in things that personalize or otherwise demarcate the entire neighborhood or subareas within it—for example, rows of plants, gates, walks, changes in texture of walks, graffiti, and so forth. Finally, they posit an affective component, consisting of a sense of mutual aid, a sense of community, and an attachment to place.

Beyond its specific contribution, Unger and Wandersman's effort is noteworthy for its combined reliance not only on community psychology but also on research and theory from social psychology, environmental psychology, and sociology. Which of these diverse social, cognitive, and affective functions of neighboring will emerge, and when, appears, according to Unger and Wandersman, to depend on the individual's rootedness in the neighborhood, satisfaction with the neighborhood, general well-being, sense of community, participation in neighborhood activities, and life stage.

Neighborhoods and Delinquent Gangs

For the most part, the literatures concerning neighboring and ganging have formed two quite independent streams. The Chicago school of sociology has studied neighborhood social disorganization, as noted earlier, and some of the gangs-as-cultures literature is neighborhood focused in some respects, but there is little more. One major and seminal exception is the gang-related, neighborhood-comparing work of Spergel (1964), *Racketville, Slumtown, and Haulberg.*[1] Spergel hypothesized that "different types of delinquent subcultures arise in and are concomitant with specific kinds of neighborhoods and social contexts" (p. 1). He studied three neighborhoods: Racketville, mostly Italian, was well organized in the pursuit of criminal racketeering and thus was termed the study's racket subculture. Slumtown, predominantly Puerto Rican, was designated as a conflict subculture, reflecting high levels of both neighborhood aggression and resident organization for gang conflict. The third neighborhood, Haulberg, was of mixed ethnicity (mostly Irish, German, Czech, and Italian) and was labeled a theft subculture because of its high levels of involvement in such behavior. Neighborhood influences on delinquent ganging behavior clearly emerged:

> Characteristic subcultures and concomitant behavioral
> systems appeared to have developed in the three
> areas. . . . Delinquent behavior was highly aggressive,
> regardless of neighborhood. However, aggressive
> orientation and activities were differently organized
> in each area. For example, the racket subculture's
> "toughness" was directly associated with preparation
> for careers in the rackets. In the conflict subculture,
> aggressive behavior was highly organized for purposes
> of group conflict. In the theft subculture, aggressive
> orientations tended to be more indirect and were
> expressed through acts of theft. (p. 61)

The nature and prevalence of gang fighting also varied among neighborhoods:

> Gang fighting in its most organized and offensive form
> was prevalent in Slumtown. It occurred less frequently
> and more defensively in Racketville, especially when
> delinquents and grownups viewed themselves as
> threatened from outside. In Haulberg, gang fighting was
> not a significant phenomenon. (Spergel, 1964, p. 46)

---

[1] A recent and relevant supplement to Spergel's 1964 study is Sullivan's (1989) comparative ethnographic examination of youth crime in three inner-city neighborhoods. Though it is not gang oriented, much of its methodology and findings nicely complements Spergel's earlier effort.

Spergel proposes that the Slumtown gangs fought primarily to gain status, this aspiration even being reflected in the high-prestige gang names they selected—Bishops, Crowns, Lords, Knights, Sultans, and so forth. Racketville gang youths, more targeted to aggression per se (however defensive in origin), chose such tough-sounding names as Talons, Tigers, Stompers, Eagles, and the like. In sum, Spergel teaches us that neighborhood does matter—in how delinquent youths develop, what delinquent careers they aspire to, how and why they form gangs, and how they need to perceive themselves. It especially matters in the antisocial behaviors they express within and outside their neighborhoods. Spergel concludes:

> The possibility existed in each of the three areas for the development of a variety of young-adult adaptations—conventional, quasi-conventional, and criminal. However, differential means structures appeared to set limits on the kinds of young-adult roles which could be played. The most extensive criminal opportunities were available in the neighborhood of the racket subculture. They stemmed from criminal organization, were safe, and offered even the young criminal operator large monetary returns. Extremely limited means of any variety were available in the conflict subculture. Here, ordinarily, young adults could enter upon careers of petty thievery and robbery and attain only low-echelon status in the rackets. In the theft subculture, it was possible for former delinquents to gain access to relatively lucrative careers as professional thieves—mainly as shoplifters and burglars.
>
> In each area, delinquent subcultures appeared to equip young people in some measure with the knowledge, skills, and attitudes required to discharge functionally relevant and distinctive adult criminal roles. (pp. 167–168)

SOCIAL NETWORK

Definitions

In the context of neighborhood, a *social network* has been defined as "the linkages that a neighbor develops with particular individuals both within and outside neighborhood boundaries"

(Unger & Wandersman, 1985, p. 146). More generally, it is "an individual's relatives, friends, and associates, the set of people with whom an individual is directly involved" (Fischer, 1982, p. 2). And, most generally, a social network is "the social relations in which every person is embedded . . . the chains of persons with whom a given person is in actual contact and their interconnection" (Boissevain & Mitchell, 1973, p. 24). A social network may be categorically defined or ego defined. The former kind consists of a set of persons distinguished by a shared characteristic or type of relationship— for instance, an extended family, the students in a given class, or a particular gang. The ego-defined social network, according to Fischer (1977), is defined with respect to a particular individual and includes only those who are actually linked to that person in a particular way—for example, the people with whom an adult plays cards or the subgroup or clique with whom a particular gang youth hangs out.

Network Characteristics

Network characteristics and their relational, communicative, and other implications have been the focus of substantial inquiry in both sociology and community psychology (Albrecht & Adelman, 1987; Fischer, 1977, 1982; Furman, 1989; House, Umberson, & Landis, 1988). As will be noted, some of these properties are dyadic—concerning the relationship between the focal person and one network member—and others are network variables, characterizing the focal person's relationship with two or more network members. A comprehensive listing of social network characteristics includes the following:

1. Density or integration: the extent to which members of a network are interconnected. The more a person's associates are associates of one another, the more dense is that person's network.

2. Multistrandedness: also known as role multiplicity. This network characteristic is the number of different ways a focal person is linked to another network member.

3. Links: the connections between two or more network members. Links may vary in intimacy, frequency, duration, source, and role multiplicity.

4. Size or range: the number of persons constituting the network.

5. Reciprocity: the degree to which the products of the network, such as social support, are reciprocally available and exchanged.

6. Symmetry: the degree of balance of power, attraction, or other network product within a link.

7. Intensity: the degree of commitment within a link.

8. Homogeneity: the degree of similarity of network members on given salient characteristics.

9. Reachability: the average number of links needed to connect two members by the shortest route.

10. Clustering: the extent to which the total network is divided into distinguishable cliques.

11. Dispersion: the range of sources from which network membership is drawn.

12. Dominant source: the single source or context from which most network membership is drawn.

13. Level: the comprehensiveness of relationships within the network. Interactional, dyadic, group, and global levels of social network relationships have been distinguished.

14. Facets: alternative ways of "carving up" network relationships. They include degree of support, degree of conflict, distribution of power, and the relative status of the particular relationship within the individual's more encompassing social network.

15. Perspective: the alternative views different persons (e.g., insiders, participants, observers, outsiders) may have of an interaction, relationship, group, or network.

Two theoretical frameworks have been offered to account for social network formation and functioning. Rogers and Shoemaker (1971) have described a convergence model in which a central role is given to the creation and sharing of meaning as network members communicate with one another. The second perspective, Hammer, Gutwirth, and Phillips' (1981) social feedback model, relies on notions of reciprocal influence and reduction of uncertainty via interactive feedback processes.

Networks and Delinquent Gangs

As with a great deal of the material in this part of the book, much in this array of social network characteristics seems tantalizingly relevant to the contemporary delinquent gang. For example, House et al. (1988) suggest that

> density, reciprocity, sex composition, and perhaps homogeneity seem to be the most promising network structure variables for future work. Networks of small size, strong ties, high density, high homogeneity, and low dispersion appear to be helpful in maintaining social identity (p. 304)

Albrecht and Adelman (1987) comment:

> Those who communicate frequently with fewer network contacts may realize a stronger sense of self-identity and community, stable norms, and more resources during uncertain periods of life. But . . . such network patterns may also be restrictive, providing limited opportunities for change and growth. (p. 52)

And Fischer (1982) concludes that

> networks are "inbred." As a consequence of—and as a further cause of—this inwardly turned interaction, people come to share many experiences, attitudes, beliefs, and values; they tend to adopt similar styles of speech, dress, and appearance; they frequent the same places and engage in the same activities; in short, they develop a common culture. (p. 6)

One significant and motivating consequence of such network density, reciprocity, communication, homogeneity, and inbreeding may be and often is enhanced social support. This major network benefit will be discussed shortly, but it is important first to note that social networks may be for better or worse. Whether a gang or otherwise, a social network may yield not only social support and its concomitants, but also social burdens. As Fischer (1982) puts it, "Our friends and relatives not only support us, they also require us to support them. They can give pain as well as pleasure" (p. 135). House et al. (1988) refer to such network-associated burdens as relational demands and conflict, and Shinn, Lehmann, and Wong

(1984) describe an array of social exchange costs. The actual or potential role of such costs in social network functioning has often been ignored and should not be—especially considering the possible value and relevance of social network theory and research for an improved understanding of delinquent gangs.

SOCIAL SUPPORT

Definitions

Recently, there has been an explosion of academic interest in the construct of social support. Perhaps the interest is due largely to its purported stress-buffering, health-enhancing potency in an era in which American society in general and community psychology in particular have been greatly concerned with stress, stress reduction, and the facilitation of wellness. Caplan (1974), an early social support theorist, defined this construct as the provision, in time of need, of information, cognitive guidance, tangible resources, and emotional sustenance. Cobb (1976) defined it more generically as "information leading the subject to believe that he/she is cared for and loved, esteemed and valued, that he/she belongs to a network of communication and mutual obligation" (p. 300). J.S. House (1981) saw social support as "an interpersonal transaction involving one or more of the following: (1) emotional concern (liking, love, empathy), (2) instrumental assistance (goods and services), (3) information (about the environment), or (4) appraisal (information relevant to self-evaluation)" (p. 39). Thoits (1982) called social support "the degree to which a person's basic social needs are gratified through interaction with others" (p. 147). According to Albrecht and Adelman (1987), "Social support refers to verbal and nonverbal communication between recipients and providers that reduces uncertainty about the situation, the self, the other, or the relationship, and functions to enhance a perception of personal control in one's life experience" (p. 19).

Shumaker and Brownell (1984); Lin (1986); and Heller, Swindle, and Dusenbury (1986) each placed special emphasis in their definitions on social support *as perceived,* especially by its recipient. Thus, social support is "an exchange of resources between at least two individuals perceived by the provider or the recipient to be intended to enhance the well-being of the recipient" (Shumaker & Brownell, 1984, p. 17). Again, social support is defined as "the perceived or actual instrumental and/or expressive provisions

supplied by the community, social networks, and confiding part-
ners" (Lin, 1986, p. 9). Finally, "a social activity is said to involve
social support if it is perceived by the recipient of that activity as
esteem enhancing or if it involves the provision of stress-related
interpersonal aid (emotional support, cognitive restructuring, or
instrumental aid)" (Heller et al., 1986, p. 467).

Social support is alive, well, and growing as a focus of professional interest, even if there is substantial diversity in beliefs about
what it is. Barrera (1986) suggests that the core ingredients across
these diverse definitions are (a) social embeddedness or a sense of
connectedness, (b) the perception of support or assistance, and (c) the
actual delivery of such support or assistance. Kahn and Antonucci
(1980) see the key elements of social support as affect (expressing
liking, admiration, respect), affirmation (expressing agreement or
acknowledgment), and aid (giving such assistance as information,
labor, time, or money). Vaux (1988) seeks to resolve the definitional
diversity by asserting that social support is best viewed as a higher
order metaconstruct comprising a number of legitimate and distinguishable subconstructs (definitions). According to Vaux, these
subconstructs, or core definitional streams, include support network resources, supportive behavior, and subjective appraisals of
support.

Some aspects of the definition of social support seem clear and
are generally agreed upon: its informational function, its affective
implications, its perceptual basis, its assistance content. Shinn et al.
(1984) and Vaux (1988) also clearly distinguish between social
networks, discussed earlier, and social support. As Shinn et al. note,
the two are frequently confused. The mere presence of others with
whom one is in a close relationship may yield support; alternatively,
however, "other people can be sources of conflict, they can strew
obstacles in one's path instead of helping one overcome them, or
their well-intentioned efforts can backfire if they do not fit one's
situation" (p. 56).

Perhaps this examination of contemporary definitions of social
support can best be summarized in the following final perspective,
one that conveys especially well the sense, the spirit, the essence of
this elusive construct:

You are the wind beneath my wings—Henley and Silbar

The line above . . . captures in a subtle but powerful
image the role that social support plays in our lives. Our
family and close friends, mentors and workmates,

acquaintances and neighbors are always there—a social medium through which we pass. Like the wind, their presence is so ordinary as often to go unnoticed. Yet like the wind beneath a bird's wing, they are an essential part of our flight—holding us up, carrying us along, providing life, allowing us to soar and to glide, giving us location and identity. . . . Social support has to do with everyday things—sharing tasks and feelings, exchanging information and affection. (Vaux, 1988, p. 1)

Expressions of Social Support

An understanding of what social support is and of the manner in which it functions will be further enhanced by a survey of its diverse expressions or concretizations. People may enact social support by listening, expressing concern, showing affection, sharing a task, caretaking, lending money, giving advice, making suggestions, and socializing (Vaux, 1988). They may provide behavioral assistance, feedback, guidance, information, comfort, intimacy, services, or lay referrals (Shumaker & Brownell, 1984). Social support is expressed through concern, assistance, valued similarity, positive interaction, and trust (Brim, 1974); emotional support, cognitive guidance, tangible assistance, and social reinforcement (Hirsch, 1980); help in mobilizing resources, managing emotional problems, sharing tasks, and providing material and cognitive assistance (Caplan, 1974); and provision of attachment, social integration, reassurance of worth, reliable alliance, guidance, and opportunity for nurturance (Weiss, 1974). Social support may be, as Berndt (1989) suggests, esteem (or emotional) support, informational support, instrumental support, or companionship support. Its avenues of expression are many and varied indeed. Which avenue is employed in a given instance appears to depend not only on the particular circumstances but also on age, gender, kinship, socioeconomic status, culture, and kindred factors relating to the person, person-environment, and relationship-centered considerations (Belle, 1989; Feiring & Lewis, 1989; Vaux, 1988; Weisner, 1989).

Consequences of Social Support

Social support provision has been held to protect individuals from the diverse negative effects of stressful circumstances (the stress-buffer model) or to act directly to enhance a sense of well-being, independently of stressful circumstances and experiences (the direct effect model). It can offer, according to Nietzel, Guthrie, and Susman (1990), (a) protective direct action, (b) inoculation, (c) appraisal guidance, (d) diversion, (e) problem-solving assistance, and (f) palliative emotional support. Social support has been held to promote satisfaction; a feeling of being cared for, respected, or involved; and a sense of attachment, belonging, or reliable alliance (Vaux, 1988). Sandler, Miller, Short, and Wolchik (1989) suggest that it may protect self-esteem by both preventing the occurrence of esteem-threatening events and moderating the negative effects of stressful events on self-esteem.

Other consequences of social support may be less beneficial and perhaps even harmful. Dependency on others may be promoted and self-reliance and tolerance for dealing with discomfort diminished (Brownell & Shumaker, 1985). Negative consequences may also befall the support giver: The cost of providing support may be too great when, as Vaux (1988) observes, the need for support is chronic, the relationship is not reciprocal, or the demand for support is high.

Juvenile Delinquents as Providers of Social Support

The social support literature has not yet substantially infiltrated nor influenced current thinking about juvenile delinquency or delinquent gangs. There is, of course, considerable theory and some research on the central role of peer relationships (including support) and family relations (including nonsupport) in the lives of delinquent youths, but to date there is little explicit use of existing information and ideas regarding social support.

Both Short and Strodtbeck (1965) and Suttles (1972) provided early speculation about the protective role of friendship networks among delinquent youths. More recently, Gillis and Hagan (1990) experimentally challenged the view that delinquent youths are typically nonsupportive of others and that, because of high egocentricity, they in fact seldom provide the aid, nurturance, or support others may need or desire. Support was measured in terms of willingness to assist crime victims who varied in their social and physical distance from the respondents. Although, as popularly believed, the delinquent youths indeed offered less support in general than did nondelinquent youths, they were more supportive of family and friends. Gillis and Hagan's conclusion brings the social support literature into direct relevance to delinquent gangs: "Delinquents' loyalty is undivided, suggesting that the social cohesion of delinquents may be more particularistic and intense than the more extensive and universalistic support given by other juveniles" (p. 30).

It appears that the contemporary delinquent gang may provide its members a strong psychological sense of community, a psychological and physical neighborhood of which they may feel a part, a social network within which to function, and social support in its diverse manifestations when and as needed. As one gang youth so fully expressed it,

> They're the only ones I can depend on, 'cause I know if I get into hassles, they'll help me. . . . The ones that are my friends, my real friends . . . they are all from M [gang name]. To us, we're like one big family. If they do wrong to my homegirl or homeboy, it's like they're doing wrong to me and it hurts me. (Gardner, 1983, p. 17)

PART III

Intervention

CHAPTER 7

Individual Level Intervention: Judicial and Therapeutic Approaches

Intervention efforts targeted to delinquent youths—both gang members and others—have taken many forms during the past several decades. Some, as this chapter details, have been oriented toward changing, primarily on an individual basis, the behavior, attitudes, or values of youths either through such court dispositions as diversion, probation, or parole or via diverse therapeutic interventions. Other efforts have been directed toward the gang as a group, as in the youth outreach or street gang work approach popular in the 1950s and 1960s (see chapter 8). A third intervention strategy, most in evidence during the 1960s and 1970s, has been the provision of social and economic opportunities via employment, educational, recreational, family, or other community interventions (see chapter 9).

This book will not treat in detail the most popular gang intervention approach in the United States of the 1980s—namely, the gangbusting, "just deserts" orientation emphasizing suppression, arrest, and incarceration. First, our purpose here is to present psychological, not police, perspectives on gang behavior. Moreover, it appears that suppression and incarceration have been, and continue to be, employed far too exclusively. It is time to make a much greater effort to answer such questions as these: After arrest and conviction, what then? Are there viable interventions that may be offered in conjunction with or as alternatives to simple incarceration for delinquent gang youths, interventions with reasonable potential for teaching those youths new, more prosocial ways of dealing with their worlds and creating new opportunities for them to do so? Are such intervention attempts likely to be appropriate for at-risk youths, those more on the fringe of gang involvement?

These are the gang intervention questions for the 1990s and beyond. We believe they will best be answered not only by the separate individual-oriented, gang-oriented, and community opportunity-oriented approaches described in this and the following two chapters, but also by a combination of such approaches. Chapter 10, dealing with intervention at the state level, illustrates just such comprehensive planning. That chapter presents the executive summary of the final report by the California State Task Force on Gangs and Drugs (California Council on Criminal Justice, 1989) and the full text of the report of the New York State Task Force on Juvenile Gangs (New York State Division for Youth, 1990). Each of these heavily gang-involved states, in its own way, urges a multi-front, multimodal, coordinated gang intervention strategy.

DEFINITIONS AND HISTORY

The first building block of a coordinated strategy is intervention at the level of the individual gang member. Intervention, as seen here, subsumes both preventive and rehabilitative activities. This definition agrees with that of Martin, Sechrest, and Redner (1981), who view prevention and rehabilitation as part of a continuum rather than as discrete strategies. The common distinction of primary, secondary, and tertiary prevention (Bolman, 1969) is relevant here. Primary prevention efforts are typically broadly applied interventions designed to reduce the incidence of a particular disorder or class of behaviors. Secondary prevention interventions are usually targeted to especially at-risk populations showing early signs of the condition in question. Tertiary prevention, equivalent to rehabilitation, consists of efforts to reduce the recurrence of or the impairment from conditions that already exist. All three levels of prevention—primary, secondary, and tertiary (rehabilitation)—are relevant to delinquent gang youths and thus will be emphasized in this chapter. In the terminology of Trojanovicz and Morash (1987), the concern will be both "pure prevention, which attempts to inhibit delinquency before it takes place, and rehabilitative prevention . . . which treats the youngster who has already come into contact with the formal juvenile justice system" (p. 199).

Intervention thus defined has had a roller coaster history within juvenile corrections. This history repeatedly demonstrates that prevailing etiological notions of offending behavior largely determine the intervention strategies that are recommended and implemented. From the Middle Ages to the 18th century, as Martin et al. (1981) ably document, crime was viewed as a sinful act and humans were seen as naturally evil. It followed that reform of offenders was considered impossible and that criminal behavior had to be countered with draconian punishments. The 18th century, the Age of Enlightenment, saw drastic changes in thinking about the roots of human behavior in general, including offending behavior. Views of sinfulness and depravity as the energizers of human behavior were largely replaced by notions of free will and rationality, and thus the development of more humane means for encouraging behavior change became possible. A spirit of reform crystallized in the United States following the Civil War, finding concrete expression in the formal adoption of rehabilitation as the goal of penology by the 1870 Prison Congress in its Declaration of Principles (Henderson, 1910). That declaration anticipated several of the core ingredients that would define correctional intervention in the following century. It urged indeterminate sentencing coupled with rehabilitative intervention; major attention to vocational and academic training; and emphasis on transitional (back-to-community), in-community, and, especially, preventive intervention efforts.

In juvenile corrections, much of this early intervention thinking was literally concretized in the establishment of reformatories and industrial training schools across the United States in the late 19th and early 20th centuries. This was followed shortly by the establishment of separate juvenile courts in almost all states "in order to protect, assist, and control rather than punish children" (Martin et al., 1981, p. 5), along with the heavy use of probation to permit those committing minor offenses to remain within the community.

Such prointervention thinking—especially that promoting community-based intervention—grew in popularity as the century drew on, receiving considerable further impetus from a number of sources. The President's Commission on Law Enforcement and Administration of Justice (1967) strongly urged renewed emphasis on primary prevention interventions designed to alter the economic and social character of American society. It also urged that ways be found and used to minimize the penetration of offenders into the (often label-creating) criminal justice system, such as decriminalization of juvenile offenses and diversion away from the system of those committing minor offenses.

Paralleling the primary prevention, decriminalization, and diversion interventions that followed was a larger effort at deinstitutionalization, along with a reliance on community-based intervention. There was growing skepticism about the effectiveness of institution-based interventions, and the deinstitutionalization of other populations, such as mentally disordered adults, was becoming widespread in the United States. In this climate, adjudicated youngsters increasingly were diverted or deincarcerated, and interventions offered became increasingly community based.

As this chapter will show later in more detail, many types of community-based programs were established: halfway houses, group homes, nonresidential therapeutic communities, day treatment centers, wilderness survival programs, special classrooms, summer camps, and, for youths already incarcerated, a variety of prerelease, work release, educational release, and home furlough reentry programs (Feldman, Caplinger, & Wodarski, 1983; Goldstein, Glick, Irwin, Pask-McCartney, & Rubama, 1989; Rutter & Giller, 1983). Community-based intervention, both philosophically and operationally, became a widespread, thriving phenomenon, embodied in hundreds of programs nationally. But roller coasters not only rise, they also fall. Many evaluations of these community-based intervention efforts conducted during the 1970s, recalling the earlier evaluations of residential treatments whose findings had helped spawn the community-based intervention movement, yielded negative or indeterminate results:

> Though the relevant literature is immense, most reviews have ended with essentially negative conclusions—"no delinquency prevention strategies can be definitely recommended" (Wright & Dixon, 1977); "with few and isolated exceptions the rehabilitative efforts that have been reported so far have had no appreciable effect on recidivism" (Martinson, 1974); "studies which have produced positive results have been isolated, inconsistent in their evidence, and open to so much methodological criticism that they must remain unconvincing" (Brody, 1976). (Rutter & Giller, 1983, p. 267)

Much of the intervention evaluation research of the 1960s and 1970s was of poor quality. It was characterized by a lack of appropriate controls, samples inadequate in both size and randomness of selection, poorly conceived and inconsistently implemented interventions, inadequate or inappropriate outcome measures, insufficient attention to minimizing threats to internal or external validity, use of inappropriate statistical analyses, and/or inattention to follow-up measurement—a veritable rogue's gallery of experimental weaknesses.

As noted, some seized upon these experimental outcomes to conclude that "nothing works" and that the era of preventive and rehabilitative intervention should be drawn to a rapid close.

Interestingly, for their own philosophical reasons, both the political left and right of the 1970s concurred and hastened the demise of intervention as a prevailing strategy. The left, on grounds of assumed infringement of the civil rights of offenders—due process, equal treatment under the law, voluntary participation, and informed consent—objected to "coerced therapy to 'correct' offenders as degrading, unsuccessful, and potentially repressive. They urge[d] the replacement of the indeterminate sentence and the rehabilitation philosophy with a 'just deserts' philosophy of fixed sentences based on the nature of the offense" (Martin et al., 1981, p. 6). The political right, giving expression to the justice model, called for greater use of severe punishment rather than rehabilitation and championed the goals of incapacitation, retribution, and deterrence (Vanden Haeg, 1975). Yet other objections to and criticisms of rehabilitation were raised. Greenwood (1986) comments:

> The declining fortune of the rehabilitative enterprise has many causes: abuses of power and overreaching of authority by judges who attempted to impose their standards of acceptable childhood behavior and morals and by correctional authorities bent on improving institutional control; excessive proselytizing and overpromising by academic theoreticians and ambitious practitioners; escalating costs for treatment; declining sympathy for offenders; and the fact that rehabilitation is hard work. (p. 1)

Thus, beset by consistently negative interpretations of efficacy evaluations, subjected to attacks from both poles of the political spectrum, and targeted by a miscellany of other objections, intervention became a battered and bruised component of the juvenile justice system.

As the 1980s progressed, rehabilitation again began to find a modicum of support and encouragement, not matching the unequivocal enthusiasm of earlier eras, but support and encouragement nevertheless. First, from the several failures of intervention, as well as from efforts that apparently were successful, came a clearer understanding of the procedural features that could lead to an effective intervention. One such constellation of features is suggested by Feldman et al. (1983):

> First, the treatment setting should be as similar as possible to the client's natural environment and, if

feasible, an integral part of it . . . it is bound to minimize client reentry problems and to maximize the likelihood that learned changes will be transferred to, and stabilize within, the client's natural environment. Second, as much as possible, clients should be able to remain in their own homes. . . . Hence, most treatment programs should not be residential ones that require a youth to live in an institution with peers who exhibit pronounced behavioral problems. Third, clients should receive maximum exposure to prosocial peers and minimum exposure to antisocial peers. Fourth, intervention programs should enable clients to perform conventional social roles and to assume maximum responsibility for their own successes or failures. Fifth, such programs should be situated in agencies that have stable financial support. (p. 34)

And Bartollas (1985) notes that "effective programs are more likely to take place when intervention is administered in humane environments, when offenders are genuinely interested in change and self-improvement in their lives, and when programs are led by dedicated staff" (p. 38). Finally, Rutter and Giller (1983) conclude:

The two main lessons which seem to emerge from these studies are: (1) interventions need to be directed to changing the child's home environment and the patterns of parent-child interaction, and (2) in so far as the focus is on the offender himself, it needs to be concerned with improving his social problem-solving skills and social competence generally, rather than just seeking to suppress deviant behavior. (p. 283)

Palmer (1976) has shown that Martinson's (1974) singularly negative conclusion that "nothing works" rested on what has been called the *one-true-light assumption* (Goldstein & Stein, 1976). This assumption, the antithesis of a prescriptive viewpoint, is that specific treatments are powerful enough to override substantial individual differences and help heterogeneous groups of youngsters. Research in all fields of intervention has shown the one-true-light assumption to be erroneous (Goldstein, 1978; Goldstein & Stein, 1976). Palmer (1976) has shown it to be especially in error with regard to aggressive and delinquent adolescents. Palmer reviewed the data from which Martinson drew his conclusion and pointed out that, in each of the dozens of studies concerned, there were homogeneous subsamples of adolescents for whom the treatments under study had indeed worked. Martinson's error lay in overlooking the fact that, when homogeneous subsamples are grouped into a heterogeneous full sample, the various positive, negative, and no-change treatment outcomes for the subsamples cancel each other out. The result is that the full sample appears no different from an untreated group. But when smaller, more homogeneous subsamples are examined separately, it becomes clear that treatments do work. The task then is not to continue the futile pursuit of the so-called one true light—the one treatment that works for all—but, instead, to discern which treatments administered by which treaters work for which youngsters.

Clearly, important beginnings have been reported in prescription-oriented research aimed at identifying which types of delinquent youths are and are not responsive to such interventions as diversion (Gensheimer, Mayer, Gottschalk, & Davidson, 1986), probation (Sealy & Banks, 1971), individual psychotherapy (Stein & Bogin, 1978), group counseling (M.Q. Warren, 1974), and behavior modification (Redner, Snellman, & Davidson, 1983). In addition to such evaluations of prescriptive efficacy, more generally positive (nonprescriptive) evidence has also emerged for a number of intervention approaches—especially the newer behavioral and multimodal procedures (Grendreau & Ross, 1987; Goldstein et al., 1989). Awareness of such apparent efficacy has been enhanced in recent years, it should be noted, by the contemporary development, and use on aggregate data concerning delinquency intervention outcomes, of meta-analytic statistical techniques (Garrett, 1985; Gensheimer et al., 1986).

Resurgent interest in intervention has included renewed focus not only on tertiary prevention (i.e., rehabilitation) but also on the intervention potential of primary and secondary prevention. Given the conservative political climate of the 1980s and 1990s, this latter focus—with its emphasis on social policy change and community program development—cannot be described as a major groundswell of correctional interest. But it is real nevertheless. One of its major features, which will perhaps prove more useful for preventive interventions yet to be developed, is the substantial amount of recent research identifying characteristics of youths at risk for delinquent behavior—those who will be best served by preventive interventions. Such youngsters often have histories characterized by (a) chronic acting out (lying, truancy, aggression, minor illegal behavior) in childhood; (b) poor parental supervision, harsh but often inconsistent discipline, and inadequate parental monitoring; (c) parental rejection; (d) high likelihood of criminality and alcoholism on the part of parents and grandparents; (e) early drug use; (f) numerous siblings; and (g) siblings with criminal records (Morris & Braukmann, 1987; Greenwood, 1986; Kazdin, 1985, 1987; Loeber & Dishion, 1983). Cautiousness is in order regarding the potential false positive effects and the labeling-associated dangers of intervening with youngsters who actuarially *might* at some future time become juvenile delinquents. Nevertheless, it is hoped that predictive information can increasingly be put to effective use in preventive intervention. The recent calls by F.L. Fox (1981), Lindgren (1987), Martin et al. (1981), and others that prevention efforts be focused on the family, the school, the workplace, and the community together provide a good beginning game plan for the implementation of this important phase of intervention.

Against the background of this overall perspective on intervention for delinquent gang youths, the following sections will present the diverse judicial and therapeutic interventions currently employed for delinquency reduction or prevention purposes.

JUDICIAL INTERVENTIONS

Diversion

Diversion is the formal channeling of youths away from further penetration in the juvenile justice system, an early suspension of the arrest-arraignment-prosecution sequence.[1] The *diversion from* component is typically embodied in "warn and release"; the *diversion to* component, in one or another resource for counseling, job placement, or other potentially constructive activity. In effect, the concept of diversion began with the very creation of the juvenile court system early in the 20th century as an effort to redirect youths away from the due process and correctional disadvantages that they incurred when they were dealt with in a justice system designed for adult offenders. In the decades following the creation of that system, diversion—of the warn-and-release variety—came into widespread informal use in the United States before it was recognized as a formal disposition in juvenile justice. Piliavin and Briar

---

[1] Closely related justice system programs include probation without adjudication, deferred prosecution, accelerated rehabilitative disposition, and deferred sentencing (F.L. Fox, 1981; Nietzel, 1979).

(1964), for example, found in one large city that 62 percent of adolescent offenders were released by the apprehending police following a brief lecture or reprimand. Black and Reiss (1970) and Lundman, Sykes, and Clark (1978) subsequently reported similar discretionary findings in other locations.

In the context of the long-term informal use of diversion, and in an effort to divert youths from the juvenile justice system for reasons very much analogous to those that had led to diversion from the adult justice system many years earlier, the 1967 President's Commission on Law Enforcement and Administration of Justice

> recommended a narrowing of the juvenile court's jurisdiction over cases and supported the use of dispositional alternatives for juvenile offenders that would avoid the stigma associated with formal processing, urging the establishment by Youth Service Bureaus of community-based treatment programs. (Gensheimer et al., 1986, p. 41)

Thus, in its formal, post-1967 incarnation, diversion was intended to mean *treatment* and not simply warn and release or avoidance of further processing within the criminal justice system. And indeed, the spirit and reality of diversion found fertile soil across the United States. Its endorsement and implementation spread rapidly and widely, aided in particular by funding earmarked for diversion programming under the Juvenile Justice and Delinquency Prevention Act of 1974.

A number of years have passed, and over 50 studies have evaluated the effectiveness of diversion efforts. What conclusions may be drawn? Romig (1978) reviewed eight of the previously completed diversion evaluations, involving over 1,000 youths. Most were referred for individual counseling, casework, or work experience. Outcome results for diversion to these modalities were uniformly negative. Romig hypothesizes that a better outcome might have resulted had youths been diverted instead to programming centered on skill development. Gensheimer et al. (1986) conducted a meta-analysis of 44 studies designed to evaluate diversion programming efficacy. The overall conclusion was that "diversion interventions produce no effects with youths diverted from the juvenile justice system" (p. 51). Yet, as both those authors and Lundman (1984) note, diversion is no less effective than other procedures that draw youths further into the juvenile justice system. Moreover, there are at least strong hints from the Gensheimer et al. meta-analysis that a more prescriptive use of diversion, emphasized with younger offenders, might well yield more positive outcomes—especially if greater attention were paid to the potency of the programming to which the youths were diverted. This latter suggestion gains strength from Grendreau and Ross's (1987) assertion that "the diversion literature parallels precisely the prison counseling literature, which was condemned as a failure, only to be reported later, however, that the services delivered were of abysmal quality" (p. 355).

How might diversion programming be improved? Several preliminary answers lie in Kobrin and Klein's (1983) enumeration of the diverse, concrete weaknesses of such programming to date:

1. Programs were often short term and low level and, in some settings, nonexistent.

2. Programs often were conducted in an atmosphere of turbulence and uncertainty.

3. The skill level of the program staff was often poor or highly questionable.

4. Program treatment strategy was often neither formulated nor articulated.

5. Administrative, legal, and other concerns were often given precedence over treatment considerations.

It is not just with regard to diversion, but also in connection with a number of the other rehabilitative and preventive interventions to be examined shortly, that effectiveness will prove to be closely tied to such implementation parameters as prescriptive utilization (to whom and by whom the treatment is offered), treatment integrity (whether the treatment as described is actually delivered), and treatment intensity (concerning dose or amount and regularity of implementation).

Probation and Parole

Probation and parole are the two most common interventions used with juvenile (and adult) offenders. Both are to-the-community dispositions. Probation, approximately six times more frequently used than parole, is administered by the judicial system and has been defined as either postponing the sentencing of an offender or pronouncing the sentence but suspending its execution while requiring the offender to meet certain conditions during a specified period. If the conditions are met, the sentence is not imposed (if postponed originally) or is considered served (if suspended originally). L.P. Carney (1977) reports that half of all criminal sentences in the United States take the form of probation, with its use most frequent for juvenile offenders, misdemeanants, and some categories of adult first-time felons. The use of probationary dispositions has accelerated especially rapidly in the 1980s and 1990s, as growing attachment to "just deserts," "get tough" penological thinking has led to the widespread overcrowding of the country's jails, prisons, and juvenile residential centers.

The origins of probation are usually traced to the efforts of a British shoemaker and social reformer, John Augustus (1784–1859), who with creativity and energy was able to establish the basic procedures of probation (e.g., background investigation of candidates, supervised activities, etc.) within the British court system. Massachusetts, in 1878, became the first state to legalize the use of probation. Its use at the federal level was enacted by statute in 1925, by which time almost all of the United States had also adopted the practice. L.P. Carney (1977) suggests a number of reasons for such widespread use of probation:

1. It maximizes the normalizing influences that are most often absent in correctional institutions but that can operate when the offender remains in the community.

2. It minimizes the psychological and physical degradations that often accompany imprisonment.

3. It is cheaper than institutional confinement, costing approximately one-tenth as much as imprisonment.

4. It is (Carney holds) a more effective correctional procedure than incarceration.

As noted earlier for diversion, the reality of the implementation of probation has proven much harsher than its promise. Caseloads are often unmanageably large; two-thirds of probated offenders are seen by probation officers with caseloads over 100, though 35 is the frequently recommended maximum (President's Commission on Law Enforcement, 1967). Probationary goals far too often focus on what probationers are not to do and use aversive controls toward this end, with insufficient attention to the building of constructive alternative behaviors. Nietzel and Himelein (1987) capture much of what is wrong with probation in its actual operation:

> Although its personnel are poorly trained in behavioral science, they have been expected to master the social casework–medical model approach. Their caseloads are unmanageably large; their clients are often indifferent if not hostile to the entire probation concept; and they face constant demands for accountability in controlling the behavior of their charges without knowledge of what techniques to use to accomplish that control. (p. 110)

Parole has been defined as "a form of conditional release of the prisoner from the correctional institution prior to the expiration of his sentence" (Tappan, 1960, p. 709) and as "the selective and supervised release of offenders who have served a portion of their prison sentence" (Nietzel, 1979, p. 193). As with probation, the stated goals of parole are the continued rehabilitation of the offender and the continued protection of the public. Unlike probation, which is a judicial function, parole is an executive activity administered by parole boards or other correctional agencies. Parole has its roots in the late 18th and early 19th century penal policies crafted by Alexander Maconochie, governor of an early British penal colony, and the related efforts of another British official, Sir Walter Crofton. Maconochie (see L.P. Carney, 1977) devised and implemented a marks system in which inmates could earn their way by means of industry and good conduct through a sequence culminating in ticket-of-leave or parole (Phase 4) and total freedom (Phase 5).[2]

Parole originated as a formal disposition for juvenile offenders in the United States with its use in 1825 at the New York City House of Refuge. This facility, and the several others like it that came into being, were established

> to teach juveniles how to read, write, and "cipher," acquire job-related skills and, most important, establish habits of obedience and conformity. . . . [M]ost were kept

---

[2] This approach foreshadowed some aspects of current practice, resembling in many particulars a levels system combined with a token economy used in a number of contemporary juvenile correctional settings.

one or two years and then released under a procedure known as "binding out" [parole as an apprentice worker to adult masters]. (Lundman, 1984, p. 113)

The use of parole with juvenile offenders spread rapidly, continuing to grow as houses of refuge metamorphosed into reform schools, and was certainly a broad and well-established disposition at both state and federal levels well before the modern era of community corrections.

Do probation and parole work? Results are mixed. Standard probation or parole supervision, across a large number of efficacy evaluations (Romig, 1978), proves every bit as effective on recidivism criteria as do a number of more expensive interventions—for example, guided group interaction, transactional analysis, psychodrama, and youth and parent lecture series. If while on probation or parole the youth is also provided certain types of behavioral intervention, such as contingency contracting, covert sensitization, and/or social skills training, he or she is likely to do better than a youth merely receiving typical case supervision (Nietzel & Himelein, 1987). A number of negative results have also been reported. A study by the San Diego County Probation Department (1971) showed no difference between imposing probation and simply closing the case after an initial interview. A similar negative finding was obtained in independent evaluations by Empey and Erickson (1972), Feistman (1966), Kraus (1974), Pilnick (1967), and Stephenson and Scarpitti (1968). Parole has not fared much better in most formal evaluations of its efficacy, with most studies reporting no significant effects on revocation, recidivism, and similar criteria (Boston University Training Center in Youth Development, 1966; Hudson, 1973; B.M. Johnson, 1965; Pond, 1970). Yet, as with diversion, there are grounds for optimism, and they lie largely in the realm of prescriptive utilization. There is evidence that probation, for example, may yield better outcomes for adolescent offenders who are neurotic (Empey, 1969), who display a reasonable level of prosocial behavior (Garrity, 1956) or social maturity (Sealy & Banks, 1971), or who are, in the terminology of the Interpersonal Maturity System, "cultural conformists" (California Department of the Youth Authority, 1967). Probation appears to be a substantially less useful prescriptive intervention when the youth is nonneurotic (Empey, 1969), manipulative (Garrity, 1956), or low in social maturity (Sealy & Banks, 1971).

Probation and parole are dispositions in which offenders are either precluded from or removed from incarceration. Their effectiveness, it must be said, will be greatly enhanced to the degree that rehabilitation and correctional specialists devote equal energy and concern to the quality of the interventions to which probationers and parolees are being removed. Matters of caseload size, probation and parole officer intervention competence, official and public commitment to rehabilitative goals, and the like will clearly determine whether probation and parole remain revolving door interventions of mixed and modest outcome or emerge as substantially more potent means for dealing with juvenile offenders.

THERAPEUTIC INTERVENTIONS

Institution-Based Versus Community-Based Intervention

The previous section explored the nature and effectiveness of a series of commonly employed judicial dispositions of delinquent youths—diversion, probation, and parole. Before examining diverse therapeutic interventions, it is useful to consider the settings —institutional and community—in which such interventions are implemented.

Since the era of the houses of refuge, through the period of the reform schools and industrial training schools and continuing into the present with the use of residential youth facilities, a substantial number of offending juveniles have been incarcerated for individual or gang-related crimes. Typically, youths so treated have been multiple recidivists or, if first or second offenders, have committed serious felonies. Even in the 1980s, with the heavier emphasis on punishment, retribution, and related "get tough" policies, the vast majority of offending youths received at least one, and usually several, juvenile court dispositions of warn and release, probation, and/or community-based placement before receiving an institutional sentence. Thus, comparisons and conclusions that might be drawn regarding the relative effectiveness of institution-based and community-based intervention must take into account major differences in seriousness and number of offenses committed.

For the most part, institution-based intervention has not fared well over the course of a long series of efficacy evaluations. To be sure, if the outcome criterion is absence of repeat offenses, there are, as the "just deserts" proponents point out, no such offenses during the period of incapacitation. But on other criteria—both proximal outcome indices such as institutional behavior, days spent in security, and number of assaults, as well as such more distal criteria as parole revocations, drug abuse, and recidivism—poor results are found for most institution-based interventions, including milieu therapy (Levinson & Kitchener, 1964), therapeutic community (Knight, 1970), self-government (Craft, Stephenson, & Granger, 1964), psychodrama (Ingram, Gerard, Quay, & Levinson, 1970), and confrontation therapy (Seckel, 1975). The reason for the repeated appearance of this outcome pattern is clearly traceable to several sources. Feldman et al. (1983) suggest that

> the factors that interfere with effective treatment in closed institutions are myriad and potent: they include severe manpower deficiencies, multiple and conflicting organizational goals, overpopulation and accompanying social control problems, prisonization, the emergence of negative inmate sub-cultures, homogenization of inmate populations, adverse labelling and stigmatization, inadequate generalization and stabilization of desired behavior changes, and finally, excessive cost in comparison with virtually all other treatment alternatives. (p. 26)

As a later section will detail, a more recent emphasis on behavioral interventions in institutional settings has tended to yield more positive outcomes, especially regarding within-institution behavior. Here too, however, inadequacy in transfer and maintenance of gain has led to a more modest, decidedly mixed outcome on distal efficacy criteria.

In spite of this preponderance of primarily negative evaluation evidence, it is important in considering institution-based intervention to note that, for philosophical reasons, and aside from concern with effectiveness for rehabilitation purposes, some are calling for the continued and perhaps increased (if differential) use of institutionalization for severe recidivists. Lundman (1984), for example, makes this observation:

> Currently, the use of training schools and other correctional facilities for juvenile offenders is again being advocated as an effective method of controlling delinquency. Some of those urging more frequent use of training schools are incapacitation theorists. They argue that there exists a small group of repetitively delinquent offenders responsible for a large amount of youth crime. . . . [T]herefore [they] hypothesize that the solution to the youth crime problem is to sentence repeat offenders to long terms in correctional facilities.

Deterrence theorists also support more frequent use of incarceration. They assert that the experience of being institutionalized alerts offenders to the painful consequences of involvement in delinquency. They also assert that punishment of particular offenders alerts other juveniles to the possibility of punishment. (p. 187)

It is indeed correct that a very small number of youths commit a very high proportion of the total delinquent offenses. Wolfgang, Figlio, and Sellin (1972), for example, found that approximately half of all offenses committed by their sample of 9,945 males in Philadelphia between their 10th and 18th birthdays were committed by but 6 percent of the cohort. A similar result was found in Columbus, Ohio, by Hamparian, Schuster, Dinitz, and Conrad (1978) and reported in their aptly named book *The Violent Few: A Study of Dangerous Juvenile Offenders*. These findings would seem to support the aspirations of the incapacitation theorists, who hold that one need only identify such multiple-recidivists-to-be as early as possible and incarcerate them both punitively and preventively for long periods. Unfortunately, philosophical and ethical considerations aside, it is well established that the ability to predict recidivistic criminal behavior is quite poor (Monahan, 1981). Thus, Lundman (1984) appropriately comments:

The inability to predict chronicity makes incapacitation as a general delinquency control strategy unacceptable. Early incapacitation means unnecessarily locking up too many offenders and spending too much money. Late incapacitation, waiting until chronicity is fact rather than prediction, controls too little delinquency. Incapacitation is thus a potentially effective delinquency control strategy in search of reliable methods of predicting chronicity. (p. 198)

For the present, therefore, selective incapacitation as an effective rationale for institutionalization as intervention must remain more a hope than a reality.

What of community-based intervention? A consideration of this approach to juvenile correction was introduced earlier; its rise reflected the negative outcomes of the institution-based intervention evaluations just described, as well as the broader deinstitutionalization movement in the United States in the 1960s. The decline of the community-based approach began in the late 1970s as a function both of continued weaknesses in intervention implementation and evaluation and of a major rightward shift in correctional thinking in the United States away from rehabilitative or preventive programming. Those championing community-based intervention hoped to avoid the prisonization, stigmatization, adverse labeling, and economic disadvantages of institutionalization and to promote effective rehabilitation.

The community-based programs initiated were many and varied. Some truly reflected nothing more than the old control-oriented philosophy of many institutions simply moved to a community setting; others sought much more fully to embody intervention in, by, and with the community; most programs fell somewhere between these extremes. Some of the more noteworthy and ambitious community-based efforts include the San Francisco Rehabilitation Project (Northern California Service League, 1968); the Positive Action for Youth Program in Flint, Michigan (Terrance, 1971); the Attention Home Program in Boulder, Colorado (Hargardine, 1968); the Philadelphia Youth Development Day Treatment Center (Wilkins & Gottfredson, 1969); the Girls' Unity for Intensive Daytime Education in Richmond, California (Post, Hicks, & Monfort, 1968); the Essexfields Rehabilitation Project in Newark, New Jersey (Stephenson & Scarpitti, 1968); the Parkland Non-Residential Group Center in Louisville, Kentucky (Kentucky Child Welfare Research Foundation, 1967); Achievement Place teaching-family homes (Phillips, 1968); the Detroit Foster Homes Project (Merrill-Palmer Institute, 1971); the Case II Project (Cohen & Filipczak, 1971); the Associated Marine Institute in Jacksonville (Center for Studies of Crime and Delinquency, 1973); the Providence Educational Center in St. Louis (Center for Studies of Crime and Delinquency, 1973); Illinois United Delinquency Intervention Services (Goins, 1977); Project New Pride in Denver (U.S. Department of Justice, 1977); the Sacramento 601 Diversion Project (Romig, 1978); LaPlaya in Ponce, Puerto Rico (Woodson, 1981); the Inner City Roundtable of Youth in New York City (Center for Studies of Crime and Delinquency, 1973); the House of Umoja in Philadelphia (Woodson, 1981); and the St. Louis Experiment (Feldman et al., 1983).

It was noted earlier that much of the research intended to evaluate the effectiveness of community-based interventions such as these was weak in many of its characteristics. The weakness of the research is clear. What is less clear is why a strong conclusion—that such interventions do not work—should have followed from weak research. Rather, it would seem that the relevant evidence, instead of being interpreted as proving lack of effectiveness, should more parsimoniously be viewed as indeterminate, generally neither supporting nor undermining a conclusion of effectiveness or ineffectiveness. As Fagan and Hartstone (1984) observe, accepting the conclusion that nothing works is premature for at least two reasons. First, the evaluation research practices have many weaknesses, and, second, a persistent problem with many studies has been the failure to implement the intended treatment approach accurately: "If the treatment was not operationalized from theory, not delivered as prescribed, or incorrectly measured, even the strongest evaluation design will show 'no impact'" (p. 208).

As community-based intervention programs have continued to be developed, implemented, and evaluated, the beginnings of a somewhat more guardedly optimistic view may be discerned. Many programs still yield poor results, but the qualities of those that appear to work are becoming clearer. In a 1987 meta-analysis of evaluation reports on 90 community-based interventions, Gottschalk, Davidson, Mayer, and Gensheimer (1987) conclude as follows:

> The median intervention lasted roughly 15 weeks and involved 15 hours of contact with the youths. A picture of not particularly intense interventions seemed to emerge. . . . The most popular types of interventions were some type of service brokerage, academic support or counseling, group therapy, and/or positive reinforcement. . . . Methodologically, these studies appear to have a number of problems. Few studies measured the implementation of treatment, included data collectors blind to the experimental hypotheses, or used random assignment to treatment, and no studies included random assignment of the service deliverer. In addition, over 20 percent of the studies reported some kind of unplanned variation in the treatment. Finally, 50 percent of the studies included no control group, or had a treatment-as-usual group, making it more difficult to estimate the true strength of the intervention. (pp. 276–277)

Yet these same authors also observe that

> treatments tended to be of short duration both in terms of intensity and length. It may be that most interventions simply were not powerful enough. This last explanation

seems to be supported by the data as shown by the
positive correlation between ES [effect size, a
standardizing index of intervention efficacy] and length
of treatment. In addition, we found some evidence of
experimenter effects in the positive correlation among
amount of intervener and service deliverer influence and
ES. . . . These findings suggest some circumstances under
which community interventions with delinquents may
have positive effects. If a strong treatment is used and
care is taken *during* the treatment to ensure that the
treatment is actually being implemented as designed,
then more positive effects may emerge. (p. 283)

This perspective and similar distillations of effectiveness-en-
hancing intervention features described earlier (Bartollas, 1985;
Feldman et al., 1983) suggest a "not proven, not disproven," more
indeterminate, and—compared to most observations—less pessimistic view of this 25-year-long series of community-based intervention programs. The following three conclusions appear to be
appropriate:

1. Because essentially equivalent recidivism rates for residential
   and community-based interventions have consistently been
   reported (Bartollas, 1985; Lundman, 1984), the latter are to
   be preferred on grounds of humaneness and expense. An
   exception would be youths for whom the more modest
   supervision of probation or the more severe supervision of
   incarceration is indicated.

2. The community intervention programs that collectively
   appear most effective are those that are most intense (frequent
   and lengthy) in delivery, best monitored to maximize
   correspondence between planned and actual procedures, and
   most community oriented—that is, most oriented toward
   "the reconstruction or construction of ties between the
   offender and the community through maintenance of family
   bonds, obtaining education and employment, and finding a
   place for the offender in the mainstream of social life"
   (Harlow, Weber, & Wilkins, 1971).

3. Given this emphasis on preparation for effective and
   satisfying within-community functioning, it appears highly
   desirable that community intervention for juvenile offenders

emphasize acquisition of the personal, interpersonal, cognitive, and affect-associated skills that are required for achieving effective family bonding, obtaining and maintaining a job, pursuing appropriate educational goals, and more generally becoming a competent, choiceful, effective individual less in need of turning to antisocial means to realize personal aspirations.

Individual and Group Psychotherapy

One-on-one treatment (psychotherapy, counseling, casework) has had a long history in the effort to rehabilitate delinquent youths. Healy (1915) and Aichhorn (1925) set the tone early. Both believed that delinquent behavior reflected deep personality disturbance within the individual and that its remediation required in-depth individual treatment. The treatment offered was largely psychoanalytically oriented. It sought, via the establishment of a favorable therapeutic relationship and evocative treatment techniques, to develop insight and—it was hoped—behavior change in delinquent patients. Such work continued over the ensuing decades, as a modest number of psychoanalytic and psychodynamic change agents pursued further individual treatment of delinquent youths (Crocker, 1955; Eissler, 1950; Friedlander, 1947; Healy & Bronner, 1936; Gladstone, 1962; Glover, 1944; Keith, 1984b; Ruben, 1957).

As characterizes psychoanalytic work with other clinical groups, most of the foregoing efforts are single or aggregate case descriptions yielding impressionistic evidence of effect. Little faith can be placed in such data, as they are notoriously open to clinical bias and spurious measurement effects. Such skepticism is buttressed by the primarily (though not totally) negative outcomes of the few evaluations of such individual treatment conducted in an investigatively more rigorous manner—for example, Adams (1959, 1961), Gutterman (1963), Jurjevich (1968), and Sowles and Gill (1970). Yet in such research, the skill of the change agent, the quality and amount of treatment actually delivered, and the presence of antitherapeutic contextual influences each subtract from the adequacy of the treatment offered, the evaluation of its efficacy, and one's faith in the definitiveness of the conclusions one can appropriately draw from the evaluation of outcomes. The most appropriate stance, it would appear, is to concur largely with Kazdin (1985), who asserts:

> The evidence leads to one major conclusion, namely, the jury is still out on the effectiveness of individual and group psychotherapies for anti-social behavior. The quality of evidence is sufficiently poor to preclude arguing for or against the efficacy of major treatment techniques. (p. 102)

Group psychotherapeutic intervention for delinquent youths is of two broad types. The first resembles in history and substance the path of individual psychodynamic psychotherapy sketched previously. A medical model is applied; the youth is seen as the locus of deficits to be corrected, whereas societal contributions are largely ignored; and treatment is evocative and insight oriented in its procedures and goals. The early work in this domain was Redl and Wineman's (1957) psychodynamic group psychotherapy and Slavson's (1964) activity group psychotherapy. A substantial number of data-based studies of these interventions and their derivations have been reported, leading Romig (1978) to this conclusion:

> To decide whether group counseling is effective in the rehabilitation of juvenile delinquents, 28 studies involving over 1,800 youths have been reviewed. . . . The results of the majority of studies were that group counseling did not result in significant behavior changes. At best, group counseling allowed for the verbal ventilation of negative feelings of institutionalized delinquents. Such emotional catharsis did at times positively affect the youths' immediate institutional adjustments. However, institutional behavior changes did not transfer outside the institution. (p. 68)

The group psychotherapeutic and counseling interventions whose outcomes are reflected in this conclusion are each examples of treatment within a group—that is, the therapeutic focus is on individual dynamics and means for changing them within a group context. A quite different set of group intervention approaches for delinquent youths may be described as treatment *by the group,* in which the agents of change are other group members rather than a centralized leader. Staff members function more as facilitators and positive models than as directors, and much of the change focus is on the individual's within-group behavior. Rather than viewing delinquent youths as sick and in need of treatment, these anti-

medical-model group approaches view them as responsible individuals capable of managing the group's conduct and learning to
change their own behavior. This philosophy was concretized in the
therapeutic community (Jones, 1953), guided group interaction
(McCorkle, Elias, & Bixby, 1958), and the positive peer culture
(Vorrath & Brendtro, 1974). These intervention approaches shared
considerable popularity during the 1950s and 1960s, benefited
from positive if impressionistic evidence of their value (Agee &
McWilliams, 1984), and saw declining use during the 1970s and
1980s as first behavioral treatment approaches and then antireha-
bilitation thinking became ascendent in juvenile corrections.

With regard to outcome efficacy of both individual and group
treatment interventions, an indeterminate, "not proven" stance
seems the most reasonable. Research evaluations have yielded
largely negative, though somewhat mixed, evidence of effectiveness.
But research procedures have been generally inadequate, hence the
"not proven" position. There is, however, an important exception
to this suspended conclusion vis-à-vis both individual and group
psychotherapy for delinquent youths: the quite promising outcome
pattern that emerges when effectiveness data are scrutinized more
segmentally and subsamples of delinquent youths are examined in
an effort to determine the differential or prescriptive effectiveness
of the treatment offered. Prescriptive intervention appears to be
especially valuable in the rehabilitation of delinquents and the
prevention of juvenile delinquency. For this reason, the following
section will examine its basis and potential in greater depth.

Prescriptive Programming

Consistently effective rehabilitative and preventive interventions are likely to be treatments that are developed, implemented,
and evaluated according to the spirit and methodology of what we
have termed *prescriptive programming* (Goldstein & Glick, 1987).
Simple to define in general terms but quite difficult to implement
effectively, prescriptive programming recognizes that different juveniles will be responsive to different change methods. The central
question in prescriptive programming with juvenile delinquents is,
*Which types of youths meeting with which types of change agents for
which types of interventions will yield optimal outcomes?* This view
runs counter to the prevailing one-true-light assumption underlying most intervention efforts directed toward juvenile offenders.
Once again, that assumption, the antithesis of the prescriptive
viewpoint, holds that specific treatments are sufficiently powerful to

override substantial individual differences and aid heterogeneous groups of people.

Both the spirit and substance of the alternative many-true-lights, prescriptive programming viewpoint have their roots in analogous thinking and programming underlying endeavors to effect change with populations other than juvenile delinquents. Examples from work with emotionally disturbed adults and children are Kiesler's (1969) grid model matching treaters, treatments, and clients; Magaro's (1969) individualization of the psychotherapy offered and the psychotherapist offering it as a function of patient social class and premorbid personality; and our own factorial, tridifferential research schema for enhancing the development of prescriptive matches (Goldstein, 1978; Goldstein & Stein, 1976). In elementary and secondary education contexts, examples of prescriptive programming include F.S. Keller's (1966) personalized instruction; Cronbach and Snow's (1977) aptitude-treatment interactions; Hunt's (1972) matching of student conceptual level and teacher instructional style; and Klausmeier, Rossmiller, and Sailey's (1977) individually guided education model.

These ample precedents, however, are not the only demonstrations of beginning concern with prescriptive programs relevant to juvenile corrections. Early research specifically targeted to juvenile delinquents also points to the value of prescriptive programming. Several early findings of successful outcomes for specific interventions with subgroups of juvenile delinquents appear to be almost serendipitous side results of studies searching for overriding, one-true-light effects, a circumstance slightly diminishing their generalizability. Nonetheless, especially given the earlier, essentially negative review of their efficacy, it is worth noting the differential effectiveness of each of the two interventions most widely used with juvenile delinquents: individual and group psychotherapy.

Individual psychotherapy has been shown to be effective with highly anxious delinquent adolescents (Adams, 1962), the socially withdrawn (Stein & Bogin, 1978), those displaying at most a moderate level of psychopathic behavior (F.J. Carney, 1966; Craft et al., 1964), and those who display a set of characteristics summarized by Adams (1961) as "amenable." Adolescents who are more blatantly psychopathic, who manifest a low level of anxiety, or who are "nonamenable" in Adams' terms are appropriately viewed as poor candidates for individual psychotherapy.

Research demonstrates that a number of group intervention approaches are indeed useful for older, more sociable and person-oriented adolescents (Knight, 1970); for those who tend to be confrontation accepting (M.Q. Warren, 1974); for the more neurotic-conflicted (Harrison & Mueller, 1964); and for acting-out neurotics (California Department of the Youth Authority, 1967). Juveniles who are younger, less sociable, or more delinquent (Knight, 1969) or who are confrontation avoiding (M.Q. Warren, 1974) or psychopathic (Craft et al., 1964) are less likely to benefit from group interventions. Some investigations of the efficacy of individual or group psychotherapy also report differentially positive results for such subsamples as the immature-neurotic (Jesness, 1965), those under short-term rather than long-term incarceration (Bernstein & Christiansen, 1965), the conflicted (D. Glaser, 1973), and those reacting to an adolescent growth crisis (M.Q. Warren, 1974).

Other investigators, studying these and other interventions, continue to succumb to their own one-true-light beliefs and suggest or imply that their nondifferentially applied approach is an appropriate blanket prescription, useful with all delinquent subtypes. Keith (1984a, 1984b) writes in this manner as he reviews the past and current use of psychoanalytically oriented individual psychotherapy with juvenile delinquents. Others assume a similarly broad, nonprescriptive stance toward group psychotherapy (Levin, Trabka, & Kahn, 1984). As already noted, this stance clearly seems nonproductive; evidence favoring prescriptive programming appears to be substantial.

The exploration of prescriptive programming to this point has focused on two of the three classes of variables that combine to yield optimal prescriptions—the interventions themselves and the types of youths to whom they are directed. But optimal prescriptions should be tridifferential, specifying type of intervention by type of client by type of change agent. This last class of variable—the change agent—merits attention. Interventions as received by the youths to whom they are directed are never identical to the procedures specified in a textbook or treatment manual. In actual practice, the intervention specified in a manual is interpreted and implemented by the change agent and perceived and experienced by the youths. The change agent looms large in this sequence. Just as it is erroneous to think that all delinquents are alike, it is likewise erroneous to ignore the differences among change agents. Supporting, if preliminary, evidence in the context of interventions with juvenile delinquents already exists for the assertion that the person who administers the intervention does make a difference. Grant and Grant (1959) report finding internally oriented change agents to be highly effective with high-maturity offenders but detrimental to low-maturity offenders. Palmer (1973) found that change agents judged high in relationship/self-expression achieved their best results with communicative-alert, impulsive-anxious, or verbally hostile–defensive youths and did least well with dependent-anxious ones. Change agents characterized by surveillance/self-control did poorly with verbally hostile–defensive or defiant-indifferent delinquents but quite well with the dependent-anxious ones.

Agee (1979) reports similar optimal pairings. In her work, delinquents and the change agents responsible for them were each divided into expressive and instrumental subtypes. The expressive group included adolescents who were overtly vulnerable, hurting, and dependent; the instrumental group included youths who were defended against their emotions, independent, and nontrusting. Expressive staff members were defined as open in expressing their feelings and working with the feelings of others. They typically valued therapy and personal growth, which they saw as an ongoing process for themselves and for the youths they treated. Unlike the expressive delinquent youngsters, though, they had resolved significant past problems and were good role models because of their ability to establish warm, rewarding interpersonal relationships. Instrumental staff members were defined as being less comfortable with feelings than were the expressive staff members. They were more likely to be invested in getting the job done than in processing feelings and were more alert to behavioral issues. They appeared self-confident, cool, and somewhat distant. Agee thus reports evidence suggesting the outcome superiority of (a) expressive-expressive and (b) instrumental-instrumental youth/change agent pairings, a finding confirmed in large part in our own examination of optimal change agent empathy levels in work with delinquent youths (Edelman & Goldstein, 1984). Clearly, these several studies of youth, treater, and/or treatment differential matching indicate an especially promising path for future planning, implementation, and evaluation of community-based intervention.

Behavior Modification:
Contingency Management Approaches

Contingency management consists basically of two core sets of procedures. The first is designed to increase or accelerate the frequency of desirable, appropriate behaviors; it is operationalized by some means of delivering positive reinforcement or removing aversive stimuli (e.g., contingency contracting, token economy) contingent upon the performance of such behaviors. The second, designed to decrease or decelerate the frequency of undesirable, inappropriate behaviors, is punishment—in the form of either the removal of positive reinforcers (e.g., extinction, time-out, response cost) or the provision of aversive stimuli (e.g., reprimands; overcorrection; unpleasant tastes, sounds, odors). Both sets of procedures have been used, often in combination, in a number of programs targeted to delinquent and chronically aggressive youths in community-based or institutional settings. Evaluations of these programs have investigated the impact of the systematic provision of diverse tangible, social, monetary, and token reinforcers (Bassett, Blanchard, & Koshland, 1975; Fo & O'Donnell, 1974, 1975; Schwitzgebel, 1967; Tyler & Brown, 1968); the use of behavioral contracting (Jesness, Allison, McCormick, Wedge, & Young, 1975); the systematic withholding or removal of such rewards via extinction (Brown & Elliott, 1965; Jones & Miller, 1974; Martin & Foxx, 1973), time-out (Bostow & Bailey, 1969; Patterson, Cobb, & Ray, 1973; White, Nielson, & Johnson, 1972), or response cost (Burchard & Barrera, 1972; Christopherson, Arnold, Hill, & Quilitch, 1972; O'Leary & Becker, 1967); and the presentation of diverse aversive stimuli, especially through verbal punishment techniques (Hall et al., 1971; Jones & Miller, 1974; O'Leary, Kaufman, Kass, & Drabman, 1970) or overcorrection (Foxx & Azrin, 1972; Foxx, Foxx, Jones, & Kiely, 1980; Matson, Stephens, & Horne, 1978). These are but a sampling of a considerably larger number of relevant investigations, a body of research reviewed by Grendreau and Ross (1987), Goldstein and Keller (1987), and Romig (1978). Each concludes that, as a group, contingency management procedures are regularly effective in altering a wide range of within-institution, within-community behaviors, at least for the short term. Their power to accelerate or decelerate behavior more distal to the intervention period (e.g., to forestall recidivism) is considerably less evident. This dual conclusion of proximal potency and longer term weakness or, at best, indeterminacy of effect, was also drawn from two comprehensive meta-analyses of behavior modification intervention programs with delinquent youths (Garrett, 1985; Redner et al., 1983). Redner et al., also echoing the earlier call for prescriptive programming, observe that

> behavioral interventions with delinquent populations seem successful, particularly with program-related and prosocial behaviors. However, one can neither specify optimal conditions for the behavioral treatment of delinquents nor claim that behavioral interventions are extremely successful in reducing recidivism for any

length of time. This area of research has consistently omitted the experimental manipulation of such potentially important variables as the role of the change agent, participant characteristics, and setting characteristics, which would allow one to make suggestions for optimal intervention conditions. (p. 218)

Behavior Modification: Cognitive Approaches

The various cognitive approaches to behavior modification have their theoretical roots in social learning theory (see chapter 3) and cognitive developmental theory (Gordon & Arbuthnot, 1987; Kohlberg, 1969, 1973). They are appropriately viewed as complementary in purpose to the contingency management approaches just considered. Platt and Prout (1987) comment:

Traditional behavioral techniques applied to correctional situations have relied heavily on a conditioning model in which contingencies are manipulated in hope of changing overt performance. Cognitive-behavioral interventions would seem to support the development of an internal locus of control by having as their goal the improvement of the adaptive personal mediational processes such as self-instruction, perspective taking, and interpersonal problem solving, all of which support self-control. These approaches seek to reorient behaviorists to focus attention upon the internal processes and their influence on overt behavior. (p. 481)

As a group, the cognitive behavior modification approaches are designed to help the client both identify and correct faulty cognitions (thoughts, expectations, perceptions, beliefs) and build a repertoire of skills in order to deal effectively with challenging and stressful situations. Some of the approaches to the identification and correction of faulty cognitions employed with delinquent youths include self-instruction training (McCullough, Huntsinger, & Nay, 1977; Snyder & White, 1979), cognitive self-guidance (Williams & Akamatsu, 1978), thought stopping (McCullough et al., 1977), stress inoculation (Novaco, 1975), cognitive restructuring (D'Zurilla & Goldfried, 1971), perspective-taking training (Chandler, 1973), impulsivity reduction training (Camp & Bash, 1975), and moral reasoning training (Gibbs, 1986). Approaches to the enhancement of (primarily interpersonal) skills have included Interpersonal Cognitive Problem Solving (Platt & Prout, 1987),

Skillstreaming (Goldstein, Sprafkin, Gershaw, & Klein, 1980), role-playing (Scarpitti, cited in Little & Kendall, 1979), modeling (Sarason & Ganzer, 1973), social skills training (Argyle, Trower, & Bryant, 1974), Life Skills Education (Adkins, 1970), and Activities for Social Development (Elardo & Cooper, 1977). Ross and Fabiano (1985) and Hollin (1989) have reviewed the efficacy evaluations of a number of these interventions. Their potency readily matches that of the contingency management behavioral approaches in short-term effectiveness and frequently exceeds it in long-term impact. Change in long-term outcome, including recidivism, has not surprisingly been most pronounced following implementation of intervention programs that combine both contingency management and cognitive plus skill-oriented components, or that are analogously multimodal (Bowman & Auerbach, 1982; Carpenter & Sugrue, 1984; DeLange, Lanham, & Barton, 1981; Feindler & Ecton, 1986; Feindler, Marriott, & Iwata, 1984; Goldstein & Glick, 1987; Hollin, Huff, Clarkson, & Edmondson, 1986).

CHAPTER 8

Group Level Intervention: Gang Outreach

A major component in the decades-long effort to intervene effectively with delinquent gangs was the detached worker movement. It rose and flourished in the 1950s and 1960s and, for reasons this chapter will make clear, has since largely died. We will define its nature and goals, describe its major programs and procedures, and consider its several evaluations. It appears that, for a number of reasons to be examined shortly, the demise of the detached worker movement was premature, and the consistently negative evidence concerning its efficacy led to the wrong conclusion. A more appropriate assessment would have been "not implemented and tested adequately" or "not proven ineffective or effective," rather than the conclusion of ineffectiveness that has been drawn.

Two major figures in gang intervention research during the past 40 years have been Irving Spergel of the University of Chicago and Malcolm Klein of the University of Southern California. As part of a career-long effort to better understand how gangs form and function, as well as to aid in developing and evaluating means to reduce gang involvement in criminal and antisocial activity, each became heavily involved in detached worker programming and evaluation. Their perspectives will set the stage for a consideration of this intervention; their evaluation attempts will be examined later.

Spergel (1965) characterizes the detached worker approach:

The practice variously labeled detached work, street club, gang work, area work, extension youth work, corner work, etc., is the systematic effort of an agency worker, through social work or treatment techniques within the neighborhood context, to help a group of young people who are described as delinquent or partially delinquent to achieve a conventional adaptation. (p. 22)

The assumption of youth agencies was that youth gangs were viable or adaptive and could be re-directed.

> Counseling and group activities could be useful in
> persuading youth gang members to give up unlawful
> behavior. The small gang group or subgroup was to be
> the center of attention of the street worker. (p. 145)

Klein (1971) defines this approach further:

> Detached work programs are grounded in one basic
> proposition: Because gang members do not ordinarily
> respond well to standard agency walls, it is necessary
> to take the programs to the gangs. Around this simple
> base of a worker reaching out to his client, other
> programmatic thrusts then take form—club meetings,
> sports activities, tutoring and remedial reading projects,
> leadership training, family counseling, casework,
> employment training, job finding, and so on. In addition,
> a community organization component is often built into
> the program. . . . The primary change mechanism is the
> rapport established between worker and gang members.
> (p. 46)

Detached work programs have historical roots in the mid-19th century, when, as Brace (1872; cited in Bremmer, 1976) reported, charity and church groups—as well as Boy Scouts, Boys' Clubs, YMCAs, and settlement houses—sought to establish relationships with and programs for urban youths in trouble or at risk. Thrasher (1927/1963) spoke of similar efforts, and the Chicago area projects of the 1930s (Kobrin, 1959) provided much of the procedural prototype for the youth outreach, detached work programs that emerged in force in the 1950s and 1960s. And blossom they did. In the fertile context of the social action movements of the midcentury United States, many cities developed and implemented such programming. The goals were diverse and ambitious. The New York City Youth Board (1960), with one of the major early programs (the Street Club Project), aspired to provide

> group work and recreation services to youngsters
> previously unable to use the traditional, existing
> facilities; the opportunity to make referrals of gang
> members for necessary treatment . . . the provision of
> assistance and guidance in the vocational area;
> and . . . the education of the community to the fact

that . . . members of fighting gangs can be redirected into constructive, positive paths. (p. 7)

At a more general level this project, and many of the detached work programs that soon followed, also had as broad goals the reduction of antisocial behavior; friendlier relations with other street gangs and increased democratic participation within the gang; increased responsibility for self-direction among individual gang members, as well as their improved social and personal adjustment; and better relations with the surrounding community.

Most detached work programs, as the movement evolved, came to the position that their central aspiration was the transformation of values: a rechanneling of the youths' beliefs and attitudes—and consequently, it was hoped, their behavior—in less antisocial and more prosocial directions. Some programs incorporated components of the provision-of-opportunity approach (Maxson & Klein, 1983), which years later was to supplant values transformation as the emphasis in gang intervention programming (see chapter 9). Others, responding to the many intrapersonal, gang, and community forces that perpetuate antisocial behavior, aspired considerably more modestly and hoped that detached work efforts would "hold the line with the individual delinquent . . . until normal processes of maturation take over" (Spergel, 1965, p. 43). As the use of detached work programs continued, and users developed a better sense of what such efforts might realistically aspire to accomplish, goal planning became both more refined and more complex. Spergel (1965), for example, described the goals of detached work programming with delinquent gangs as fourfold:

1. *Control.* The first goal is to saturate an area with detached work services, offering them to all gangs in conflict in the area. In addition to the services and their consequences, such saturation of effort yields surveillance and control opportunities that may themselves be conflict reducing.

2. *Treatment.* To the degree that the antisocial behavior of delinquent gang members is viewed as resulting at least in part from psychological disturbance, successful counseling or therapeutic intervention becomes an appropriate goal for the detached worker. In the 1950s and 1960s, such intervention was based largely on psychoanalytic notions and often took the form of expressive/cathartic interactions aimed at anxiety reduction and the development of more effective personal controls.

3. *Opportunity provision.* This class of program goals addresses the limited access to and use of educational, employment, and recreational resources often characteristic for delinquent gang youths. Programming, in this view, should aim both to develop and make available such resources and to aid youths in making use of them.

4. *Value change.* Via a variety of means, this goal—as noted earlier—entails a reorientation or rechanneling of values from antisocial to prosocial, both in the individual gang member and in the adults and organizations in the surrounding community whose norms may be supportive of delinquent, criminal behavior and beliefs.

PROGRAMS AND PROCEDURES

Four detached work programs have become especially well known and will be the focus of this section. The prominence of these programs—the New York City Youth Board Project, the Roxbury Project, the Chicago Youth Development Project, and the Group Guidance Project—reflects both their scope and the attention their evaluations have drawn.

The New York City Youth Board Project began in 1950 with 11 workers assigned to the gangs in two Brooklyn neighborhoods. Eight years later, the project employed 85 workers dealing with 100 gangs in all boroughs of New York City. Some detached workers were assigned to specific gangs, others to particular areas, and still others to local settlement houses or community centers. The workers' operating strategy is expressed in their credo that "street club members can be reached and will respond to sympathy, acceptance, affection, and understanding when approached by adults who possess those characteristics and reach out to them at their own level" (New York City Youth Board, 1960, p. 6).

The following steps reflect the project's operating procedures:

1. *Establishing contact and developing initial relationships.* Workers typically establish contact through a combination of "hanging around," direct introduction, agency referral, referral by a serviced group, and self-referral or self-introduction. Marginal worker participation in gang/clique/youth activities and conversations is the typical vehicle for beginning a worker-youth relationship. Thanks to this participation, "one develops relations through offering

and providing services, by sharing information regarding one's self, by meeting the members' suspicions and tests and dealing with them understandingly" (New York City Youth Board, 1960, p. 128).

2. *Structuring roles and gaining rapport.* The worker communicates the array of potential roles and services associated with his position partly by what he says to target youths but mostly by his actions, such as arranging recreational facilities; learning names, likes, and dislikes; securing employment; or making court appearances. Gang member suspicions must be allayed, questions answered, personal information shared. Gradually, self-disclosure begets self-disclosure, and rapport begins to build:

> The group begins to share with the worker something of its past history and introduces him to new members. Personal problems are confided to the worker. He may be introduced to parents. He is invited to participate in their activities. . . . There is a reduction of hostility. . . . At the conclusion of this step, the group will have experienced the worker as an understanding, warm, friendly, feeling person, genuinely interested, concerned, and respectful of them as a group and as individuals. (New York City Youth Board, 1960, pp. 132–133)

In addition to the difficult, rapport-building task of repeatedly dealing with gang member suspicion and testing, this stage of intervention is complicated by the need to communicate to the youths the idea that the worker values and respects them—but not their delinquent behaviors.

3. *Forming dependable relationships.* In an interpersonal world too often bereft of reliable and nurturing adults, the worker's continuing and dependable service to the youths often is a powerful relationship force. The worker, in various ways, capitalizes on this connectedness toward prosocial ends:

> The worker attempts to help individuals and the group set limits and take responsibility for their own behavior. He aids in improving intra-group relations, helps to increase their satisfaction from socially acceptable activities, to handle their negative and hostile feelings more constructively,

and to attain an enlarged concept of their
community. He helps in improving relations with
other peer groups and with other adults in the
community. The worker, during this extended
period, becomes an integral part of the gang
members' daily living. (New York City Youth
Board, 1960, p. 144)

During this phase of detached work, the worker is actively
involved with individual members regarding counseling,
prison and court matters, and educational and employment
concerns, and with the gang as a whole regarding meetings,
dances, parties, trips, and team activities.

4. *Closing relationships.* In collaboration with the gang, the
   worker establishes a schedule for the termination of services.
   The youth-worker attachment often is quite strong.
   Anticipated termination may lead to real or threatened
   relapse, regression, or reinvolvement in antisocial
   behavior—in part, efforts to maintain worker involvement.
   Eventually, the group sees itself as ready for termination,
   perhaps following trial separations, and program involvement
   is ended.

A second prominent detached work program, the Roxbury
Project (Miller, 1970), was conducted in Boston between 1954 and
1957. It involved 400 youths who were members of 21 gangs; 205 of
them were served by the seven participating detached workers. The
project's aims and procedures closely paralleled those of the New
York project. As in New York, the major intervention component
was detached work, in this instance supplemented by family
casework, work with local citizens' groups, and a serious effort to
enhance interagency relations.

The third program, the Chicago Youth Development Project
(Mattick & Caplan, 1962), was conducted by the Chicago Boys'
Clubs between 1960 and 1966. Although detached work was the
program's main feature, it targeted community involvement and
organization substantially more than did the Roxbury Project.
Unlike the other programs just described, it served both delinquent
and nondelinquent youngsters.

Finally, the Group Guidance Project (Klein, 1968b) was sponsored by the Los Angeles County Probation Department between
1960 and 1965. Its four participating gangs took part in individual
and group counseling, weekly group meetings, outings, sports,

remedial reading, and tutoring. The program sponsored a parents' club as well as other worker-initiated and youth-initiated activities. Workers frequently acted as brokers, mediators, or interpreters, intervening not only *with* the youths, but also *for* them with teachers, police, probation and parole officers, juvenile court personnel, employers, and others. Like the other detached work programs, the Group Guidance Project was primarily a transformational effort, designed mainly to "change gang member values, attitudes and perceptions through counseling and group activities" (Spergel, 1965, p. 155).

Spergel (1965), who has examined a number of such detached work programs, provides the following comprehensive and more or less sequential organization of their collective implementation procedures.

1. *Introduction.* Via self-introduction, introduction by a previous worker, or introduction by a member of the community, the worker and the gang meet. The youths' initial response will depend in part on how they perceive the worker: as a police-like agent of control; as a member of a social agency, perhaps a welfare worker; or accurately for the role(s) the worker intends to enact. And, if the worker is perceived accurately, youth response may vary according to community perception—whether having a worker is status enhancing (the gang is seen as bad enough to need one) or status diminishing (the gang prefers to avoid the delinquent label).

2. *Observation and orientation.* This is the structuring stage of the youth-worker relationship. The worker, capitalizing on one major advantage of being detached from agency to street, begins to observe target youths in their natural, neighborhood contexts. As opportunities arise or can be created, the worker begins, by word and deed, to orient both the youths and their significant others (parents, community figures, etc.) to his possible roles and functions.

3. *Meeting group tests.* Gang members test and retest the worker. Such testing may include displays of suspicion, ostracism, verbal abuse, and even physical aggression. Spergel (1965) comments:

   Testing takes many forms. For example, at first the youngsters may deliberately fabricate stories

> of fights or planned criminal activities, requests
> for help with jobs or problems at school. They
> are interested mainly in the way [the worker]
> responds to hypothetical situations. . . . The
> worker is also tested in a very personal way. The
> group wants to know why he is a street worker
> and what his personal ambitions are. . . . The
> group wants to know how far they can push him
> and in what way they can make him angry.
> (pp. 76–77)

4. *Helping the group solve a problem.* The initial testing ends,
   and the worker-youth relationship may be considered
   established, suggests Spergel (1965), when the worker helps
   the group deal successfully with a problem that it sees as
   significant: "Helping to solve a problem may be as simple as
   teaching the members how to shoot a basket, how to conduct
   a dance, or helping youngsters transfer from one school to
   another" (p. 79).

5. *Dealing with a sense of deprivation.* An early and often
   continuing task for the worker is helping alleviate the
   youth's sense of estrangement from community, perhaps
   from family, and from significant others. Gang youths often
   pessimistically fear further deprivation, including eventual
   loss of the worker. The resulting emotional climate can
   substantially influence both the tone of worker-youth
   interactions and the likelihood of positive outcomes.

6. *Setting appropriate standards.* The overriding purpose of
   detached work programs, it will be recalled, is to help gang
   youths develop prosocial values and behavior and relinquish
   antisocial norms and actions. The behavior and perceived
   values of significant adults with whom the youths interact
   loom large in this challenging effort:

   > The worker who is warm and friendly, who has gained
   > the respect and admiration of group members, may be
   > used as a role model. His behavior, attitudes, and beliefs
   > may become their standards. . . . [C]hanges in certain
   > patterns of behavior occur in a generalized, nonplanned
   > way because of the worker's positive relationship with the
   > members. (Spergel, 1965, p. 84)

7. *Decision making.* In the belief that it both increases a sense
   of satisfaction and encourages conventional behavior, the

worker strongly promotes a democratic decision-making process. The group is urged to assume maximum responsibility in the control of its own acting out behavior.

8. *Advice and normative controls.* These are straightforward, instructional communications from worker to youth. On occasion, the communications may go beyond mere advice and admonitions regarding the consequences of planned delinquent behavior and the value of conforming to more conventional norms and actions.

9. *Compelling conformity to conventional standards.* Under extreme circumstances—for example, when the worker or someone else is under direct threat of violence—the worker may have to compel behavioral compliance through his own actions, with the aid of other staff, or with police assistance.

10. *Other worker-initiated procedures.* Depending on an almost limitless array of behaviors and events originating with gang members, significant others, and environmental factors, the detached worker may be called upon for an exceedingly broad range of additional procedures and services. These may include planning and supervising diverse gang programming, contriving circumstances that minimize the possibility of intergang fighting, encouraging the gang's segmentation into conventional and delinquent subgroups when such a polarization naturally emerges and cannot be avoided, providing direct instruction in conventional behaviors (e.g., what to say, when, and to whom), and much more.[1]

Given the diverse multifaceted demands and procedures that constitute the detached worker's job, it is no wonder that J.R. Fox (1985), in an article aptly titled "Mission Impossible? Social Work Practice With Black Urban Youth Gangs" described the qualifications of the worker in this way: "dedicated, abundant energy, a sense of fun, good and quick intelligence, courage, inventiveness, ability to relate to suspicious teenagers, a degree of comfort with authority, and a firm set of values rooted in his own experience, all seem essential" (p. 26).

---

[1] Additional detailed descriptions of detached gang work are provided by Bernstein (1964); Crawford, Malamud, and Dumpson (1950); and J.R. Fox (1985).

EVALUATION RESULTS

The New York City Youth Board Project, though its scope and duration were extensive, was never formally evaluated. The Roxbury Project was evaluated by means of a variety of effectiveness criteria and a number of comparison groups. Results on a series of intermediate criteria were favorable: Worker relationships with gangs were established; recreational, educational, and occupational interests were stimulated. However, on the project's ultimate criterion, inhibition of law-violating or morally disapproved behavior (Quicker, 1983b), no significant between-condition differences emerged. The Chicago Youth Development Project represented another apparent outcome failure on delinquency reduction criteria. Results indicated that an intensive worker-youth relationship was not, as had been predicted, positively related to a prosocial outcome. In fact, the youths who claimed to be closest to their detached workers were most in trouble with the police. The Los Angeles Group Guidance Project was also fully evaluated, and it too proved to be a seemingly inadequate approach to rechanneling the values and behavior of delinquent gang youths. Gang member delinquency actually increased over the course of the project's life, especially for youths who received the fullest worker attention.

It is not often the case in social science research that such a clear confluence of results (positive or negative) emerges, and thus it is not surprising that gang researchers more or less unanimously concluded that the detached work approach should not be pursued further. Klein (1968b), in particular, urged this step. He claimed that the consistently negative results were largely due to the manner in which detached work programming attended primarily to the gang as a group and less to its individual members, thus enhancing gang cohesiveness, perpetuating and not rechanneling the gang and drawing new recruits to its membership. Klein's programmatic response to these conclusions, the more individually oriented, cohesiveness-reducing, gangbusting Ladino Hills Project (see chapter 9), did succeed in reducing the absolute level of delinquency, mostly because the gangs diminished in size. This seemed to Klein and others to be the evidential nail in the detached work program's coffin.

Negative evidence notwithstanding, there apparently is more to the evaluation story to be told. As suggested at the outset of this chapter, it seems that detached work programs—all of them— suffered from at least one, and typically several, failures of implementation. In each instance, both program plans and evaluation procedures seem adequate, but not the manner in which worker activities were actually conducted. If this is the case, program effectiveness remains indeterminate and conclusions regarding outcome efficacy must be suspended. There are five reasons for taking this position: (a) failure of program integrity, (b) failure of program intensity, (c) absence of techniques relevant to delinquency reduction, (d) failure of program prescriptiveness, and (e) failure of program comprehensiveness.

Program Integrity

Program integrity is the degree to which the intervention program as actually implemented corresponds to the program as planned. As noted in the report from the New York State Task Force on Juvenile Gangs (New York State Division for Youth, 1990):

> If youth at risk of gang involvement are to be served adequately, it is critical that programs developed be actually implemented according to planned program procedures. Too often, mostly as a result of too few personnel or inadequate funding, programs of apparent substantial potential are actually implemented inadequately. (p. 44)

Failure of program integrity, as thus defined, appears to have been a relatively common characteristic of the detached work programs examined earlier. The New York City Youth Board Project, according to Gannon (1965), repeatedly suffered from high staff turnover, monumental red tape, low staff morale, worker role confusion, and a number of other, kindred threats to program integrity. In the Chicago Youth Development Project, "the workers found their jobs so demanding [that] they tend to swallow up the whole life of the person holding them" (Quicker, 1983b, p. 69). And addressing even more directly the correspondence between intervention plan and implementation, Klein (1968b) notes with regard to the Group Guidance Project that its worker counseling policy component was confused, its planned parent groups component largely nonexistent, and its psychiatric intervention component inflexible. In addition, its supervisory plan, meant to promote program integrity, was severely inadequate in actual implementation: Program supervisors wound up spending less than 30 minutes

per worker per week in field supervision and observation. Responding to this fact, Klein comments that

> action in the street scene means, almost inevitably, lower
> levels of line supervision. . . . For the researcher, this
> supervisorial gap poses serious problems of data validity,
> discrepant views of the action, feedback mechanics, and
> proper implementation of program . . . procedures. In
> other words, there is little control, and certainly less than
> is found in most action-research settings. (p. 235)

Program Intensity

The intensity with which an intervention is delivered is its
amount, level, or dosage. The New York State Task Force on
Juvenile Gangs made this observation on program intensity:

> In general, it will be the case that "the more the better,"
> whether referring to amount of youth contact with the
> intervenors; amount of counseling time, recreational
> time, or job skills training time; or amount of family or
> community involvement in programming for youth.
> (New York State Division for Youth, 1990, p. 44)

On this criterion of project adequacy, the detached work programs
considered here do not do well. Worker-youth ratios were an
acceptable 1 to 29 in the Roxbury Project, an unacceptable 1 to 78
in the New York City Youth Board Program, and a quite impossible
1 to 92 in the Chicago Youth Development Project. Such disproportionate caseloads usually meant that workers rarely met youths
individually and almost always met them in groups. As Mulvihill et
al. (1969) comment on this problem:

> How would a rational worker go about meeting and
> maintaining rapport with as many as a hundred
> youngsters much of whose lives are street oriented? Being
> on the street himself is not sufficient; too many boys are
> missed that way. The worker has little choice but to
> encourage group gatherings. (p. 1455)

These gatherings, as Dumpson (1949) noted in connection with the
New York City Youth Board Project, can mean dealing with as
many as 50 youths at a time!

Klein's (1968b) data on the intensity of the Group Guidance Project are most telling on this topic. The project's detached workers, it seems, were in reality only partly detached. They spent 25 to 50 percent of their time (on average 38 percent or about two-fifths) in the project office and a considerable amount of time (on average 25 percent) alone (traveling, hanging around gathering spots). Thus, almost two-thirds of their typical working day was not spent with project youths. Klein pointedly comments:

> Whether one looks at this as an hour and a half a day,
> a day a week, or ten weeks out of a year, this is a
> fascinating piece of information. Gang workers in
> this project spent one-fifth of their time with gang
> members. . . . With 50 to 100 gang members in the
> neighborhood, and eight hours a week spent in contact
> with them, how much impact can reasonably be
> expected? It may be like squeezing blood out of a turnip
> to think that an average of five minutes per week per boy
> could somehow result in a reduction of delinquent
> behavior. (p. 163)

So much for intervention intensity!

Absence of Delinquency-Relevant Techniques

Well-designed evaluations of intervention programs often include both proximal and distal measures of the intervention's effectiveness. The former are tied directly to the content of the intervention: If remedial reading was the intervention, has the youth's reading level advanced? If social skills training was provided, is the youth more socially skilled? If the intervention taught the skill of interviewing for employment, how does the trainee actually behave in a mock or real interview? Improvement on distal or more derivative outcome criteria is usually possible only if prior improvement on the proximal or more immediate criteria has first taken place. Thus, grade point average might well be a distal criterion of effectiveness in a remedial reading intervention whose proximal criterion was change in reading level. Similarly, level of self-esteem might be the derivative criterion in a social skills intervention, and actual job attainment could be the distal measure in the instance of employment interviewee training. In the evaluation of detached work programs, a variety of appropriate proximal measures have been employed, but the criterion of distal effectiveness (and the programs' raison d'être) has consistently been change in delinquent behavior. Combined outcome evidence is fairly supportive of the proximal effectiveness of detached work but, as noted earlier, consistently unsupportive of its distal effectiveness thus defined.

Though the effectiveness of delinquency-altering techniques has improved since the era of detached work programming (see chapter 7), it is still largely inappropriate to predict that any intervention targeted to behavior, attitude, or value A will be so potent that, in addition to changing A, it will also have significant impact on derivative criterion B. Available delinquency interventions are simply not that powerful. Klein (1968b), in examining the outcome of his Group Guidance Project, comments in this regard:

> Another weakness derives from the general lack of knowledge in the entire field of delinquency prevention, and the worker is the unfortunate bearer of this burden. I refer here to the lack of specific techniques for dealing with specific forms of delinquent behavior. An exception is the control of gang fighting in which worker visibility, the provision of face saving alternatives, and truce meetings are accepted procedures for avoiding territorial raids and retaliations. Unfortunately, few techniques exist that are comparably effective with theft, rape, malicious mischief, auto theft, truancy, and so on. This lack of specific behavior related techniques forces the worker to fall back upon general intervention procedures such as individual or family counseling, group activities, job development, and so on, procedures which at best have only an indirect relationship to delinquency producing situations. (p. 150)

In the Group Guidance Project, a diverse array of 241 activities (usually group) were conducted over the 2-½ years of the program's life, an average of 2 activities per week. In spite of the activities' diversity, their contents were such that the evaluators concluded:

> It was clear from our observations that the special activities were seldom used directly . . . for delinquency prevention. Any major positive impact on delinquency

would have to be indirect, through self-discovered lessons about fair-play, the value of prosocial activity, and so on. (Klein, 1968b, p. 169)

These absence-of-technique conclusions, in addition to eliciting admiration of Klein and his research team for both their research acumen and their remarkable candor, should, one hopes, serve as both insight and stimulus: insight regarding the need for more direct and potent delinquency interventions; stimulus for the effort to produce them.

Program Prescriptiveness

As delinquency reduction techniques are developed, become available, and are implemented with both program integrity and intensity, they must also be applied prescriptively. The detached work programs examined here, as is true of the vast majority of delinquency intervention programming of all kinds, were not used in a differential, tailored, individualized, or prescriptive manner. The historical and evidential case for prescriptive intervention was considered in depth in the discussion of individual interventions (see chapter 7). Suffice it to say that the success of such interventions as detached work seems likely to be substantially enhanced to the degree that the worker's techniques and characteristics are well matched with the qualities of the participating youths. Valuable leads in this regard already exist. They include notions urging different approaches to core versus marginal gang members (Yablonsky, 1967); to leaders versus followers (Needle & Stapleton, 1982); to older versus younger youths (Spergel et al., 1989); to youths from theft, conflict, or racket subcultures (Spergel et al., 1989); to youths with varying degrees of aggressiveness and gang involvement (Klein, 1968b); and to youths classified as clique leaders, cohesiveness builders, or recruits (Klein, 1968b). Moreover, different approaches may be chosen in response to diverse worker qualities. This last prescriptive ingredient is largely ignored but, we believe, is especially relevant for outcomes. Spergel et al. (1989) comment on the importance of matching the skills of the worker with the needs of the group:

> For example, the worker who is particularly effective in setting limits should be assigned to a group which has great difficulty in controlling its aggressive impulses; a

worker who is skilled at individual and group treatment
should work with a group requiring therapeutic help; a
worker who is talented at opening up and developing
community resources for socioeconomically deprived
youths should be assigned to a group needing access to
appropriate opportunities. (p. 29)

For prescriptive programming, the key question—a complex
one—is, Which types of youths in which types of gangs being
served by which types of detached workers will experience which
types of prosocial outcomes?

Program Comprehensiveness

All of the detached work programs considered here shared the
intent to provide not only the main intervention components
associated with worker-youth relationships, but also comprehensive, multilevel programming to both individual youths and the
systems of which they were a part. The New York City Youth Board
Project had broad aspirations:

It has been asked whether it is most productive to work
with the group, with the individual in the group, or with
the community itself, and through changes in the
community, bring about changes in the group.
Traditionally the work of the Street Club Project has
been focussed on . . . the group, the neighborhood and
the individual members themselves. This stems from our
conviction that delinquency is caused by a multiplicity of
factors—both individual and social—and that an
effective approach to the problem should incorporate
both of these areas. (New York City Youth Board, 1960,
p. 118)

Given the long, formative, and frequently antisocial life histories of
many gang youths and the level of contemporary reinforcement
they receive for persisting in antisocial behavior, this aspiration to
multipronged intervention seems most appropriate. Yet detached
workers in the programs implemented were overworked and under-
trained, and they had few resources at their disposal. Most of what
was available to them was youth oriented, not system oriented, in
aims and substance. Thus, rather than comprehensiveness of intervention, what actually emerged

targeted specific gangs and gang youth. It was not integrated into other service or community development approaches occurring at the same time. It concentrated on the development of worker–gang member relationships and recreational and group activities in somewhat isolated terms. It was a fairly unidimensional approach. (Klein, 1968b, p. 52)

These several shortfalls in intervention implementation—regarding program integrity, program intensity, delinquency reduction techniques, prescriptiveness of implementation, and program comprehensiveness—characterize not only the four detached work programs examined in this chapter but also other similar programs: El Paso (Quicker, 1983b), the YMCA Project in Chicago (Spergel et al., 1989), San Francisco's Youth for Service Project (Klein, 1968b), and others. Given this reality, an examination of the nature and efficacy of detached work programming must conclude, as was true for individual interventions with gang youths, that "the relevant evidence, instead of being interpreted as proving lack of effectiveness, should more parsimoniously be viewed as indeterminate, generally neither supporting nor undermining a conclusion of effectiveness or ineffectiveness" (Goldstein, 1990, p. 87).

CHAPTER 9

Community Level Intervention: Opportunity Provision

Gang intervention programming, whatever its major thrust, has always given at least some attention to enhancing extra-gang opportunities available to gang youths. But in some eras, it has been decidedly minor attention. During the decades of detached work programming, for example, primary emphasis was consistently placed on the worker-youth relationship and on attempts to alter youth behavior by gang reorientation and value transformation, with relatively little effort directed toward system change (e.g., the enhancement of work, school, or family opportunity). A number of factors were among the major antecedents and stimulants of the next phase of gang work, opportunity provision: awareness of the incompleteness or asymmetry of the previous perspectives, the purported effects of the detached worker approach in increasing gang cohesiveness and delinquency, and the general promotion within the United States of diverse social legislation. Spergel et al. (1989) describe the new approach as

> a series of large scale social resource infusions and efforts to change institutional structures, including schools, job opportunities, political employment . . . in the solution not only of delinquency, but poverty itself. Youth work strategies were regarded as insufficient. Structural strain, lack of resources, and relative deprivation were the key ideas which explained delinquency, including youth gang behavior. The structures of social and economic means rather than the behavior of gangs and individual youth had to be modified. (p. 147)

The proposed relevance of the opportunity-oriented strategy to gang youths in particular is expressed well by Morales (1981): "The gang is a symptom of certain noxious conditions found in society. These conditions often include low wages, unemployment, lack of recreational opportunities, inadequate schools, poor health, deteriorated housing and other factors contributing to urban decay and slums" (p. 4). Quicker (1983b) echoes this view, pointing even more directly to the need for improved opportunities:

> The development of gangs stems primarily from environmental causes. It appears that the legitimate opportunity system is closed to most lower class boys who, having internalized middle class norms of success, are frustrated by their inability to succeed in socially prescribed ways. Joining with other boys, similarly frustrated, they form gangs which provide some of them access to that illegitimate opportunity system (an illegal economy) where they are able to at least partially realize their aspirations. (p. 11)

A similar view is expressed by Klein (1968b) in response both to the apparent failure of his detached work Group Guidance Project and the subsequent greater success of his opportunity-oriented Ladino Hills Project. Klein comments:

> One of the difficulties encountered by many past programs stems from the enormous complexity of the gang problem. It has been assumed that a problem deriving its existence from a multitude of sources (family, community, economic deprivation, individual deficiencies, etc.) must be dealt with on all levels. Yet most gang programs have been of the detached worker variety, a form of intervention for which this multilevel approach is inefficient at best, and in reality almost impossible. Detached workers can have relatively little impact on individual character disorders or psychological deficiencies, family relationships, poverty, educational and employment disadvantages, community disorganization and apathy, and so on. (p. 238)

The need for provision of practical and esteem-enhancing opportunities, of course, was apparent as far back as Thrasher's (1927/1963) work and earlier. What was different in the late 1960s and 1970s was the country's willingness to respond to this need with a broad programmatic effort. Dozens of varied programs followed to address the need for opportunities. Following is a roughly chronological sampler of programs oriented in particular to gang youths:

- Mobilization for Youths (Cloward & Ohlin, 1960; Miller, 1974), which offered vocational guidance and the opportunity to gain small business work experience

- Spergel's (1965) street gang project, which included substantial involvement with gang members' families, employers and employment services, public school personnel, and a variety of youth agencies

- Klein's (1968b) Ladino Hills Project, whose resource workers (rather than detached workers) sought to provide participating gang youths with employment, improved school opportunities, and enhanced access to recreational, health, and welfare resources

- Baca's 1970 and Citywide Mural Project (Gardner, 1983)

- The 1973 New York Police Probation Diversion Project (Gardner, 1983), providing special education and substance abuse prevention programming

- Krisberg's (1974) Urban Leadership Training Program, which attempted to train gang leaders for careers in community service

- DeLeon's (1977) corporation- and police-initiated scouting troops

- Haire's (1979) Rampart gang study mobilizing a unified school district to provide expanded educational opportunities

- The Hire-a-Gang-Leader program (Amandes, 1979), which taught an array of job-seeking and job-keeping skills and provided actual employment opportunities

- The Ocean Township Youth Volunteer Corps (Torchia, 1980), which offered both community service and diverse recreational possibilities to adjudicated gang youths

- Willman and Snortum's (1982) Project New Pride and Gang Employment Programs, and Falaka's House of Umoja (Gardner, 1983), all of which emphasized job training and employment opportunity programming

- Project SAY (Save-A-Youth), developed by Willis-Kistler (1988), offering a full array of family, school, and recreational opportunities

- Thompson and Jason's (1988) school and after-school Project BUILD (Broader Urban Involvement and Leadership Development)

- The employment-oriented Community Access Team (California Youth Gang Task Force, 1981), Youth Enterprises of Long Beach (Quicker, 1983b), and SEY Yes (Quicker, 1983b) programs

- The school-oriented GREAT (Gang Resistance and Training; Los Angeles Unified School District, 1989), PREP (Preparation Through Responsive Education; Filipczak, Friedman, & Reese, 1979), and Gangs Network (college option generating; Needle & Stapleton, 1982) programs

- The family-oriented Family and School Consultation Project (Stuart, Jayaratne, & Tripoldi, 1976) and the Aggression Replacement Training project (Goldstein et al., 1989)

PRESCRIPTIVE EVALUATION

With very few exceptions (e.g., Klein, 1971; Thompson & Jason, 1988), programming aimed at providing opportunities for gang youths has not been systematically evaluated. There is no concrete evidence whether, or to what extent, gang youths in general or subgroups of gang youths take advantage of the diverse opportunities provided by such programs. Thus, it is unknown whether they benefit, either in proximal, opportunity-specific ways, or more distally in terms of termination of gang membership, reduction of delinquency, or future life path. There is no shortage of affirming impressionistic and anecdotal support— including a 45-city survey seeking the views of law enforcement and other agencies on the effectiveness of opportunity enhancement and other gang intervention approaches (Spergel et al., 1989)—but its heuristic value is limited, especially for determination of future programming.

Klein's (1968b) Ladino Hills Project is an important exception; its careful evaluation sets a standard to which others should aspire. Especially noteworthy is its prescriptive feature, a systematic effort to develop a typology of gang youths to identify categories that are responsive to different patterns of programming, including provision of opportunities. Strong support for such a strategy has been presented elsewhere in this book; suffice it to say here that Klein's (1971) initial success in this attempt well deserves replication and elaboration by others. His gang member categories (clique leaders, cohesiveness builders, recruits, and best bets) make both intuitive and empirical sense.

Whether implemented prescriptively or not, the strategy of providing opportunities should be responsive to the urging of Spergel et al. (1989) that the opportunities be accompanied by sufficient support and organization. These authors comment that

> a general design for improved living in particularly deprived lower-class areas should be based on three concepts: opportunity, service, and organization. . . . Since the provision of basic social and economic opportunities is not enough . . . a variety of significant social supports, through services, must be developed to insure that the expanded opportunities which become available . . . are utilized. Social work, as well as psychological, psychiatric, health, and other community services, must be amply provided to many parents and children so that the basic opportunities are appropriately appreciated and used. . . . Even the provision of expanded opportunities and services may still not be enough to prevent social ills and to rehabilitate problem families and their children. Expanded opportunities and services must be efficiently organized. Too often, problem youngsters and their families are shunted from agency to agency. . . . [M]any programs in deprived neighborhoods lack quality, imagination, and flexibility. Untrained and poorly supervised personnel are presented with intolerably heavy and difficult assignments which they cannot handle effectively. Stereotyped and inferior practices at schools and agencies are little better than no teaching at all. (pp. 173–174)

The effectiveness of opportunities provision is thus seen as a joint function of the opportunities themselves, the manner in which they are provided, and the way they are coordinated, organized, or interrelated. Similar thinking regarding the context, content, and relationship of opportunities provided will also be evident in the next chapter, which illustrates a multifaceted, comprehensive orientation to gang intervention.

OPPORTUNITY WITHDRAWAL AND THE RISE OF DETERRENCE/INCARCERATION

As the 1970s drew to a close, America got tough. As described in chapter 2, a combination of the heavy influx of drugs, increasing violence, purported failure of rehabilitative programming, and the rise of political and judicial conservatism combined to usher in the era of deterrence/incarceration and begin ushering out the provision of social, economic, and educational opportunity. Opportunity provision is not gone, but it is much less frequently the centerpiece of gang intervention programming. Social control—surveillance, deterrence, arrest, prosecution, incarceration—has largely replaced social improvement as the preeminent approach to gang youths in the United States:

> A philosophy of increased social opportunity was
> replaced by growing conservatism. The gang was viewed
> as evil, a collecting place for sociopaths who were beyond
> the capacity of most social institutions to redirect or
> rehabilitate them. Protection of the community became
> the key goal. (Spergel et al., 1989, p. 148)

The deterrence/incarceration strategy came to guide the gang-related actions not only of law enforcement personnel but of others also. In Philadelphia's Crisis Intervention Network program, in Los Angeles' Community Youth Gang Services, and in other similar crisis intervention programs that sprang up across the country, the resource worker—who had replaced the detached worker—was in turn replaced by the surveillance/deterrence worker. Working out of radio-dispatched automobiles and assigned to geographical areas rather than to specific gangs, surveillance/deterrence workers responded to crises, focusing on rumor control, dispute resolution, and, most centrally, violence reduction. Maxson and Klein (1983) convey the essence of this strategy, contrasting it with the earlier value transformation approach:

> The transformation model fostered social group work in
> the streets with empathic and sympathetic orientations
> toward gang members as well as acceptance of gang
> misbehavior as far less of a problem than the alienating
> response of community residents and officials. By
> contrast, the deterrence model eschews an interest in
> minor gang predations and concentrates on the major

ones, especially homicide. The worker is, in essence, part of a dramatically energized community control mechanism, a "firefighter" with a more balanced eye on the consequences as well as the cause of gang violence. Success is measured first in violence reduction, not in group or individual change. (p. 151)

Indeed, it is a primary responsibility of society's officialdom to protect its citizens. Gang violence in its diverse and often intense forms must be monitored, deterred, and punished. But much more must be done. Gang youths are *our* youths. They are among us now, and, even if they are periodically incarcerated, most will be among us in the future. We deserve protection from their predations, but they deserve the opportunity to lead satisfying and productive lives without resorting to individual or group violence. Punishment may be necessary, but punishment fails to teach new, alternative means to desired goals. Implementation of the deterrence/incarceration model may indeed be needed in today's violence-prone United States, but it is far from sufficient. What is needed and, we hope, appears to be emerging is a less unidimensional and more integrative gang intervention model, one with at least the potential to supplant exclusive use of deterrence/incarceration. We term it the Comprehensive Model; it is similar in spirit and in most particulars to Spergel et al.'s (1989) Model B, which incorporates and seeks prescriptively to apply major features of programming centered on detached workers, opportunities provision, and social control.[1] It is a multimodal, multilevel strategy; its successful realization requires that substantial resources, of diverse types, be employed in a coordinated manner. A previous study has documented the manner in which aggressive and antisocial behavior derives from complex causality and, hence, will yield most readily when approached with targeted interventions of equivalent complexity (Goldstein, 1983). The same is true for gang aggression and antisocial behavior. Efforts in both California and New York State, described in the following chapter, give full philosophical and concrete expression to this comprehensive gang intervention strategy.

---

[1] Spergel et al. (1989) comment that this model "assumes that the gang problem may be only partially amenable to police suppression. Gang interventions must be defined in broader terms. The youth gang suppression strategy must be incorporated as part of an interagency community collaborative approach which also gives due attention to prevention and social intervention" (p. 173).

CHAPTER 10

State Level Intervention: Comprehensive Planning

As much of this book makes clear, the delinquent gang problem in the United States is major and growing. Efforts to better understand its scope and nature, and to intervene effectively to reduce its consequences, have reached beyond individual agency or community concern to command attention at the government level in several states. California and New York, for example, each formed task forces composed of academic, police, youth agency, educational, government, and other experts concerned with the problem of gangs. The task forces were charged with probing matters of cause, magnitude, demographics, and trends in gang formation and behavior, and offering recommendations concerning both prevention and remediation. This chapter presents the executive summary of the final report by the California State Task Force on Gangs and Drugs (California Council on Criminal Justice, 1989) and the entire text of the report of the New York State Task Force on Juvenile Gangs (New York State Division for Youth, 1990). Though, as will be seen, the nature of gangs differs considerably between the two states—in longevity, organization, territoriality, typical size, and other respects—both reports recommend quite similar comprehensive intervention strategies. Preventive and rehabilitation efforts, it is urged, need be targeted to the youth, the gang, the community, and the larger society—a comprehensive strategy thoroughly consistent with that offered by this book. Both reports articulate this strategy and concretize its intervention implications with specific programming information, thus making an especially valuable contribution to a contemporary understanding of delinquent gangs and their management.

GANG AND DRUG IMPACT ON CALIFORNIA: REPORT OF THE CALIFORNIA STATE TASK FORCE ON GANGS AND DRUGS

Purpose of the Task Force

The California Council on Criminal Justice (CCCJ), at the direction of Governor George Deukmejian, convened the State Task Force on Gangs and Drugs to recommend statewide policy and legislative proposals to address the growing threat of gangs and drugs.*

Background

Gang involvement in drug trafficking has expanded to dramatic proportions, bringing with it a reign of terror brought on by battles for sales territories and profits.

The gang and drug problem is not new to the state of California. In 1981, then–Attorney General George Deukmejian examined the criminal justice implications of gang violence. In 1985, the California Council of Criminal Justice convened the State Task Force on Youth Gang Violence to examine the growing problem of violent crimes committed by youth gangs throughout the state. This body developed numerous legislative and administrative recommendations for targeting both the prevention and suppression of youth gang violence.

In 1988, the State Task Force on Gangs and Drugs was reconvened to focus on the specific issues and concerns relating to the growing involvement of gangs in narcotics trafficking. This Executive Summary provides an overview of the public hearing process, describes the impact of gangs and drugs as experienced in the various regions of the state, and presents a Summary of Findings and a Summary of Recommendations that address the concerns and needs of local communities and local, state, and federal agencies.

It is the objective of this Task Force Report to provide a thorough understanding and specific plan of action to combat the violence of gang drug-traffickers and to prevent negative gang and drug influences on the youths of tomorrow.

---

* This section presents the executive summary of *State Task Force on Gangs and Drugs: Final Report* by the California Council on Criminal Justice, 1989, Sacramento, CA: Author.

Summary of Public Hearings

The State Task Force on Gangs and Drugs investigated the problem of gangs and their involvement in drug-trafficking and associated violence. Understanding that this is not a problem unique to any one community, the Task Force held hearings throughout the state to hear testimony from representatives of small and large cities and counties, schools, social services agencies, government, businesses and industries, community organizations, and a broad range of criminal justice agencies.

The public told the Task Force of the need for immediate solutions to the expanding violence and terror and of the public outcry for stricter sentencing and treatment of drug-trafficking gang members. The Task Force listened to testimony from concerned citizens and gang members on the nature of gang- and drug-related violence, and on the effect that this form of terrorism has on our communities. Most criminal justice agencies are overwhelmed by the excessive caseloads, jail and prison overcrowding, and continuing violence on the streets. Yet, throughout the hearings, criminal justice officials spoke of the success of interagency task forces in the investigation and prosecution of gang drug-traffickers, stressing the importance and the value of vertical prosecution. (*Vertical prosecution* refers to a technique whereby one attorney handles all prosecution of a case from filing through sentencing.)

Judicial and other criminal justice representatives addressed the need for more efficient court processes and consistent sentencing and probation conditions for the gang and drug offender. Representatives from community organizations, service agencies, and criminal justice entities stressed the overriding need for long-term solutions to the gang and drug problem through prevention and intervention programs. A majority of those who testified recommended a school-based, prevention education program starting with preschool and kindergarten and continuing through to the highest secondary grades.

In addition to the public hearings, the Task Force conducted written surveys of district attorneys, chiefs of police, sheriffs, and probation officers to solicit their ideas. The Task Force also received extensive written testimony.

The Task Force members have developed these Findings and Recommendations after hearing 7 days of testimony and carefully analyzing the results. Through examining this issue from various geographical, agency, and personal perspectives the Task Force has gained an in-depth understanding of the pervasiveness of the gang and drug problem, and a full appreciation of the needs of the individual communities in addressing these problems.

Summary of Findings

1. Some communities are literally held captive by the violence, intimidation, and decay resulting from drug-trafficking by gangs.

2. Gang involvement in drug-trafficking has increased with the advent of crack cocaine, and gang members are operating with an increased level of sophistication and violence for the purpose of seizing and maintaining profitable drug territories.

3. Specialized law enforcement prevention, intervention, and suppression approaches, coordinated with other criminal justice agencies, schools, businesses, and community organizations, are effective approaches in addressing the gang and drug problem.

4. Prosecution units specializing in gang and drug cases, using vertical prosecution techniques in coordination with other criminal justice entities, are successful in targeting and incarcerating serious gang and drug offenders.

5. Intensified, specialized supervision of gang and drug probationers/parolees is a successful approach in monitoring their activities and enforcing compliance with probation/parole conditions.

6. Specialized treatment of gang and drug offenders within correctional facilities is successful in monitoring their activities and decreasing violence in the institutions.

7. A statewide information system is needed for law enforcement to investigate and suppress gang- and drug-related criminal activities.

8. Present California laws are not strict enough to address the activities of serious gang and drug offenders. Probation restrictions are not standardized nor consistently applied throughout the state.

9. Present court proceedings and criminal procedures are so lengthy and cumbersome that it is impossible to provide speedy trials.

10. The present training provided to the judiciary does not prepare judges to deal with serious gang and drug cases.

11. Federal agency support is necessary to address the growing sophistication, mobility, and violence demonstrated by today's drug-trafficking gangs.

12. Gang crime suppression activities also improve the ability of law enforcement to suppress other crimes.

13. Local police and sheriffs' departments presently do not have the effective resources to suppress gang and drug crimes.

14. The new California statute for asset forfeiture will sunset in 1994, diminishing the ability to seize the gains of gang and drug dealers in the future.

15. The Serious Habitual Offender (SHO) Program funded by the Governor's Office of Criminal Justice Planning (OCJP) is an effective method for early identification of juvenile offenders in order to refer them to intensive counseling and intervention, which may deter them from ongoing delinquent or gang- and drug-related behavior.

16. The present capacity of local and state correctional facilities is inadequate to ensure the incarceration of serious gang and drug offenders.

17. The flow of narcotics into this state has increased in the past few years.

18. Current law does not hold parents or guardians responsible for the costs of detaining or incarcerating their children.

19. Early prevention, education, and intervention are effective methods in keeping youths away from gangs and drugs.

20. Employment opportunities are an attractive and effective means of keeping youths away from gangs and drugs.

21. Juvenile gang and drug offenders state that the juvenile justice system is a "joke" and poses no significant threat or deterrent to committing crimes.

22. Schools furnish the most effective means for providing gang and drug prevention education.

23. Local community-based programs, which involve the cooperation of individuals in the community, businesses, schools, religious organizations, and law enforcement and

government agencies, are essential to combat the intimidation of the community from gang and drug violence and to prevent gang and drug activities.

24. Parental and adult role models play a vital role in a child's attitude toward gangs and drugs.

25. Many drug treatment programs do not address the unique problems associated with gang-related substance abuse.

26. Penal Code Section 1000 diversion procedures are abused by gang members to avoid prosecution for narcotics trafficking.

Summary of Recommendations

Law Enforcement Recommendations

1. Establish or consolidate gang and narcotics enforcement activities within a single, specialized gang and narcotics enforcement unit.

2. Provide ongoing training to the appropriate officers on methods of gang and drug enforcement, patrol, and investigation, as well as on the need to integrate specialized operations with patrol and investigations.

3. Coordinate gang and drug enforcement and prevention within an interagency task force, including schools, prosecution, probation, corrections, and community organizations.

4. Coordinate efforts with fire marshals and health inspectors to abate crack houses (or other facilities used as gang gathering places) by enforcing local health, fire, building, and safety codes.

5. Recruit officers, both men and women, from a representative cross section of ethnic groups, possessing bilingual skills and sensitivity to special language or cultural needs.

6. Coordinate law enforcement efforts with business and community organizations as well as with outreach and awareness programs to encourage community participation and victim/witness cooperation.

7. Notify parents or guardians of their children's gang affiliations.

8. Increase the number of peace officers in law enforcement agencies to enhance patrol and field operation staffing, placing more officers on the street to protect the community and to suppress gang- and drug-related crime.

9. Establish a Serious Habitual Offender (SHO) Program within each law enforcement agency to coordinate with prosecution and probation operations in targeting the most serious offenders for apprehension, prosecution, and incarceration.

10. Establish a community advisory group within all law enforcement departments to coordinate and select community-based organization programs that will most effectively provide community service, prevention, intervention, and community mobilization programs that are necessary to address the gang and drug problem.

Prosecution Recommendations

1. Establish vertical prosecution units focused on gang and drug offender cases.

2. Target first-time gang and drug offenders for stricter prosecution to discourage their criminal behavior.

3. Provide training to specialized prosecution units on the unique aspects and methods of gang and drug case prosecution.

4. Participate in or encourage the development of local multiagency task forces directed toward the apprehension, prosecution, and incarceration of gang and drug offenders.

5. Request the courts to place no bail holds on serious gang and drug offenders who may pose a danger to the community, victims, or witnesses.

Corrections Recommendations

1. Continue intelligence coordination between corrections and enforcement agencies.

2. Establish, under the direction of the California Department of Corrections and the Department of the Youth Authority, minimum-security state correctional facilities to house appropriate offenders in vacant or unused military facilities (as provided by the U.S. Department of Defense) to alleviate

overcrowding and to permit the incarceration of violent, drug-dealing gang offenders. Inmates confined in these facilities should be assigned to work on job skills training that supports the renovation and maintenance of the grounds and buildings.

3. Continue present programs within correctional facilities to classify and segregate gang members, and to provide for tattoo removal and assistance in returning the gang members to the community.

4. Implement gang drug treatment and prevention programs within correctional institutions and as an element of preparation for release on parole/probation.

5. Continue to provide correctional officers with training in gang and drug offender supervision, classification, and investigative techniques.

6. Modify construction standards for local jails to allow for quicker and less expensive facility construction without sacrificing safety and security.

7. Establish, under the direction of local jail corrections authorities, minimum-security county correctional facilities to house appropriate offenders in vacant or unused military facilities (as provided by the U.S. Department of Defense) to alleviate overcrowding and to permit the incarceration of violent, drug-dealing gang offenders. Inmates confined in these facilities should be assigned to work on job skills training that supports the renovation and maintenance of the grounds and buildings.

8. Recruit officers and agents, both men and women, from a representative cross section of ethnic groups possessing bilingual skills and sensitivity to special language or cultural needs.

Probation/Parole Recommendations

1. Continue to establish specialized vertical probation and parole supervision units with reduced caseloads, focusing on the gang drug-trafficking offender.

2. Develop standardized gang control probation and parole conditions in conjunction with the courts and paroling authorities to be used statewide that will preclude continuing gang and drug involvement and will provide enhanced ability for parolee/probationer tracking. Require that the

conditions be listed on an identification card that must be carried by the probationer/parolee at all times and be presented to any peace officer on request. The card must also include the name of the probation or parole officer and a 24-hour contact phone number for that agency.

3. Establish a centralized statewide registry to maintain information on all probationers and parolees, listing the specific probation and parole terms and conditions that apply to each individual.

4. Implement gang and drug probation and parole programs to more effectively manage gang parolees and probationers.

5. Provide training to specialized probation and parole supervision personnel on the aspects of and methods for gang and drug offender supervision.

6. Recruit officers/agents, both men and women, from a representative cross section of ethnic groups possessing bilingual skills and sensitivity to special language or cultural needs.

Judicial Recommendations

1. Establish, through the California Center for Judicial Education and Research (CJER) and the State Judicial Council, a training program for judges to inform them of the unique aspects of gang and drug cases.

2. Establish regional courts to hear cases pertaining to a designated geographic/community area so that judges may become more aware of, and sensitive to, the crime problems occurring within a specific community.

3. Establish specialized courts, within larger communities, hearing only cases involving gangs and drugs so that judges may become more aware of the complex nature of the specific legal interpretations, criminal behavior, and sentencing requirements relating to these cases.

4. Ensure that gang and drug offenders violating their probation are returned to the judge who sentenced them.

5. Establish special night court sessions within either regional or specialized gang and drug case courts in order to offer a convenient time for juvenile offenders to attend court with their parents or guardians.

6. Develop, through the State Judicial Council and the Chief Probation Officers Association, uniform, statewide standards for setting probation conditions for serious gang and drug offenders.

Executive Recommendations

1. Consider the creation, through an executive order, of a Statewide Narcotics Enforcement Coordination Task Force.

2. Direct the California National Guard to concentrate surveillance and reconnaissance efforts along the California-Mexico border.

3. Direct the Governor's Office of Criminal Justice Planning to survey community-based organizations in order to establish a clearinghouse of information on successful models for prevention, intervention, and community mobilization programs and on methods for obtaining funding for such programs.

4. Direct the Commission on Peace Officer Standards and Training to provide instruction for law enforcement officers regarding the history, function, and safe handling of assault-type weapons. Also direct the Governor's Office of Criminal Justice Planning to provide prosecutors with similar training.

5. Establish a computer-based information system for compiling and organizing municipal, county, and statewide gang data, including gang-related narcotics trafficking intelligence.

Legislative Recommendations

1. Enact legislation that would provide stricter treatment of juveniles who commit serious crimes. The Task Force recommends the following changes to the Welfare and Institutions Code:

   a. Amend the Welfare and Institutions Code, including Section 707, as well as Section 190 *et seq.,* of the Penal Code, to mandate that any 16- or 17-year-old juvenile who is charged with a serious "Proposition 8" felony, as defined in Section 1192.7 of the Penal Code, or who is charged with the sale or possession for sale of any controlled substance, or who is charged with any offense involving the use of any type of firearm or possession of a firearm at the time of commission or arrest, shall be automatically tried as an adult and subject to the imposition of an adult sentence;

b. Amend Welfare and Institutions Code Section 707, as well as Section 190 *et seq.,* of the penal Code, defining the crime of murder and its punishment to mandate that 16- or 17-year-old juveniles charged with the commission of special circumstances murder be subject to the term of life imprisonment without the possibility of parole;

c. Amend Section 707 of the Welfare and Institutions Code to provide, in cases involving other felony offenses, that juveniles 16 years of age or older involved in gang activity as defined by Penal Code Section 186.2 are reputably presumed to be unfit for treatment by the juvenile court, and are suitable to be tried as adults; and

d. Further amend the Welfare and Institutions Code to provide that 14- and 15-year-old minors who are charged with the commission of special circumstances murder are to be tried as adults and, upon conviction, shall serve a minimum term of 20 years, including automatic transfer from the Department of the Youth Authority to the Department of Corrections upon the age of 21 years.

2. Enact a comprehensive Racketeer Influenced and Corrupt Organization Act (RICO) statute similar to the existing federal provision.

3. Amend the state narcotics asset forfeiture laws to:

a. Eliminate the 1994 sunset clause from the statute language and make it identical to existing federal forfeiture provisions.

b. Provide for the forfeiture of any vehicle used in a drive-by shooting.

c. Commit an amount from the Asset Forfeiture Fund to the Gang Violence Suppression Program budget within the Governor's Office of Criminal Justice Planning.

4. Enact legislation to establish policy to provide stricter treatment of offenders who use weapons:

a. Amend Subdivision (a) of Section 245 of the Penal Code by adding a provision that would make assault with a machine gun punishable by a mandatory term of life imprisonment with the possibility of parole;

b. Amend Subdivision (a) of Section 245 to provide for a mandatory term of 4, 8, or 12 years of imprisonment for assault with a high-capacity, semiautomatic firearm;

c. Amend the Penal Code by adding a mandatory sentence enhancement section covering murder, shooting into a dwelling or vehicle, kidnapping, robbery, escape, or witness intimidation that would enhance the sentence for the underlying felony as follows:

- Use of a machine gun by a principal—an additional term of 5, 10, or 15 years.

- Use of a high-capacity semiautomatic firearm by a principal—an additional term of 3, 4, or 5 years.

- Any principal armed with a machine gun—an additional term of 3, 4, or 5 years.

   Sections 1203.06 and 12022.5 of the Penal Code, which together compose California's "Use a Gun—Go to Prison" law, require that personal use of a firearm receive a mandatory state prison sentence and the most severe sentence enhancement;

d. Amend Section 1385 of the Penal Code to prohibit a judge from striking any sentence enhancement for misuse of a machine gun or high-capacity semiautomatic firearm;

e. Amend the Penal Code to provide that the punishment for an ex-felon who possesses a machine gun will be a mandatory term of 4, 8, or 12 years, and a term of 3, 6, or 9 years for possession of a high-capacity semiautomatic firearm by an ex-felon;

f. Amend the Penal Code to provide that carrying a semiautomatic firearm and an easily accessible, loaded high-capacity magazine for that specific semiautomatic firearm in an automobile be a felony punishable by a term of 1, 2, or 3 years;

g. Amend Section 12220 of the Penal Code to provide a term of imprisonment of 3, 4, or 5 years for illegal possession of a machine gun; and

h. Amend the Penal Code to provide that the intentional conversion of a firearm into a machine gun shall be punished by a term of imprisonment of 3, 4, or 5 years.

5. Amend Section 666 of the Penal Code by adding Section 11550 of the Health and Safety Code to the list of those violations that may be charged as an alternative felony/misdemeanor if the defendant has suffered a prior conviction for violation of Section 11550 or any of the offenses enumerated in Section 666.

6. Amend Section 11353.5 of the Health and Safety Code so that it conforms with Title 21 of the United States Code, Section 845a, relating to the distribution or manufacturing of drugs in or near schools and colleges.

7. Enact legislation that would eliminate, by constitutional amendment, postindictment preliminary hearings in cases in which the defendants have already been indicted by a grand jury.

8. Enact legislation to enable and to fund the Governor's Office of Criminal Justice Planning in administering a training program for prosecutors, law enforcement officers, and the judiciary regarding the investigative functions of a criminal grand jury.

9. Enact legislation that would allow hearsay testimony in the preliminary hearing.

10. Revise the provisions of the Penal Code and the Rules of the Court relating to sentencing in order to limit a trial court's discretion to grant probation to narcotics traffickers.

11. Enact legislation, through constitutional amendment, that would require judicial officers to consider the protection of the public in setting bail or allowing a defendant to be released on his or her own recognizance in all criminal prosecutions.

12. Enact legislation that would amend Section 1078 of the Penal Code to provide for judicial *voir dire* of prospective jurors in criminal trials.

13. Enact legislation that would amend the California Constitution to allow *voir dire* of prospective jurors in open court, in capital cases.

14. Enact legislation that will expand the designation of Enterprise Zones and Economic and Employment Incentive Areas in order to provide increased economic development and job opportunities within gang-affected communities.

15. Enact legislation to eliminate heroin and cocaine addiction and drug sales from any consideration for diversion to Penal Code Section 1000 drug programs and allow the program to concentrate on the drug users who can benefit from the education and counseling concepts that are intended by these programs.

16. Enact legislation to place on the ballot a constitutional amendment that will require parents to be responsible for the costs of detaining their children within juvenile facilities.

17. Enact legislation to mandate that the Department of Corrections develop and implement a comprehensive narcotics treatment, education, and diversion program for inmates in all of its penal institutions.

18. Enact legislation to amend the current provisions of the state's electronic surveillance law to parallel the federal statute.

19. Enact legislation that will provide for the forfeiture of any leasehold, and attendant deposits, where there has been illegal narcotics-related activity in the leased or rented property.

20. Enact legislation to provide adequate funding for the expansion of the prison system and/or any California detention facility, including secure facilities for juvenile offenders.

21. Amend Penal Code Section 594 (Vandalism) to make gang-related graffiti, regardless of the dollar amount of damage, an alternate misdemeanor or felony with increased penalties.

22. Enact legislation to implement a statewide curfew law and to recommend that communities with current curfew ordinances make a renewed, concentrated enforcement effort in the area of juvenile curfew violations.

23. Enact legislation to require that the State Department of Education, the Governor's Office of Criminal Justice Planning, and the Department of the Youth Authority

develop and implement a statewide mandated gang and drug prevention program within all public schools in the state to:

a. Teach social values and self-esteem to youths, commencing with kindergarten;

b. Teach social responsibility and, most importantly, family values and parenting skills;

c. Teach students in all grades how to avoid involvement with gangs and drugs;

d. Train teachers and administrators on how to implement this curriculum, and how to detect and intervene with gang- and drug-related or "at risk" behavior; and

e. Mandate the California State Commission on Credentialing to require all teachers and administrators to complete the gang and drug prevention program as a requirement for certificate renewal.

24. Enact legislation to establish Juvenile Justice Centers within individual communities throughout the state.

25. Enact legislation to fund and establish Juvenile Assessment Centers through the Governor's Office of Criminal Justice Planning, the California Department of the Youth Authority Youth Services Bureau, the probation authority, and the juvenile court to screen juvenile status offenders. The process must take appropriate action within the current 6-hour time limit in which the juvenile can be legally detained.

26. Enact legislation to mandate that the State Department of Education establish a program to require testing of all juveniles in primary grades to determine physiological or psychological learning disabilities.

Federal Agency Recommendations

1. Increase the availability of federal resources to state and local gang- and drug-related case investigations.

2. Increase public awareness of the Internal Revenue Service's (IRS's) cash transaction reporting requirements for businesses, and enforce compliance with these regulations.

3. Increase the use of federal "cross designation" of local police officers and prosecutors to allow local authorities to use the federal system.

4. Coordinate Immigration and Naturalization Service (INS) investigations with state and local authorities to identify known offenders who may be suitable for deportation proceedings and also to increase the seizure of narcotics illegally imported across our borders.

5. Coordinate federal agency investigations with state and local authorities to identify opportunities for interdiction. Use military forces and their resources to interdict more effectively the flow of illegal narcotics into our country.

6. Conduct a nationwide investigation of gang relationships with international narcotics traffickers. Establish, through the Federal Bureau of Investigation (FBI), a nationwide data base for drug-trafficking case information.

7. Continue funding to support victim/witness protection and relocation.

8. Continue and expand funding to Head Start–type programs.

9. Adopt federal legislation that provides mandatory sentences for gang members, their associates, or others who cross interstate lines for the purpose of conducting gang-related drug activities.

10. Provide vacant or unused military facilities that would be suitable for the confinement of adult or juvenile inmates to the California Department of Corrections, the California Department of the Youth Authority, or local governments.

Local Government Recommendations

1. Expand gang intervention programs to prevent continuing gang and drug involvement.

2. Set local government budget priorities to allocate funds to gang and drug prevention and enforcement programs.

3. Direct the Community Redevelopment Agency to develop job-generating, inner-city projects to develop residential communities and business/industry zones within affected communities.

School Program Recommendations

1. Establish a required gang and drug prevention program, coordinated with local law enforcement, community, and business organizations.

2. Provide and require, for continuing certification, training for administrators and teachers to raise awareness of the gang and drug problem, and outline prevention education curricula.

3. Provide components in the school prevention education program to enhance parental awareness of gang and drug problems, and refer parents or guardians to community support groups.

4. Coordinate with community-based organizations and law enforcement agencies to develop and implement a parental skills training program.

5. Establish and enforce codes within the schools to prohibit the display of gang "colors" and the use of pagers or car phones on school grounds.

6. In cooperation with local government and state agencies, expand after-school, weekend, and summer youth programs to appeal to broader based groups, especially in the age range of 10 to 18 years.

7. Establish a program within all school systems to require the testing of juveniles in primary grades to determine physiological or psychological learning disabilities.

Community-Based Organizations Recommendations

1. Identify and recruit successful community members and business persons to serve as role models and mentors to youths.

2. Seek support from local businesses and industries for employment training and placement programs.

3. Provide for community mobilization and involvement through Neighborhood Watch programs to encourage citizen participation and victim/witness cooperation.

4. Encourage parental responsibility, establish parental support programs to increase awareness of gang and drug problems, and provide 24-hour hot lines and counseling. Enhancing parental skills is critical to mitigating the gang problem.

5. Establish, in coordination with local law enforcement agencies and the schools, a parental notification program to inform parents or guardians when their children are involved in gang and drug activity.

6. Establish, in coordination with religious organizations, a prevention and intervention program utilizing role models and mentors for counseling youths.

7. Establish prevention and intervention programs in communities with special language or cultural needs.

8. Implement programs to encourage teenagers to serve as role models and to participate in community development programs.

Business and Industry Recommendations

1. Expand opportunities for business development through the state's Enterprise Zones.

2. Engage in "adopt a school," youth sports team sponsorship, inner-city job placement, and executive volunteer job training and counseling programs.

3. Develop training programs and work experience opportunities for youths, targeting both gang members and potential gang members.

Media Recommendations

1. Cover all aspects of the gang and drug problem, including the success of intervention and prevention programs.

2. Provide public service announcements and programming for public education on gang and drug prevention and parenting responsibilities.

3. Ensure that gang-related reporting does not glorify the gang culture or attribute acts to any one gang by name.

REAFFIRMING PREVENTION: REPORT OF THE NEW YORK STATE TASK FORCE ON JUVENILE GANGS

Introduction

A serious juvenile gang problem currently exists in the United States.† Although the appearance, fading, and reappearance of such law-violating youth groups have been recurrent phenomena in American history, the 1980s have brought a new and more virulent level of such activity. The wide availability and profitability of diverse and potent drugs, changing American traditions that permit and at times encourage increased use of aggression, and a broad array of disadvantageous social and economic conditions have each contributed importantly to this heightening of juvenile gang existence activity. Several recent surveys, national or in states other than New York, have sought to specify more fully the causes of such gang development; the scope and nature of their size, membership, and activity; and means for their prevention, deterrence, and remediation (Huff, 1989; Needle & Stapleton, 1982; Philibosian, 1986; Quicker, 1983b; Spergel, 1989). These efforts combine to underscore the following:

1. The difficulty in defining what constitutes a gang, and the manner in which the definitions put forth differ from one region of the country to another

2. The diversity and intransigence of causes currently purported to give rise to gang formation and activity, and the manner in which such causal thinking must determine remediation efforts

3. The crucial need for carefully formulated strategies or statements of guiding philosophy to help determine and direct such remedial efforts

4. The need for the development, support, and implementation of effective remedial programming aimed at prevention, deterrence, and rehabilitation

---

† This section presents the complete text of *Reaffirming Prevention: Report of the Task Force on Juvenile Gangs* by the New York State Division for Youth, 1990, Albany, NY: Author.

5. The need for such programming to go beyond youth-directed efforts to include effective systems change intervention directed to family life, schools, the employment market, and other significant components of the context in which gang members live and gangs flourish

The New York State Task Force on Juvenile Gangs was organized in the fall of 1989 to be responsive to these earlier conclusions. To ensure both depth and diversity of gang-relevant expertise, the Task Force included several youth agency administrators serving the needs of at-risk youths; police gang unit directors; New York State Division for Youth program and local service administrators; faculty from relevant academic disciplines (social work, criminology, sociology, psychology); and representatives of the New York City Board of Education, the New York City Department of Corrections, the New York State Department of Education, and the New York State Division of Criminal Justice Services. In addition to the rich, gang-relevant knowledge and experience thus reflected, a major and successful effort was made to similarly reflect the regional and ethnic diversity characteristic of New York State. Our goal in broad terms was to ascertain the juvenile gang pattern currently existing in New York State and to formulate both programmatic and strategic recommendations designed to ameliorate this pattern in ways that would serve both New York State's citizens and the gang youths themselves. In order to concretize these goals, we set ourselves the following specific tasks, the results of which constitute the body of the present report:

1. Define the term *gang* as it is reflected in the behavior and relationships of juveniles in New York State.

2. Describe the current gang demographics of New York State, including estimates of the numbers of gangs and participating youths, member characteristics (age, gender, ethnicity, etc.), growth patterns over time, drug and violence involvement, and other salient characteristics.

3. Formulate a comprehensive, utilitarian perspective on youth gangs to serve as a guiding philosophy for the state's dealings with juvenile gangs. Such a strategic statement, as well as both the programmatic and strategic recommendations to which it gives rise, should be reactive to gangs as they exist and proactive to the positive needs of both youths at risk of gang activity and the general citizenry. It should lay a philosophical

groundwork for system change and youth change intervention, and, because gang youths display different levels of involvement in antisocial behavior, concern itself with prevention and remediation issues.

4. Select and recommend to New York State for expanded implementation a small number of effective programs to prevent or remediate antisocial gang behavior and promote alternative prosocial behavior. Program recommendations should be based upon professional expertise and experience, as well as on input obtained from a panel of gang-involved youths. Programs recommended should be the best available in terms of their demonstrated effectiveness and demonstrated responsiveness to the constructive needs and aspirations of both gang-involved youths and the citizens of New York State.

5. Develop and present to New York State a sequence of strategic recommendations designed to enhance the quality and effectiveness of existing and potential programming for youths at risk of gang involvement. These recommendations should be collectively designed to generate, implement, and sustain the best possible programming for such youths, and do so in a manner fully responsive to the real-world opportunities and constraints inherent in their family and community environments.

Definition

As the nature of juvenile gangs in the United States has changed over recent decades, so too have the formal definitions of *gang* put forth:

The gang . . . has been viewed as a play group as well as a criminal organization (Puffer 1912; Thrasher 1927/1963); also as malicious and negativistic, comprising mainly younger adolescents (A.K. Cohen, 1955); or representing different types of delinquent subcultural adaptation (Cloward and Ohlin 1960). Definitions in the 1950s and 1960s were related to issues of etiology as well as based on liberal, social reform assumptions. Definitions in the 1970s and 1980s are more descriptive, emphasize violent and criminal characteristics, and possibly a more conservative philosophy of social control and deterrence (Klein and

Maxson 1989). The most recent trend may be to view gangs as more pathological than functional and to restrict usage of the term to a narrow set of violent and criminal groups. . . . Definitions determine whether we have a large or small, or even no problem, whether more or fewer gangs and gang members exist, more or fewer arrests are to be made, and which agencies will receive funds to deal with the problem in one way or another. (Spergel, 1989, p. 14)

At the current time, gang definitions vary greatly from region to region, from one gang-relevant professional group to another, and among academic disciplines. To some extent this definitional diversity reflects true differences in the actual nature of the juvenile groups involved in different parts of the country; in other instances the differences appear to be a result of the wearing of differing professional or academic glasses when observing the same phenomenon. The Task Force, reflecting both its varied professional perspectives as well as the realities of gang composition and behavior in New York State, defined *gang* as follows:

An ongoing identifiable group of adolescents (highly organized or loosely structured) which, either individually or collectively, has engaged in or is considered likely to engage in unlawful or antisocial activity that may be verified by police records or other reliable sources and who create an atmosphere of fear and intimidation within the community. *Exclusion:* Gangs or groups that initially come together for the sole purpose of furthering a business enterprise.

Note that unlike the more structured, long-lived, territorial, colors-oriented gangs more typical of Los Angeles, and even Chicago, the typical New York State gang is a loose association of irregularly antisocial youths, often anonymous, more nomadic than territorial, and of shifting or changeable leadership. As one Task Force member with many years of experience with gangs aptly put it, "These groups are like pick-up basketball teams. They live all over the city and come together at school. They meet on a subway platform, a leader steps forward, and they're off and running."

The following excerpt from a recent report by the Youth Gang Intelligence Unit of the New York City Police Department assists further in elaborating the Task Force's definition of *gang:*

There are serious law-violating youth groups in the City
of New York. However, many of them do not fall under
the classic category of gangs. But that does not mean
they are not causing community and police problems and
violating laws. The traditional New York City youth gang
with a structured organization is becoming a thing of the
past. What we generally see are small groups known as
posses or crews or just disorderly groups of law violating
youth, with no real or identifiable leadership. There are
no "colors," tattoos or identifiable clothing to indicate
what gang or group they belong to or graffiti identifying
"turf" claimed by them. Members can belong to more
than one group, posse or crew. Most of the units are
short-lived. The constant intermixing of members in
different groups results in their disintegration and the
establishing of new groups being placed under
investigation. New York City gangs and/or groups tend to
be individual groups with little or no affiliation with
other gangs or groups. Turf depends for the most part on
where the group gathers. There are no clubhouses, so
they usually hang out near schools or subway stations
which are near the school, or at a transfer point on the
way home. The gangs or groups are not controlling their
home or neighborhood area or using it as a place to be
protected. Membership in gangs tends to be about 25
and loosely knit. (New York City Police Department,
1988, p. 3)

Finally, an optimal current definition of youth gangs in New
York State is also more fully clarified by mention of what such gangs
are not. It is common in the United States to assume that a central
defining feature of gang structure and behavior is organized involvement in illegal drug-trafficking and that, in a real sense,
juvenile gangs are drug organizations. Such, however, is largely not
the case in much of New York State. The New York City Police
Department's report comments in this regard:

In New York City, drugs are controlled by organized
crime groups. Young, weak, undermanned and poorly
organized street gangs cannot compete with the older,
more powerful and violent groups. The fragmented street
gangs do not have the network or the power to distribute
or control drugs on a large scale. What we see are the

drug organizations employing youths in various aspects
of their drug business. They are employed as steerers,
lookouts, dealers, enforcers or protectors from robbers
and other drug organizations. The primary difference
between a drug organization and a youth gang is that in a
drug organization all members are employees while youth
gang membership only requires affiliation. We do not see
our youth gangs becoming drug organizations. (New York
City Police Department, 1988, p. 4)

Demographics

The specific demographics of gang membership and activity in
the major New York State population centers are as follows:

New York City

Number and membership. Currently there are 37 active street
gangs with a membership of 1,036 and another 51 gangs under
investigation with an alleged membership of about 1,020.

Activities. At present the gangs and groups do not have clubhouses but frequent certain areas of the city. During the week and
particularly during the school day, these gangs are seen at schools
and on the transit system. Turf tends to be where the group occupies
space at any given time. Most of the gangs or groups are not based in
their neighborhoods. Activity from the nonneighborhood groups
tends to be profit oriented, whereas neighborhood activity tends to
be more assault oriented.

Growth patterns. Organized street gang activities in New York
City have decreased from the 1970s, when gang incidents and
arrests were recorded in the thousands. The last 5 years, gang
arrests have averaged about 160 a year. During this same period,
the number of associate arrests (arrest of more than one person,
which could indicate group activity) has averaged about 19,500.
Youth arrests and associate arrests continue to be high, whereas
identifiable gang arrests are relatively low and stable. Indications
are that today's antisocial and criminal youths prefer anonymity
from identifiable groups and no permanent association with any
one group.

Drug and violence patterns. Drug-trafficking and drug abuse
continue to be a serious problem in New York City. In the city drug

traffic is usually controlled by organized criminal groups comprised of adults. The fragmented youth gangs do not have the network or the power to control or distribute drugs on a large scale. Youth violence in New York City tends to be concentrated in and around the schools and transit systems. Most of the activity is committed from Monday through Friday from 8 A.M. to 7 P.M. The number one activity during this time is robbery accompanied by assault either near a school or on a transit facility.

Other characteristics. Other characteristics of gang member demographics include the following.

1. Age: Gang members range in age from 13 to 23.

2. Gender: Most are male; some are female.

3. Ethnicity (by gang organization):

	Male	**Female**
Hispanic	13	0
Black (one Black gang with a Black female chapter)	8	0
White	6	0
Chinese	3	0
Vietnamese	1	0
Hispanic/White	4	0
Hispanic/Black	1	0
Hispanic/Black/White	1	0
Total number of gangs	37	0

4. Recruitment: At present recruitment is typically initiated by those wanting to belong to the gang. The exception to this would be the Asian gangs, which still heavily recruit through fear and strong-arm tactics. There seems to be no ritual to get into the gang or dues to pay after admission.

5. Leadership: Although most groups claim not to have a leader, some names have surfaced as the heads of some of New York City's gangs. Today's gangs are not organized and structured like the gangs of the 1960s and 1970s. Today, gangs are loosely organized with little structure, if any. Activity can be initiated by any member of the group at any time.

Buffalo

In the Buffalo area there are no active, structured juvenile gangs known at this time. There are various related types of law-violating youth groups, such as street posses, teams, and crews identified by street names (e.g., Box Street Boys) and neighborhood locations (e.g., Fruit Belt Posse, Uptown Boys, Downtown Boys). The leadership of these groups usually depends on what is happening in the neighborhood at a given time and may change from week to week. Usually, law-violating youth groups appear at times of opportunity when a victim is available and circumstances are right.

Rochester

There are approximately 11 gangs in the Rochester area, involving an estimated 215 youths. Members range from 13 to approximately 25 years of age and are primarily Black males. Females are also members but currently are generally inactive. Gang membership appears to have decreased during 1989. Most crime committed by gang members is perpetrated by individuals acting alone or in small groups. In addition to committing such crimes as assault, burglary, and drug use, gang members have recently become active in the sale of narcotics.

Syracuse

It is estimated that almost 200 youths are members of the four juvenile gangs that currently exist in Syracuse. Membership levels appear to have grown in 1989, after approximately 7 years of little or no gang activity. As in the other New York cities, gang membership is concentrated in the low-income areas. In Syracuse, gang youths—usually 14 to 18 years old—are primarily Hispanic, with some observed gang activity involving both Black and White juveniles.

Albany

Albany's gang activity is reported to be different in some major respects from that in most other New York urban centers. A large concentration of youths aligned with the "five percent Nation–Muslim Sect" has been observed. Juvenile members of this organization are increasingly involved in the organized sale of narcotics. Albany also has a small number of White supremacy youth gangs (skinheads), who have been involved in crimes of arson and vandalism.

Mt. Vernon

Four known gangs exist in the city of Mt. Vernon, with an approximate membership of 80 youths. In addition, 15 other possible gangs are under investigation. Gang membership is primarily African-Americans and Jamaicans, aged 13 to 16. Leadership appears to fluctuate, and organization is loosely knit. Gang activity has emerged mainly in the last 2 years and consists largely of drug selling, assault, car theft, and extortion. Much of the gang activity occurs in or near the city's one senior high school.

Other Cities and Counties

A number of New York State population centers report no substantial organized gang problems at the current time. Unorganized, unruly, law-violating youth groups are present, however, in most of these centers. These locations are the city of New Rochelle, city of Utica, city of Yonkers, Nassau County, Suffolk County, and Westchester County.

Philosophical Foundations

Decade of the Child

In January 1987, Governor Mario M. Cuomo declared a "bold and broad commitment" to the children of New York State when he proclaimed the Decade of the Child. In his State of the State message to the legislature Governor Cuomo remarked:

New York's children are in danger. They are threatened by poverty, inadequate education, even terrible physical and mental abuse. The statistics are frightening:

- In 1980, one in five New York children lived in poverty; by 1984, the population had grown to one out of every four; for minority children, one out of two are poor

- Over 500,000 children have no health care coverage

- More than 24,000 children dropped out of New York City's High Schools in 1985

- Over 760,000 young adults are believed to be functionally illiterate.

Too many children bear children; too many children lack decent and safe housing; too many children receive inadequate education. They are our future. We have no time to lose.

For most of this century, New Yorkers called for public assistance to low-income families and children because it was the right and compassionate thing to do. Over the last generation, we began to understand that the provision of effective, efficient and accountable public services to assist low-income families and children was essential to our own self-interest. Today, it is even more evident that public and private efforts on behalf of families and children are no longer just a matter of self interest, they are a matter of economic survival in the twenty-first century. The problem is pervasive and deep. It demands nothing less than a bold and broad commitment of government at all levels, in partnership with the whole community. With that in mind, we must make a commitment to our children, in every conceivable way. Not just this year, not just next year: we must make the next ten years, the Decade of the Child! (p. 3)

Division for Youth Mission

The New York State Division for Youth has as its stated purpose preventing delinquency through positive youth development. As such, the agency is most concerned with youngsters from birth through age 21 and particularly with those programs and services that have impact upon their normal growth and development. The agency is mandated to provide prevention services to youths as well as direct (re)habilitative care for those youths adjudicated through family courts as either juvenile delinquents (JDs) or persons in need of supervision (PINS), as well as for those youths designated Juvenile Offenders (JOs) by adult courts.

Prevention

Caplan (1964), a community mental health specialist whose work has been applied to other human service areas, defined three categories of prevention: (a) primary—those prevention activities that attempt to reduce the number of disorders or problems of all types in the community, (b) secondary—those prevention activities that attempt to reduce the duration of disorders or problems, and (c) tertiary—those prevention activities that attempt to reduce the damage that may result from the disorders or problems. Bolman (1969) amplifies these categories in ways directly relevant to the goals of the present Task Force:

Primary prevention attempts to prevent a disorder from occurring. Secondary prevention attempts to identify and treat at the earliest possible moment so as to reduce the length and severity of disorder. Tertiary prevention attempts to reduce to a minimum the degree of handicap or impairment that results from a disorder that has already occurred. (p. 208)

The work of the Task Force, and its recommendations as embodied in this report, bear most directly upon primary prevention (to reduce the likelihood of gang involvement for at-risk youths not yet involved) and secondary prevention (to reduce the personal and societal consequences of involvement for at-risk youths peripherally or irregularly involved). There is concern for, but also somewhat less emphasis upon, tertiary prevention (of relevance to youths deeply and regularly involved in organized gang activity). We believe prevention, particularly primary prevention, is a process that attempts to change the conditions that create problems for youths within our society. Toward that end, to the extent that New York State is able to create systems, develop programs, and institute services that change the conditions creating the need for youths to be involved in gang activity, we will be able to implement the Governor's vision of the Decade of the Child.

Youth Development

Youth development is central to the Division for Youth's mission and at the heart of the Task Force's aspirations for youths at risk of gang involvement. Youth development refers to those programs and services that are necessary to ensure positive growth. By positive growth, we mean those constructive activities that a youth engages in that enhance the youth's feelings of self-worth, self-confidence, and self-esteem. At the very least, certain core factors need to be addressed in order to ensure positive growth and development. These include but are not limited to the following:

Health. A primary requisite for successful youth development is adequate levels of health care. Many of the youths involved in gang activity are not afforded appropriate preventive medical interventions. Often these youths do not have health education opportunities, such that they do not have a basic understanding of hygiene and disease prevention and control. In addition, basic medical care is oftentimes not available to them should they become ill.

The family/community. The literature in child development stresses the effects the family has on a child's life, especially during the formative years. The family and community are both essential to a child's moral, social, spiritual, emotional, physical, and intellectual development. The extent to which youngsters learn social rules, employ prosocial behaviors, internalize moral development, and structure values is directly related to their interactions with family and community members.

Education and training. Youths' positive development is directly correlated with their involvement in school. Youngsters who successfully participate in and complete their education have greater opportunities to develop into constructive, participating citizens. Data indicate that one-third of all New York State youths who enter high school never graduate. As such, they lack the basic literacy to function adequately within contemporary society. Thus, these youths, including those who ultimately are at risk of becoming gang members, often do not find jobs, retain employment, or develop work ethics that produce fully functioning citizens.

Leisure. The constructive use of leisure time and the appropriate knowledge of and access to recreational activities are basic to positive youth development. Many of the youths who participate in gang activities never develop recreational skills to use constructively in their leisure time. As such, having fun is defined by the group, in this case the gang, and often involves antisocial and criminal activity.

Youth Vulnerability

There are many encumbrances that interfere with the positive development of youths. Three of them—racism, poverty, and lack of cultural acceptance—are prepotent and deserve primary attention.

Racism. One of the major factors that increases youth vulnerability is racism. Racism is a most insidious social plague. The intrusion of racism into the normal growth and development of young people makes them highly vulnerable to its pervasive negative effects. We are most concerned with two of its manifestations: personal and institutional.

Personal racism involves attitudes individuals hold and subsequent behaviors they perform that are prejudicial and discriminatory. Personal racism involves name calling, bias-related violence, overt physical oppression, sexual harassment, and a plethora of other activities that affect certain classes or categories of people. The effects of personal racism upon those who are its victims include the development of low self-esteem, feelings of hopelessness and helplessness, and the acquisition of those aggressive behaviors that often characterize living within a hostile environment.

Institutional racism is the systematic denial to a group of people of the power, privilege, and prestige available within an existing culture or society. The effects of institutional racism include issues of access to power (social and economic), resources, and affiliation. Such limited access to power is a direct result of the fear and reluctance of those who are in power to relinquish their positions. Indirectly, people who are in power fear role reversal and thereby fear becoming victims themselves. The fact that certain classes of people are denied access to the in-group and its resources often leads those very same individuals to form groups of their own, often antiestablishment in nature, which are then characterized by the established groups as antisocial. Such groups include gangs, posses, or clubs.

Poverty. Poverty is so broadly oppressive in its consequences that it often leads youths to develop a pervasive attitude of hopelessness relative to both their present and future lives. Beyond depriving youths of basic shelter and food, poverty limits their opportunities to participate in constructive leisure activities, purchase goods and services, or develop responsible patterns of economic behavior. The conditions of poverty debilitate the very essence of positive youth development in that young people find it difficult to meet basic needs, both physical and psychological. This ultimately leads to self-effacing feelings—a lack of pride, self-worth, and esteem for self and/or others. In essence, the conditions of poverty often inhibit young people from pursuing their dreams. For some groups of youngsters, a lack of economic independence leads to antisocial activities and negative peer groups.

Lack of cultural acceptance. Awareness and acceptance of, and pride in, one's cultural heritage also lie at the very foundation of positive youth development. Racism, poverty, and a widespread perception that at-risk youths are "culturally deprived" or "culturally disadvantaged" erode this foundation. Rather than enhancing youths' sense of origin, history, language, and values, society too often perpetuates their purported deficiencies, minority status, and lack of a strong sense of culture. How, under such vulnerability-promoting circumstances, can youths develop into confident and productive adults, with an adequate level of personal self-esteem and cultural identity? Must we continue to permit gang identification and involvement to be the main and often only opportunity for many youths to find such esteem and identity? The Task Force believes otherwise and wishes to underscore the especially potent role we believe cultural acceptance can play in decreasing youth vulnerability.

Although racism, poverty, and a lack of cultural acceptance have overarching impact on the growth and development of youths, there are several other factors that affect how successful or unsuccessful youths may be as they seek to effectively negotiate their environments. These include the following:

Inadequate support networks. Youths need a cadre of people, both adults and peers, who can relate to them, help them solve problems, be supportive in times of stress, and intervene with and for them when crises occur. These support networks can also provide positive adult role models and opportunities for youths to help one another. In essence, it is the support network that provides the extended family and community within which the young person develops and prospers. The development of positive self-concepts, the feelings of confidence and competence, are often reflected in the groups with which the youth identifies and the community in which the youth lives. Oftentimes a strong support network provides alternatives to ineffective family units or negative influences that lead youths to antisocial and criminal behaviors.

Unequal access to resources and services. Even if programs, services, materials, and goods are available at adequate levels, equal access to these products by youths who are at risk of gang involvement is unlikely. Partly because of economics and partly due to lack of skill, these youths are often unable to adequately and successfully take advantage of programs and services. Furthermore, even when programs and services are available within their own communities, problems negotiating public transportation or not having transportation available at all often impede access.

Negative media influences. Television, movies, radio, and music have had a profound effect upon youth development. The advent of more liberal societal norms and the frequent promotion of drugs, sexual activity, and violence in every form of our media have created a generation of young people who are exposed to certain behaviors before they have matured, developed their own value systems, or explored alternatives. The media have also trained our young people in the quick, fast-paced use of all the glitter of modern technology without attending to their basic developmental needs as children. As such, the quick-fix, get-rich-fast, don't-work-hard ethic is often ingrained in our New York State children at a very tender age. Television in particular frequently has a negative impact on the activities in which youths participate and influences their everyday behavior in antisocial, egocentric directions.

Aggression. We live in an often hostile society in which aggression is learned at a very young age and is all too often immediately and richly rewarded. We teach our children, through media and actual direct experience, that the bigger, tougher, meaner persons usually get what they want, when they want it. This attitude is often practiced and supported in our homes, schools, and communities. Thus, by the time children reach second grade, they have often already learned to take, harass, and intimidate in order to survive and get their basic needs met. Such learned behavior—when combined with racism, poverty, and a failure of cultural acceptance; limited access to positive youth development programming; and influences from the media—often makes this generation of youths an easy target for the pervasive gang activity we now experience.

Youths at Risk

Youths who are involved with gangs or are at the periphery of gang activity often are unable to imagine a positive future. They describe their futures pessimistically. Many do not believe they will reach middle age. As such, their life script is brief, often volatile, without constructive aspiration. These youths do not dream hopeful dreams but rather fantasize pessimistic scenarios.

Youths who are at the periphery of gang activity. There are three distinct factions of youths at the periphery of gang activity. The first consists of those who tend to be younger in age than the youths who have actually committed themselves to gang activity. Their involvement in gang activity is often a result of impulsive, unplanned behavior prompted by peer pressure. These youths gain a false sense of prestige and power from their participation in the gang activities and are often motivated simply by the thrill of occasional participation in antisocial or criminal behavior. When these youths do become involved in criminal behavior, they tend to participate in crimes against property and generally do not participate in crimes that cause physical injury to others. In addition, these youths tend to be followers rather than leaders. If given attractive alternatives to gang activity, they are most likely to channel their energy into activities that do not involve antisocial or criminal behavior. These youths appear to have at least one positive role model, at home or elsewhere, with whom they are close. These role models seem to be able to exert just enough positive influence to limit the youths' antisocial activity to occasional, spontaneous incidents. If caught in criminal activity and processed through the criminal justice system, these youths will often find the negative aspects of their experience enough to discourage future gang activity.

The second faction consists of youths who are undomiciled or whose homes are unavailable to them. These youths are often labeled "the throw-aways" because no one wants them. They are left to fend for themselves on the streets. Often they are older (16 or over), unschooled, and untrained. In order to survive, they turn to antisocial, gang activity. In part, the gang meets their need for family, provides shelter, and, more importantly, offers earning power.

The third faction consists of youths who, primarily because of hoped-for economic advantages, are attracted to adult gangs involved with lucrative drug dealing. In turn, drug gang leaders find it especially convenient to use young people to distribute drugs and act as lookouts and couriers for drug monies because juvenile laws are more lenient. Youths potentially can make hundreds of dollars a day, which makes the economic lure of these gangs irresistible. Unfortunately, many of these youths become the primary means of support for their families and create yet other problems within their family units. Indeed, the economic potential of being involved in drug gang activities provides these young people with alternatives to the abject poverty and limited socioeconomic environments in which they live.

Youths who are gang members. Young people who are fully integrated into gangs usually have been involved with antisocial criminal behavior for several years. They often have juvenile records and have spent some time out of their communities incarcerated in Division for Youth facilities or other custodial institutions. Often these youngsters have been labeled by their schools' special education committees as emotionally disturbed, behaviorally disordered, or developmentally delayed. Whatever the label, however, these youths are often as much as 5 years below grade level in math and reading. They have already developed a value system that incorporates a paramilitary style, a rigidity of thought and action, and a lack of regard for property and life. These youths are often capable of destroying property and hurting people with malice and little feeling of remorse.

Summary

In summary, it is this Task Force's philosophical position that New York State—its leadership and its citizenry—must energetically and creatively respond to the overridingly negative life circumstances of many of its youths—namely, (a) inadequate access to such central youth development resources as health services, supportive family and community networks, education, and constructive recreation and (b) the debilitating and denigrating consequences of racism, poverty, and the lack of cultural acceptance. Our continuing vital focus should reflect a greatly heightened concern not only with at-risk and currently active gang youths but also with the diverse and pervasive social pathologies just enumerated that daily impinge upon such youths.

Program Recommendations

A major survey was conducted by all Task Force members in order to identify high-quality intervention programs for at-risk youths that we might collectively recommend for support and perhaps expanded implementation in New York State. Task Force members were asked to independently and then collectively consider (a) existing programs, (b) programs that previously existed but had been phased out, and (c) programs that never existed but that are nevertheless attractive in conceptualization.

Spergel's 1989 national survey of gang intervention strategies employed in 45 United States cities revealed that five strategies of intervention were the basis for agency programs dealing with the gang problem. They included community organization (e.g., community mobilization and networking); social intervention, focusing on individual behavioral and value change; opportunity provision, with special focus on improved basic education, training, and job opportunities for youths; suppression, emphasizing arrest, incarceration, and close monitoring and supervision of gang members; and organizational development and change, or the creation of special organizational units and procedures.

In considering and selecting programs worthy of recommendation, the Task Force sought to be fully responsive to the diversity of such national gang intervention programming, both because such programming reflects valuable professional expertise and because of our shared belief that effective programming will often be multilevel programming (i.e., targeting intervention efforts not only toward the youths themselves but simultaneously to the community and larger society of which they are a part).

Two other selection criteria helped shape our program recommendation decisions. In our view, effective programming is prescriptive in both its planning and implementation. Both program substance and delivery must be differentially responsive to the developmental levels, motivational patterns, learning styles, and community beliefs and traditions of the youths served. To the extent possible, programming for at-risk youths and current gang members should also be fully community based (i.e., developed in the community, for the community, and by the community). Just as this Task Force sought information from and explored its planned recommendations with a large panel of current gang youths, program developers must be in a full feedback loop with those persons constituting the context in which such programming will be employed: the community of which the youths are a part.

Finally, gang intervention efforts have been shown to be most effective when the agencies offering programs work in close and continuing coordination. Program providers, administrative leaders, law enforcement and prosecutorial personnel, and academics must meet, coalesce, and develop services for youths conjointly and cooperatively. The programs described in the next section are the fruits of this survey and screening effort. We recommend each as being potentially very effective and worthy of continued, expanded implementation for youths at risk of, or currently involved in, juvenile gang activity.

Youth Options Unlimited (Bronx and Brooklyn)

Adolescents involved with the Family Court—persons in need of supervision (PINS) and juvenile delinquents (JDs)—are typically among the most educationally needy children in New York City. They tend to be significantly below age-appropriate grade and skill levels and have histories of school-related behavioral and/or emotional problems and truancy. Although most of these youngsters remain at home during their court cases and most case dispositions do not specify out-of-home placement, more than 3,000 children are detained each year, and even more are placed after adjudication in longer term residential facilities. When they return home, they have the added problem of going back to schools that may not be eager to have them and that may not have met their needs adequately in the past.

An interagency subcommittee composed of the agencies responsible for or concerned with court-related children—the Department of Juvenile Justice (DJJ), the State Division for Youth (DFY), the Office of the Coordinator of Criminal Justice (OCCJ), and the Mayor's Office of Youth Services—has been working for several months with the Board of Education to design a program specially targeted to this difficult-to-serve and high-risk group.

Youth Options Unlimited (Project YOU) is an educational program administered by the alternative high school programs of the New York City Board of Education. For the 1989–1990 school year the program will be in two sites: Mission Society in the Bronx and Bushwick Youth Center in Brooklyn. From 150 to 300 youngsters will be served. About half of the students will be court-related; the other half will be referred by community school districts and will share many of the educational problems of court-related youngsters. Project YOU's mixed population will decrease the negative impact of labeling court-related students and will provide an educational option for students whose educational needs are difficult to meet in currently operating school programs. Project YOU is an interim educational service with the goal of placing most of its students in other educational programs within 1 year. Project YOU's academic program will be organized around "career choice" clusters paralleling course offerings of the Division of High Schools. This would permit students to enter the same cluster in their next school, facilitating continuity of educational services and minimizing disruption. Project YOU will offer course work up to the 10th-grade level and GED preparation for older students, with the goal of helping students make an appropriate choice of a high school, a part-time job, and/or full-time vocational training.

The Vocational Occupational International Cultural Exchange–Puerto Rico (Manhattan)

The Vocational Occupational International Cultural Exchange (VOICE) is an extension of the New York City Vocational Training Center, an alternative vocational high school of the New York City Board of Education. VOICE was designed to provide the high-risk disadvantaged student with an opportunity to participate in a cultural exchange program. By providing a setting that will allow disadvantaged students to give of themselves, it is believed that they will return not only with an appreciation of another culture but with greater self-esteem and higher goals. Projects identified allow the participating students to demonstrate their skills while aiding those who are less fortunate. The project identified for VOICE–Puerto Rico is the construction of an early childhood school.

Lower East Side Preparatory School (Manhattan)

The Lower East Side Preparatory School (LESP) has its origins in the free school movement of the 1960s. It went under the auspices of the Board of Education in September 1973. The school is a reflection of the diverse cultural and social backgrounds from which the 600-plus population is drawn (58 percent Asian; 32 percent Black, Hispanic, White). As one of New York's 17 alternative high schools, it serves two very distinct groups of students. Transfer, referral, and walk-in students from the larger comprehensive high schools opt to enroll for a myriad of reasons: superintendent suspensions, school phobia, overage for grade level, no credits, parental choice, anonymity of the larger comprehensive high schools, desire to separate from negative peer influences, and so forth. Newly arrived Asian immigrants over 17 years of age have chosen the program because of the extensive ESL/bilingual program and because they would not be able to get a high school diploma in a neighborhood high school.

The average student remains at LESP for 2-½ years. In order to enable these older students to accumulate credit towards a diploma, a variety of programs are offered: P.M. school, shared instruction, executive internship, part-time co-op, concurrent options. In addition, a 3-week academic program, Camp Success, is held at Pace University's Pleasantville campus and provides students with the unique opportunity to earn high school credit in six different subject areas while experiencing college life on a firsthand basis. More than 75 percent of the graduates go on to college. New York Working, a full-time school-based employment center with a professional job developer, secures part-time and summer employment for students while assisting them with career training and counseling.

With the instructional program as the focal point, ongoing staff development, assisted by Project Basics under the Urban Coalition's Center for Educational Leadership (CEL), addresses current research-based teaching methodologies, such as peer evaluation and coaching, cooperative learning, critical thinking, learning styles, and so on. In recognition of the expanding role of inner city schools, LESP has actively recruited and incorporated the participation and assistance of private industry, universities, and colleges. Exemplary partnerships have been established with American Home Products; British Petroleum of America; Irenecs, Inc.; Borough of Manhattan Community College; Pace University; Hunter University; the City-Kids Foundation; the Foreign Policy Association; and the Chinese-American Planning Council. LESP is one of only three high schools in the UFT's restructuring, school-based management initiative, "Schools of Tomorrow . . . Today," which empowers teachers and administrators to collaboratively develop, administer, and evaluate the educational program.

The 91.1 percent graduation and the 84.3 percent attendance rates, as well as the 14 percent decrease in dropout statistics, resulted in LESP's designation as a Chancellor's Rewarding Success School and reaffirms LESP's commitment to meet the needs of the at-risk student.

Ranger Cadet Corps (Manhattan)

The Block Banner Proposal intends to reactivate Harlem's famed Ranger Cadet Corps, a youth group that was in operation from 1965 to 1972. During that period, the Rangers were organized from 25 volunteer members into a cohesive unit of 1,000 resident youngsters. Involved in various community and civic awareness projects, they were mobilized for school demonstrations, clean-up drives, parades, and recreational outlets. The members were instilled with a feeling of pride in their accomplishments, pride in themselves, and pride in their unit.

The Cadet officers will work closely with the school and parents in order to correlate behavior patterns at home that are in conflict with training procedures or appropriate community demands.

Rochester Youth Outreach Program (Monroe County)

The Youth Outreach Program was established by the Rochester Police Department to (a) hire and train youth outreach workers, (b) afford the Rochester Police Department the opportunity to establish better community relations with the younger members of the community, (c) respond to the needs of area youths in a proactive rather than reactive manner, (d) reach youths involved in organized groups or gangs who have or may become involved in illegal or disruptive behavior, and (e) refer youths involved with gangs to agencies that can assist them with specific problems.

Over the 3-year period of the program, there have been many accomplishments and successes. Outreach workers have been successful in referring group members to various community agencies for help with personal problems (i.e., drug abuse, school, work, etc.). With input from the workers, the Rochester Police Department Teens on Patrol Program has hired over 60 teens who had been identified as youth group members over the last 3 years. The workers have also been instrumental in warning the department about planned confrontations between rival groups, and major problems have been averted. In addition, workers have become known in the community. On several occasions they have been called upon to speak to groups of teens about involvement with gangs and have acted as positive role models for many area youths.

Rochester Youth Service Corps (Monroe County)

The Rochester Youth Service Corps is a community of out-of-school youths, aged 18 to 23, that performs priority human service and physical work projects while integrating corps members into the active lives of their communities and empowering them to improve the quality of their own lives and to secure meaningful, productive, long-term employment. Its goals are as follows:

- To market the corps widely throughout the community as an exciting opportunity to serve the community and enhance corps members' lives

- To recruit youths who represent the racial, ethnic, cultural, and economic diversity of the local community and who include both high school graduates and dropouts

- To select projects that represent priorities identified by the broad community and that cannot be conducted with existing community resources

- To enhance educational opportunities, to increase academic achievement, and to establish learning as a lifelong activity for each corps member

- To establish individual educational goals for each corps member that correspond with his or her functional academic level at admission to the corps and with the corps member's future career goals and interests

- To identify, with entering corps members, the specific support services each needs to participate successfully in corps activities and to secure and sustain competitive employment at the end of corps participation

- To identify community resources that are available to support corps members during and after corps participation and to link the corps program with these resources

- To assist corps members in identifying individual short-, medium-, and long-range career goals that are compatible with their interests, skills, and economic needs

- To assist corps members in developing training and employment plans that will lead to the attainment of their career goals

- To prepare corps members to meet the realistic expectations (in terms of job behaviors and attitudes and entry-level job skills) of employers

- To empower each corps member, upon program completion, to secure employment compatible with his or her interests, skills, career goals, and economic needs

Youth Dynamic Alternatives for Rehabilitation Through Educational Services (Brooklyn)

The primary objective of Youth Dynamic Alternatives for Rehabilitation through Educational Services (Youth DARES) is to offer positive alternatives to at-risk youths and their families. The 61st Precinct Youth Program is the core of Youth DARES. It provides educational, counseling, and crisis intervention services. The components of the 61st Precinct Youth Program are:

- *Project BEST* (Begin Excelling Starting Today), composed of an alternative high school, general equivalency diploma (GED) classes, educational therapy, and school advocacy. The high school educates students who have not met with success in a traditional school setting.

- *Family Mediation Project,* which fosters open communication in families that are experiencing

internal strife. Families meet with one of the trained
mediators to discuss problems and, most important, to
derive their own solutions.

- *Court Advocacy Project,* offering alternatives to
  incarceration for criminally involved youngsters. Very
  often, youths are probated by the courts to the agency
  for educational and counseling services.

- *Counseling Project,* which provides direct counseling to
  youths with emotional or other problems. If necessary,
  youngsters with severe psychological problems are
  referred to one of the many mental health clinics with
  whom a networking arrangement exists.

- *Recreation Project,* providing basic recreational
  activities for young people. Programs operate out of
  local public schools.

Boys and Girls Clubs of America (Statewide—Buffalo, Rochester, Syracuse, Albany, Binghamton, and New York City)

Boys and Girls Clubs of America, Inc., is a youth development
agency with primary focus upon youths from disadvantaged life
situations. Boys and Girls Clubs of America is a member-affiliated
organization with over 1,500 organizations located in the urban
centers of cities across the nation. Boys and Girls Clubs organizations are facility centered, delivering a wide range of programs and
activities designed to enhance emotional, social, and vocational
opportunities for youths. These programs include:

- *Project Smart Moves,* designed to deter abuse of
  substances and delay the onset of sexual
  experimentation

- *Targeted outreach,* designed to assess, intervene with,
  and monitor the activities of youths determined to be
  high-risk and envelop them in positive alternatives

- *Keystoning,* designed to promote leadership
  development through participation in a
  social/citizenship development–formed group with peer
  leadership and service to club and community as
  primary foci

- *Gang prevention,* with a specialist to provide resources, information, and training to local Boys and Girls Club organizations regarding means for preventing gang involvement

- *Delinquency prevention strategy,* which provides training to local organizations to assess their programmatic responses and help staff positively intervene on behalf of high-risk youths

Young People's East Harlem Resource Center (Manhattan—Implemented by Youth Action Program of East Harlem and Block Nursery, Inc., of New York City)

The Youth Action Program, a 3.5 million dollar grassroots organization with a staff of 50 employees, is an educational and community organizing program helping inner city, at-risk young people take responsibility for improving their communities and their lives. It is based on the premise that teenagers have clear ideas about what is wrong in the world and about how things could be improved. Youth Action draws out these ideas and provides resources and technical assistance for implementation. Community improvement projects are designed and governed by volunteer youths and are administered by adults accountable to the youth governing committees. Participants are also provided with counseling, homework assistance, and vocational and leadership activities.

Requirements for membership in the Resource Center include remaining drug and alcohol free, refraining from negative behavior, and formulating short- and long-term goals.

Delinquency Prevention Through Youth Involvement (Manhattan—Implemented by Hotline Cares, New York City)

This program recruited, trained, and involved youth volunteers aged 12 to 21 in providing assistance to other youths and families. Services included crisis intervention through telephone and walk-in counseling, emergency food and financial assistance, information and referrals, advocacy, street outreach to troubled youths, and drug abuse prevention activities.

Hotline's youth volunteers developed a sense of responsibility, discipline, and self-awareness, which in turn improved their ability to solve personal problems and enhanced their potential for personal growth.

Junior High School Alternative Program (Suffolk County—Implemented by Colonial Youth Center, Mastic Beach)

This project is designed to decrease juvenile delinquency in one of Suffolk County's most turbulent communities. The target population is a group of at-risk students, aged 14 to 16, who have been assigned to an alternative education program in the junior high school. Programs and services teach specific skills and lead to increased self-confidence, resulting in a reduction in recidivism and a return to the mainstream of the school.

Services are coordinated through collaboration with the school, police, probation, social services, youth bureaus, and other agencies that are involved in meeting the needs of these students. Every student has the opportunity to participate in the center's ongoing Peer Leadership Program. In addition, students design and implement a community service project.

Brownsville Community Neighborhood Action Center, Inc., Youth Training and Employment Programs (Brooklyn)

- *Adolescent Vocational Exploration Program.* The Adolescent Vocational Exploration Program is designed to service youths aged 14 to 17 who are in need of extraordinary support due to environmental, economic, or personal circumstances. This program is an innovative attempt to link career awareness with educational support and to combine involvement with the private sector through field visits, speakers, and use of vocational exploration placements. The New York State Education Department provides the curriculum format and program evaluation that allows successful participants to receive up to one regents' credit for their participation in the summer classroom component, combined with the fall components of counseling, advocacy, and support services.

- *Youth Work Skills Program.* The Youth Work Skills Program serves participants who are out of school, are economically disadvantaged, and have a reading score at or below fifth-grade level as measured by a standardized achievement test. The program is funded by the New York State Department of Labor to improve young people's basic educational skills, job-seeking capabilities, and employability through the provision of basic skills remediation, work-site training, and support and counseling services. Preference is given to homeless youths and adolescent parents.

- *Youth Training and Employment Program.* The Youth Training and Employment Program is an after-school program funded by the Special Legislative Grants Unit of the New York State Division for Youth. The program, designed to service youths aged 14 to 20 who are in school, focuses on career awareness, educational remediation, employment training, job training, interview techniques, job placement, and public speaking.

- *Juvenile Justice Prevention Program.* The Juvenile Justice Prevention Program is designed to provide service to 20 high-risk youths aged 12 to 21 to decrease the number of youths involved in the criminal justice system and serve as an alternative to incarceration.

Rheedlen Foundation (New York City)

Rheedlen is a comprehensive service program focusing exclusive attention on the problem of truancy among the young by serving both children and their families. There are six program sites: a main building on the Upper West Side of New York City and five sites located within school buildings in Central Harlem and the Clinton (Hell's Kitchen) area of Manhattan. Workers make hundreds of home visits each week to pick up children and take them to school and to medical and eye examinations. Rheedlen also provides after-school remedial lessons in reading, math, and socialization skills; emergency food and shelter; crisis intervention; recreational services; field trips; parental counseling; and escort services. In addition, it provides a quiet place to do homework, a safe place to be after school, and a sense of belonging.

Project Reach (Manhattan)

Project Reach, under the auspices of the Chinese-American Planning Council, is a community-based crisis counseling and advocacy center serving approximately 200 young people, aged 12 to 21, from the Chinatown–Little Italy/Two Bridges community, as well as from Queens, Brooklyn, Staten Island, and the Bronx. The project deals with young people who are running away from home, dropping out of school, hiding out with gang groups, seeking out support in premature sexual relationships, or attempting suicide. Still others face problems surrounding coming out as lesbian or gay, deciding about an unwanted pregnancy, dealing with a sexually abusive relative, or coming to grips with a parent who is dying of AIDS. At Reach, the attempt is made to provide a safe and supportive space where young people can begin to identify and work together to resolve their own problems.

Gangs are an everyday reality for many young people, both females and males, in this community. The fact that an overwhelming number of young people who come to Reach have been incarcerated (21 percent), court-involved (22 percent), runaways (27 percent), truants/dropouts (50 percent), substance users and abusers (36 percent), in violent conflict with parents (53 percent), or depressed and suicidal (23 percent) places these young people and their peers at great risk for gang involvement. Of the crisis caseload, 37 percent involves young people who are in, close to, or dependent on local street and youth gangs. Fortunately, Project Reach's "open-door policy" has enabled young people in this community to see Reach as neutral territory where assistance and support are available. At present, Project Reach is the only drop-in center servicing the needs of Asian-American youths in New York City.

Inner City Roundtable of Youth (Manhattan)

The Inner City Roundtable of Youth (ICRY) is a youth service organization established in 1975 to help deal with a wide array of personal and community problems associated with gang-involved and at-risk youths. Its initiatives include drug abuse advisory and treatment activities, alternative vocational training projects, programs focused on prevention of and alternatives to incarceration, and interventions oriented toward homeless, runaway youths as well as AIDS and AIDS-related problems.

Much of the work of ICRY is based upon an entrepreneurial model, developing youth-community-run venture enterprises as employment and career incentives and as a means toward youth empowerment.

Unitas Therapeutic Community (Bronx)

The Unitas Therapeutic Community in the Fox Street neighborhood of the Bronx is found wherever young people are—at home, in the schoolyard, in the street. Unitas is often dubbed the "clinic of the street," a public recognition of the fact that it is not tied to one setting or style but rather exists and operates in and among the young people themselves and those adults who work with them.

Unitas teaches young people how to nurture, challenge, and help one another. In the process, it creates sustained support and understanding that are often lacking or insufficient elsewhere. Conceptually, Unitas is grounded in a systems approach to the delivery of services. It taps existing peer, family, and community support networks and works with these to provide services to youths. A wide range of treatment modalities are used, including individual, family, group, and art therapy as well as remedial education. Bilingual-bicultural staff (many of them young adults from the neighborhood who grew up with the program) provide services, and emphasis is placed on involving the nuclear and extended family in the therapeutic process.

Ulysses Youth Unlimited Program (Tompkins County)

Ulysses Youth Unlimited Program was the first drop-in, multi-service center to be developed in a rural community and has been the model for other rural programs. Over its 15-year history, the program has employed youth workers who, in addition to planning activities at the youth center located in a church basement, have reached out to youths on the street and in the high school.

The goals of this program are as follows:

- To provide constructive leisure-time activities to youths in the target population

- To provide youths opportunities for education concerning adolescent issues such as peer relations, sexuality, self-esteem, substance use, and family life

- To provide youths opportunities for employment education, employment experience, and career exploration

- To provide parents of youths opportunities to receive information, education, and support services concerning parenting issues

Huntington Family Center Teen Services (Onondaga County)

Huntington Family Center's Teen Department serves youths between the ages of 12 and 18 in a variety of capacities that enrich socialization, education, and recreation. Programs available in the teen department include the following:

- *Educational component,* consisting of a truancy program; tutoring; a homework club; a computer literacy program; educational seminars focusing on topics such as drug and substance abuse, sexuality, teen suicide, and job-seeking skills; and a teen advisory council made up of active teens who take responsibility for recruiting teens into programs and for planning special events and fund-raisers. Two teens from the advisory council serve as representatives on the Huntington Board of Directors.

- *Recreation component,* including the Huntington Drop-In Center and Game Room, open on a daily basis; weekly field trips; and special events such as roller skating, camping, tournaments, dances, and trips.

- *Skill development component,* consisting of special interest groups in such areas as arts and crafts, ceramics, pottery, woodworking, cooking, sculpting, and weight lifting.

- *Sports component,* offering seasonal leagues in such sports as football, basketball, volleyball, softball, and bowling. In addition, the Teen Department holds an annual sports banquet.

- *Computer literacy program,* providing young people aged 10 to 14 the unique opportunity to become more familiar with computers and their various uses. Young people who participate in the program learn LOGO and BASIC computer languages and are exposed to various forms of software.

Officer Correct/Youth ID Program (Manhattan)

The Officer Correct/Youth ID Program was developed by the New York City Department of Correction as an educational tool to provide information on crime and drug prevention, safety precautions, and career development. The program is administered by specially trained correction officers who have firsthand knowledge of crime, its causes, and the circumstances that lead individuals to be placed in our correctional system.

The program is conducted at the Correction Academy. In preparation, staff visit students in the classroom and give a presentation on the Department of Correction. They discuss the role of a correction officer, how the department functions within the criminal justice system, and briefly describe what a typical day in a detention facility would be like. A date is then scheduled for the academy visit.

Transportation to the academy is provided by the department. Upon arrival, the youngsters are greeted and engaged in a discussion about the importance of staying in school, drug education and prevention, and career development. A unique "loss of freedom" educational tool is used as a crime preventative: Each student is allowed to spend time in a mock jail cell to observe the reality of incarceration. From an outside video monitor, they see themselves in the cell as a recording of jail sounds plays in the background. A staff member then conducts a group discussion on the "loss of freedom" experience. The students are encouraged to participate in the discussion and express their thoughts and feelings about what they have seen, heard, and experienced.

At the end of the day, all group members are sworn in as junior correction officers and given an Officer Correct Button, a certificate of achievement for having participated in the program, and a photo ID card.

The Community Schools Program (Statewide)

Initiated by the Board of Regents of New York State in 1987, the Community Schools Program is a statewide attempt to enhance the reciprocal relationship that ideally can exist between a school and its surrounding community. The 20 schools that currently constitute this program are typically located in communities whose resources have not been adequate to deal with the level of community deterioration they have experienced. Youth enhancement, school growth, and community renewal, therefore, are closely related program aspirations. They are pursued via efforts to develop and support the following community school characteristics:

- A developmental curriculum that assures progress in basic academic skills and provides challenge and enrichment

- An instructional program that increases time on task through flexible use of time beyond the conventional school day: afternoons, evenings, weekends, summers, and so on

- School buildings that are open and accessible to children from early morning through the evening, at least 6 days per week, all year

- Elementary programs that begin in early childhood (at least pre-K) and secondary programs that provide intensive and sustained support throughout early and late adolescence

- A school that acts as broker for health, nutritional, and social services, making them accessible on the school site to children and their families

- Schools that serve as a site for educational, cultural, and recreational activity for children, their families, and the community at large

- Productive linkages with nearby community colleges, other higher education institutions, businesses, community-based organizations, cultural institutions, churches, temples, and other agencies and institutions

- Parents who are actively involved in school affairs, helping with their own and other children and pursuing their own education

- A diversified program team, including teachers, teaching assistants and/or aides, parents and/or other adult mentors, and college-age students

- Administrators capable of exercising educational leadership and of coordinating a wide variety of educational, social, health, recreational, and other services

- Principals, teachers, and other staff members sharing in the planning of the school program and enjoying substantial autonomy in carrying out their decisions

- A staff that continually seeks ways to improve and extend its program in the interests of children

- Instruction that makes creative use of the new learning technologies

- School buildings that provide a clean, safe, and friendly environment conducive to effective teaching and learning and that are adequately equipped

Strategic Recommendations

Prevention

Both preventive and rehabilitative programming for youths at risk of gang involvement are valuable and necessary. Given the major difficulty in competing with the substantial financial rewards often received by youths already heavily involved in drug-related gang activities, the Task Force recommends that programming attention be devoted to primary and secondary preventive efforts seeking to preclude or reduce such gang involvement.

Prosocial Behaviors

Programming for youths at risk of gang involvement should emphasize the teaching, development, and continued use of constructive, prosocial behaviors that help youths lead effective, satisfying, and socially valuable lives. Programming singularly devoted to changing youth behavior by punitive, sanctioning means should be discouraged.

Comprehensive Orientation

Programming for youths at risk of gang involvement must be both youth- and system-oriented. Too often have such youths alone been targeted for intervention efforts, with program failure the result. Family-oriented youth programming must seek to influence the entire family system, of which the youth is a part. School-oriented programs must seek to alter both the youth's approach to school and the school's approach to the youth. Job-oriented programs must seek not only to enhance the youth's job-related skills and motivations, but also to increase training for and availability of appropriate employment.

Coordination

The diverse youth care, educational, employment market, criminal justice, and other agency personnel who initiate and implement comprehensive programming for youths at risk of gang involvement must function as a coordinated body. In-place networking systems for the sharing of appropriate information, willingness to put youth concerns ahead of turf concerns, and creative use of time and energy in order to combine and build upon one another's professional contributions are requisites of successful coordination efforts.

School-Based Programming

The public school, as a convenient and central physical site and as an often turf-neutral location, is a particularly desirable locus of effective programming for youths at risk of gang involvement. The Task Force especially wishes to stress the likely value of school-based programming—for youths and their families—conducted at times in addition to the typical class day (e.g., after school, evenings, weekends). Optimally, in our view, schools can function as "community hubs," offering attractive and valuable programming during the very hours of the day and evening in which youths are most likely to get into trouble.

Community-Based Programming

Optimal programming for youths at risk of gang involvement will be planned and implemented at the level where people are most aware of and most able to be responsive to the real-world needs and aspirations of such youths. We believe that the youth's own community is the optimal level and would urge that all such programming involve major and continuing input from members of the youth's own geographic, ethnic, and socioeconomic community. Such involvement should draw upon not only purported leaders but also youths themselves.

Youth Input

The enhanced availability of potentially effective programming for youths at risk of gang involvement will not be of value unless such youths view it as relevant to their lives and aspirations, and are thus motivated to seek it out and participate. Such perceived relevance and optimal motivation is substantially more likely to occur to the degree that at-risk youths are sought out and encouraged to speak out regarding their own appraisals of such programming. The Task Force has done so with approximately 100 youths and has found their input to be consistently useful. It is recommended that a systematic means be developed for obtaining such youth perceptions regarding programming and related matters and that these means be utilized in the future on a regular and continuing basis.

Prescriptiveness

Although it seems but a truism to assert that different youths benefit from different programs, program implementors often act otherwise and employ but one program or type of program with many diverse types of youths. The Task Force, in contrast, strongly recommends a prescriptive orientation to program development and implementation in which the unique needs of culturally diverse youths are taken into account and responded to in the form of different programs, different program combinations and sequences, and different program implementors. These choices will depend upon program-relevant youth characteristics, as well as the characteristics of their peers, families, communities, and the program-providing agency.

Staff Training

Increased time, energy, creativity, and funding need to be devoted within New York State to the selection and training of skilled youth care workers. This need is particularly salient for workers dealing with youths at risk of gang involvement. Such youths are often minimally motivated for program participation, difficult to involve by traditional means, and may engage recurrently in illegal behaviors. To function effectively with such youngsters, such programs require especially high levels of staff member empathy, cultural sensitivity, and program-relevant skills. Judicious staff selection and heightened levels of staff training are necessary to rise to these programmatic challenges.

Program Integrity

If youths at risk of gang involvement are to be served adequately, it is critical that programs developed be actually implemented according to planned program procedures. Too often, mostly as a result of too few personnel or inadequate funding, programs of apparent substantial potential are actually implemented inadequately. For example, the major evaluations in the 1950s and 1960s of the detached worker approach to gang delinquency reduction were all negative. Compared to unserved youths, those who—at least on paper—were receiving the services of a detached worker committed as many or more delinquent acts. The programs were deemed a failure, ignoring the crucial fact that huge caseloads and major administrative demands meant that worker and youth actually met but a few minutes per week. There must, therefore, be program plan–program implementation integrity.

Program Intensity

Not only is it necessary for effective programming that the intervention as planned correspond to the intervention as actually administered (i.e., program integrity), so too must there be heightened concern with the level, amount, or dosage of the intervention (i.e., program intensity). In general, it will be the case that "the more the better," whether referring to amount of youth contact with the intervenors; amount of counseling time, recreational time, or job skills training time; or amount of family or community involvement in programming for youths.

Constructive Gang Functions

While deploring the illegal activities in which many gang youths participate and while recognizing that such activities form much of the basis for the existence of the Task Force, we also recognize that gang involvement may at times serve a number of constructive, positive functions in the lives of participating youths. Self-esteem, peer acceptance, increased pride, feelings of empowerment and hope, social skills, and a sense of family lacking elsewhere in the youths' world may each be enhanced. New York State's primary effort must be directed toward reducing the level of illegal gang activity currently operative. Recognizing, and in some instances even encouraging, the constructive features of such involvement is not incompatible with this goal.

Evaluation

Too often, programming for youths at risk of gang involvement takes on a life of its own, independent of its effectiveness in changing youth behavior. Programs continue in the absence of evaluation altogether or with the "support" of inadequate, largely anecdotal evaluation. The Task Force wishes to underscore the crucial need for all youth programming to be rigorously, systematically, and independently evaluated, using quantitative or qualitative research methodologies, to assess each program's objective efficacy in changing the behavior, attitudes, and/or values of the youths it is designed to serve.

CODA

Gangs on Gangs

This book has been a journey into the psychology of delinquent gangs: the psychology that is and the psychology that could be. Extrapolation has been our central vehicle—from clinical, developmental, social, and community psychology. We have asked what these subdisciplines of psychology may have to offer our search for a fuller understanding of delinquent gang formation and behavior, and all have provided preliminary answers. This process has yielded relevant extrapolations from research on (a) clinical intervention; (b) adolescent peer group and identity formation; (c) group dynamic cohesiveness, conflict, norm setting, groupthink, and phase sequence; and (d) communities, networks, neighborhoods, and social support. The future will reveal whether this attempt has been fruitful, either theoretically or in the applied sense. Its potential, however, seems substantial both a priori and in light of its demonstrated value in a different, if procedurally parallel, major attempt to extrapolate from one broad domain of psychology to the applied concerns of another (Goldstein, Heller, & Sechrest, 1966).

Although we have thus sought to draw on a wide range of psychological theory and research for gang-related implications, the selections collectively are but a sample, and our attempts at extrapolation from them are but a procedural model. Many other bodies of psychological literature may also yield useful information related to gangs. But however broad and rich the extrapolatory base of psychological domains drawn upon, and however comprehensive an intervention is in terms of skilled staffing, provision of opportunities, and energetic deterrence/incarceration, it seems likely to fail unless its strategic planning and tactical implementation involve major, sustained, and seriously acknowledged gang member involvement. An accurate and heuristic understanding of gang structure, motivation, perception, aspiration, and both routine and dramatic behavior cannot be obtained from the outside looking in. Such understanding depends on substantial input from gang members themselves. But such input is not easily acquired. As Hagedorn and Macon (1988) observe:

> We are in the absurd position of having very few first hand studies of, but numerous theoretical speculations

about, juvenile gangs. . . . One reason is that the vast
majority of sociologists and researchers are white, and
gangs today are overwhelmingly minority. (pp. 26–27)

Black, Hispanic, Asian, and other minority youths do indeed
constitute a large portion of contemporary gang membership in the
United States. They bring to their gang participation diverse and
often culture-specific motivations, perceptions, behaviors, and beliefs. The meaning of aggression; the perception of gang as family;
the gang as an arena for acquiring status, honor, or "rep"; the gang's
duration, cohesiveness, and typical and atypical legal and illegal
pursuits; its place in the community—these features and many
more are substantially shaped by cultural traditions and mores. A
rich literature describes in depth the cultural patterns and perspectives of our country's ethnic and racial subgroups: Black (Beverly &
Stanback, 1986; W.K. Brown, 1978; Glasgow, 1980; Helmreich,
1973; Keiser, 1969; Kochman, 1981; Meltzer, 1984; Silverstein &
Krate, 1975; J.L. White, 1984); Hispanic (Horowitz, 1983; Mirande, 1987; Moore et al., 1978; Quicker, 1983a; Ramirez, 1983; Vigil,
1983; Vigil & Long, 1990); Asian (Bloodworth, 1966; Bresler, 1980;
Chin, 1990; Kaplan & Dubro, 1986; Meltzer, 1980; President's
Commission on Organized Crime, 1985; Vigil & Yun, 1990; R.W.
Wilson, 1970); and others (Hagedorn & Macon, 1988; Howard &
Scott, 1981; Schwartz & Disch, 1970). Especially useful in much of
this culture-clarifying literature is the opportunity it provides to
view the structure, dynamics, and purposes of delinquent gangs
through the cultural lenses of their members, as well as the support
it implies for the crucial role of gang member input for effective
programming.

The literature also helps researchers to move in their thinking
from the typical perception of gang youths as broadly deficient and
in need of remediation to what Gonzalez (1981) has described as a
more appreciative perspective. The latter view recognizes that
many qualities and behaviors of gang members, seen as weaknesses,
deficiencies, or maladaptive behaviors in more mainstream perspectives, have their own appropriateness, survival value, and
potential to enhance self-esteem. As Mirande (1987) notes,
"Whereas the correctional perspective viewed those being studied
as objects, the new [appreciative] perspective treats them as subjects and assumes their definition of the situation" (p. 198).

Input from youths must be energetically and sensitively sought
but employed with caution when obtained. As noted in chapter 1,
Hagedorn and Macon (1988) urge caution in the acceptance and

processing of information provided by gang members. For a variety of self-protective reasons, some quite realistic and others not, such information may contain exaggerations, minimizations, or other inaccuracies. In a similar vein, Kleiner, Holger, and Lanahan (1975) describe anticipated distortion of information obtained from gang members, a result of "anxiety over being identified, fear of reprisal, fears for the security of the gang, [and feeling] uncomfortable talking to middle-class Whites" (p. 394).

It would be a mistake, however, to place too much of the responsibility for the misinformation transmitted, for the wall of miscommunication and mistrust erected, on the gang youths themselves. It is clear that workers and youths alike have contributed to the wall's construction. Moore et al. (1978) capture well this sense of shared responsibility in their study *Homeboys, Gangs, Drugs, and Prison in the Barrios of Los Angeles:*

> There were also divergent values, including at least four between the [gang member] addict-convicts and the academic researchers. The first was a mutual distrust of project goals. Addict-convicts fear that academic research may further stereotype them and thereby reinforce already destructive institutional arrangements, for the ultimate profit of only the researcher. Academics fear that addict-convicts cannot identify with contributing to knowledge as a goal. Second, there was mutual fear of manipulation. Addict-convicts find it hard to believe in the sincerity of the academic researcher, and that any academic person can know anything of real value about the prison experience and the criminal justice system. Third is the common academic distrust . . . of the convict's capacity to manipulate any situation to his own, potentially illegal or illegitimate goals. Fourth is a mutual distrust of long-range commitments. (p. 184)

Others, too, may have a stake in unknowingly or intentionally distorting the accuracy of gang-related information. Hagedorn (1990) observes:

> Gang problems are a prime modern example of what C. Wright Mills termed "official definitions of reality": public issues framed by the powerful to serve their own interests. In order to get beneath and behind media images—to see in what ways they may be true, in what ways false, and in what ways they serve those with

something to gain—we need studies that see the world as gang members see it. Methods of research that rely on official statistics or official channels of access are necessary but not sufficient if we are to fully understand the reality of modern gangs. (p. 244)

Yet, in spite of such hindrances (originating with youths, workers, public officials, or a combination) to obtaining accurate and valuable input from delinquent youths about themselves, their lives, and their gangs, successes do exist. There are a few highly informative, primarily qualitative research reports on the phenomenology of gang membership, juvenile delinquency, and kindred topics. Included in these are C.R. Shaw's (1930/1966) *The Jack-Roller: A Delinquent Boy's Own Story;* Strodtbeck, Short, and Kolegar's (1962) *The Analysis of Self-Descriptions by Members of Delinquent Gangs;* Bennett's (1981) *Oral History and Delinquency: The Rhetoric of Criminology;* W. Brown's (1983) *The Other Side of Delinquency;* Hanson, Beschner, Walters, and Bovelle's (1985) *Life With Heroin: Voices From the Inner City;* Roberts' (1987) *The Inner World of the Black Juvenile Delinquent;* Williams' (1989) *The Cocaine Kids;* and our own recent effort, *Delinquents on Delinquency* (Goldstein, 1990).

In the same vein, there also exist several informative interview studies of unreported delinquent behavior (Gold, 1970; Kratcoski & Kratcoski, 1975; Kulik, Stein, & Sarbin, 1968; Short & Nye, 1957) and of the employment of delinquents as paid experts on delinquency in studies of experimenter-subject psychotherapy (Schwitzgebel & Kolb, 1964; Slack, 1960).

In keeping with the extrapolatory spirit of this book, it is likely that valuable phenomenological insights regarding juvenile gangs may also be obtained from ex-delinquents and ex–gang members who abandoned their criminal careers without outside intervention (Jenkins & Brown, 1988; Mulvey & LaRosa, 1986; Shannon, 1988), as well as from youths growing up in gang-prone areas (characterized by poverty, high crime, serious school dropout rate, major drug use, etc.) who do *not* become gang members. Examples of the latter kind of information are Williams and Kornblum's (1985) *Growing Up Poor;* Ross and Glasser's (1973) *Making It Out of the Ghetto;* Monroe and Goldman's (1988) *Brothers: Black and Poor—A True Story of Courage and Survival;* and recent research on youths described as vulnerable but invincible (Werner & Smith, 1982), resilient (Goldstein, 1988b), superkids (Pines, 1979), or as simply nondelinquent though growing up in high-delinquency environments (Fagan, Piper, & Moore, 1986).

The title of this coda, "Gangs on Gangs," alludes to the likely value of input from gang youths for more fully and accurately studying delinquent gangs, understanding their functioning, and formulating possible interventions. But the spirit of "gangs on gangs" may also fruitfully be applied to the intervention process itself. It is not only outsiders—whether detached workers, resource workers, deterrence workers, or members of a traditional helping profession—who may seek to reorient gang youths in more prosocial directions. Gang and gang-prone youths may do so themselves. The Guardian Angels and their precursors, the Rock Brigade and the Magnificent 13 (Edelman, 1981; Sliwa, 1987); the Harlem Ranger Cadet Corps (New York State Division for Youth, 1990); the Black Crusaders (Helmrich, 1973); the Brown Berets (Moore et al., 1978); Brothers Gaining Equality Through Excellence ("BGE, a Positive Alternative," 1989); the Nighthawks (Hagedorn & Macon, 1988); the Federacion de Barrios Unidos (Vigil, 1988); the Puerto Rican Young Lords (Hagedorn & Macon, 1988); the East Harlem Youth Action Program (Heller, Price, & Hogg, 1988); and the Chicago ex-convict self-help groups (aka Chicano culture groups) discussed by Moore et al. (1978) are examples of prosocial intervention efforts originated and conducted in whole or in major part by the target youths themselves.

Psychology and kindred disciplines persistently study the negative (disease, crime, psychopathology, aggression, etc.) and how it may be corrected. Rarely is the focus on strength and its facilitation. Yet such disease-model thinking has increasingly been tempered by wellness-model approaches in recent years. In this prosocial spirit of emphasizing and promoting wellness, and in spite of the often justified pessimism of many respected gang experts (e.g., Klein, 1971; Miller, 1970; Short, 1974) regarding the malleability of many gang youths, we strongly urge less exclusive focus in gang research and intervention on law-violating groups and much more attention to those that, by their own efforts or with the value-transformation assistance of others, become sometime, part-time, or even full-time law-abiding or even law-promoting youth groups. Quicker (1983a) has written in this same prosocial spirit in his exploration of Chicano gangs as "working class sororities," whose behavior usually displays those qualities—trust, loyalty, helpfulness, friendship, and so forth—"that would make most Girl Scout leaders proud" (p. 76). Like Quicker, we do not wish to minimize the actual and potential antisocial behavior of gang youths. Their actual and potential prosocial behavior deserves similar attention.

References

Abadinsky, H. (1979). *Social service in criminal justice.* Englewood Cliffs, NJ: Prentice-Hall.

Adams, G.R., & Gullotta, T. (1989). *Adolescent life experiences.* Pacific Grove, CA: Brooks/Cole.

Adams, S. (1959). *Effectiveness of the Youth Authority Special Treatment Program: First interim report* (Research Report No. 5). Sacramento: California Department of the Youth Authority.

Adams, S. (1961). *Assessment of the psychiatric treatment program, Phase I* (Research Report No. 21). Sacramento: California Department of the Youth Authority.

Adams, S. (1962). The PICO Project. In N. Johnson, L. Savitz, & M.E. Wolfgang (Eds.), *The sociology of punishment and correction.* New York: Wiley.

Adkins, W.R. (1970). Life skills: Structured counseling for the disadvantaged. *Personnel and Guidance Journal, 49,* 108–116.

Agee, V.L. (1979). *Treatment of the violent incorrigible adolescent.* Lexington, MA: Lexington.

Agee, V.L., & McWilliams, B. (1984). The role of group therapy and the therapeutic community in treating the violent juvenile offender. In R.A. Mathias, P. DeMuro, & R.S. Allison (Eds.), *Violent juvenile offenders.* San Francisco: National Council on Crime and Delinquency.

Aichhorn, A. (1925). *Wayward youth.* New York: Viking.

Aichhorn, A. (1949). Some remarks on the psychic structure and social care of a certain type of juvenile delinquent. In *Psychoanalytic study of the child* (Vols. 3–4). New York: International Universities Press.

Akers, R.L. (1985). *Deviant behavior.* Belmont, CA: Wadsworth.

Albrecht, T.L., & Adelman, M.B. (1987). *Communicating social support.* Newbury Park, CA: Sage.

Alexander, F., & Healy, W. (1935). *Roots of crime.* New York: Knopf.

Altman, J., & Zube, E. (1987). *Neighborhood and community environments.* New York: Plenum.

Amandes, R.B. (1979). Hire a gang leader: A delinquency prevention program that works. *Juvenile and Family Court Journal, 30,* 37–40.

American Humane Association. (1986). *The national study of child neglect and abuse reporting.* Denver: Author.

American Psychiatric Association. (1987). *Diagnostic and statistical manual of mental disorders* (3rd ed. rev.). Washington, DC: Author.

Amir, Y. (1969). Contact hypothesis in ethnic relations. *Psychological Bulletin, 71,* 319–342.

Arbuthnot, J., & Gordon, D.A. (1987). Personality. In H.C. Quay (Ed.), *Handbook of juvenile delinquency.* New York: Wiley.

Argyle, M., Trower, P., & Bryant, B. (1974). Explorations in the treatment of personality disorders and neurosis by social skill training. *British Journal of Medical Psychology, 47,* 63–72.

Arnold, W.R. (1966). The concept of gang. *The Sociological Quarterly, 7,* 59–75.

Asbury, H. (1971). *The gangs of New York.* New York: Capricorn. (Original work published 1927)

Aultman, M.G., & Wellford, C.F. (1978). Towards an integrated model of delinquency causation: An empirical analysis. *Sociology and Social Research, 63,* 316–327.

Ausbel, D. (1974). *Theory and problems of adolescent development.* New York: Grune & Stratton.

Baca, C. (1988, June). *Juvenile gangs in Albuquerque.* Paper presented at the meeting of the Coordinating Council of the Albuquerque Police Department, Albuquerque, NM.

Bahr, S.J. (1979). Family determinants and effects of deviance. In W.R. Burr, R. Hill, F.I. Nye, & I.L. Reiss (Eds.), *Contemporary theories about the family: Research-based theories.* New York: Free Press.

Baker, R.K., & Ball, S.J. (1969). *Mass media and violence.* Washington, DC: U.S. Government Printing Office.

Bandura, A. (1969). *Principles of behavior modification.* New York: Holt, Rinehart & Winston.

Bandura, A. (1973). *Aggression: A social learning analysis.* Englewood Cliffs, NJ: Prentice-Hall.

Bandura, A. (1978). Learning and behavioral theories of aggression. In I.L. Kutash, S.B. Kutash, & L.B. Schlessinger (Eds.), *Violence: Perspectives on murder and aggression.* San Francisco: Jossey-Bass.

Bandura, A. (1986). *Social foundations of thought and action.* Englewood Cliffs, NJ: Prentice-Hall.

Barrera, M. (1986). Distinctions between social support concepts, measures, and models. *American Journal of Community Psychology, 14,* 413–445.

Bartollas, C. (1985). *Correctional treatment: Theory and practice.* Englewood Cliffs, NJ: Prentice-Hall.

Bass, B.M. (1960). *Leadership, psychology, and organizational behavior.* New York: Harper & Row.

Bass, M. (1981). *Stogdill's handbook of leadership.* New York: Free Press.

Bassett, J.E., Blanchard, E.B., & Koshland, E. (1975). Applied behavior analysis in a penal setting: Targeting "free world" behaviors. *Behavior Therapy, 6,* 639–648.

Baumeister, R.F., & Hutton, D.G. (1987). Self-presentation theory: Self-construction and audience pleasing. In B. Mullen & G.R. Goethals (Eds.), *Theories of group behavior.* New York: Springer-Verlag.

Bayh, B. (1975). *Our nation's schools—A report card.* Washington, DC: U.S. Government Printing Office.

Beck, S. (1987). Research issues. In V.B. VanHasselt & M. Hersen (Eds.), *Handbook of adolescent psychology.* Elmsford, NY: Pergamon.

Becker, H.S. (1963). *Outsiders: Studies in the sociology of deviance.* Glencoe, IL: Free Press.

Bell, R.B. (1981). *Worlds of friendship*. Newbury Park, CA: Sage.

Belle, D. (1989). *Children's social networks and social supports*. New York: Wiley.

Bender, T. (1978). *Community and social change in America*. New Brunswick, NJ: Rutgers University Press.

Benne, K.D., & Sheats, P. (1948). Functional roles of group members. *Journal of Social Issues, 4*, 41–49.

Bennett, J. (1981). *Oral history and delinquency: The rhetoric of criminology*. Chicago: University of Chicago Press.

Berkowitz, L. (n.d.). *When the trigger pulls the finger*. Washington, DC: American Psychological Association.

Berkowitz, L., & LePage, A. (1967). Weapons as aggression-eliciting stimuli. *Journal of Personality and Social Psychology, 7*, 202–207.

Bernard, J.S. (1972). *The sociology of community*. Glenview, IL: Scott, Foresman.

Berndt, T.J. (1989). Obtaining support from friends during childhood and adolescence. In D. Belle (Ed.), *Children's social networks and social supports*. New York: Wiley.

Bernstein, K., & Christiansen, K. (1965). A resocialization experiment with short-term offenders. *Scandinavian Studies in Criminology, 1*, 35–54.

Bernstein, S. (1964). *Youth on the streets*. New York: Association Press.

Beverly, C.C., & Stanback, H.J. (1986). The Black underclass: Theory and reality. *The Black Scholar, 17*, 24–31.

BGE, a positive alternative to gangs. (1989, July 10). *Newsweek*, p. 48.

Bigelow, B.J., & LaGaipa, J.J. (1975). Children's written descriptions of friendship. *Developmental Psychology, 11*, 857–858.

Binder, A. (1987). An historical and theoretical introduction. In H.C. Quay (Ed.), *Handbook of juvenile delinquency*. New York: Wiley.

Black, D., & Reiss, A.J. (1970). Police control of juveniles. *American Sociological Review, 35*, 63–77.

Bloch, H.A., & Niederhoffer, A. (1958). *The gang: A study in adolescent behavior*. Westport, CT: Greenwood.

Bloodworth, D. (1966). *The Chinese looking glass*. New York: Dell.

Bobrowski, L.J. (1988). *Collecting, organizing and reporting street gang crime*. Chicago: Chicago Police Department.

Bogardus, E.S. (1943). Gangs of Mexican-American youth. *Sociology and Social Research, 28*, 55–66.

Bohman, M., Cloninger, C.R., Sigvardsson, S., & vonKnorring, A.L. (1982). Predisposition to petty criminality in Swedish adoptees: I. Genetic and environmental heterogeneity. *Archives of General Psychiatry, 39*, 1233–1241.

Boissevain, J., & Mitchell, J.C. (1973). *Network analysis: Studies in human interaction*. The Hague, Netherlands: Mouton.

Bolitho, W. (1930, February). The psychosis of the gang. *Survey*, pp. 501–506.

Bolman, W.M. (1969). Toward realizing the prevention of mental illness. In L. Bellak & H. Barten (Eds.), *Progress in community mental health* (Vol. 1). New York: Grune & Stratton.

Boston University Training Center in Youth Development. (1966). *Educational counselors: Training for a new definition of after-care of juvenile parolees*. Boston: Boston University Press.

Bostow, D.E., & Bailey, J.B. (1969). Modification of severe disruptive and aggressive behavior using brief time-out and reinforcement procedures. *Journal of Applied Behavior Analysis, 2,* 31–37.

Bowlby, J. (1949). *Why delinquency? Report of the conference on the scientific study of juvenile delinquency.* London: National Association for Mental Health.

Bowman, P.C., & Auerbach, S.M. (1982). Impulsive youthful offenders: A multimodal cognitive behavioral treatment program. *Criminal Justice and Behavior, 9,* 432–454.

Bremmer, R.H. (1976). Other people's children. *Journal of Social History, 16,* 83–103.

Bresler, F. (1980). *The Chinese mafia.* New York: Stein & Day.

Brewer, M.B. (1979). The role of ethnocentrism in intergroup conflict. In W.G. Austin & S. Worchel (Eds.), *The social psychology of intergroup conflict.* Pacific Grove, CA: Brooks/Cole.

Brim, J.A. (1974). Social network correlates of avowed happiness. *Journal of Nervous and Mental Diseases, 158,* 432–439.

Brody, S.R. (1976). *The effectiveness of sentencing—A review of the literature* (Home Office Research Study No. 35). London: Her Majesty's Stationery Office.

Brown, B.B., Eicher, S.A., & Petrie, S. (1986). The importance of peer group ("crowd") affiliation in adolescence. *Journal of Adolescence, 9,* 73–96.

Brown, P., & Elliott, R. (1965). Control of aggression in a nursery school class. *Journal of Experimental Child Psychology, 2,* 103–107.

Brown, R. (1976). *Children and television.* Newbury Park, CA: Sage.

Brown, R.M. (1980). Crime, law, and society. In T.A. Gurr (Ed.), *Violence in America: The history of crime.* Newbury Park, CA: Sage.

Brown, W. (1983). *The other side of delinquency.* New Brunswick, NJ: Rutgers University Press.

Brown, W.K. (1978). Black gangs as family extensions. *International Journal of Offender Therapy and Comparative Criminology, 22,* 39–48.

Brownell, A., & Shumaker, S.A. (1985). Where do we go from here? The policy implications of social support. *Journal of Social Issues, 41,* 111–121.

Buckley, W. (1967). *Sociology and modern systems theory.* Englewood Cliffs, NJ: Prentice-Hall.

Burchard, J.D., & Barrera, F. (1972). An analysis of timeout and response cost in a programmed environment. *Journal of Applied Behavior Analysis, 5,* 271–282.

Burgess, R.L., & Akers, R.L. (1966). A differential association–reinforcement theory of criminal behavior. *Social Problems, 14,* 128–147.

Bynner, J., O'Malley, P., & Bachman, J. (1981). Self-esteem and delinquency revisited. *Journal of Youth and Adolescence, 10,* 407–441.

California Council on Criminal Justice. (1989). *State Task Force on Gangs and Drugs: Final Report.* Sacramento, CA: Author.

California Department of the Youth Authority. (1967). *James Marshall Treatment Program.* Unpublished manuscript.

California Office of Criminal Justice Planning. (1987). *Report of the State Task Force on Youth Gang Violence.* Sacramento, CA: Author.

California Youth Gang Task Force. (1981). *Community access team.* Sacramento, CA: Author.

Camp, B.W., & Bash, M.A. (1975). *Think Aloud Program group manual.* Unpublished manuscript, University of Colorado Medical Center, Boulder.

Camp, G.M., & Camp. C.G. (1985). *Prison gangs: Their extent, nature and impact on prisons.* South Salem, NY: Criminal Justice Institute.

Campbell, A. (1984). *The girls in the gang.* Oxford: Basil Blackwell.

Caplan, G. (1964). *Principles of preventive psychiatry.* New York: Basic.

Caplan, G. (1974). *Support systems and community mental health: Lectures on concept development.* New York: Behavioral Publications.

Carney, F.J. (1966). *Summary of studies on the derivation of base expectancy categories for predicting recidivism of subjects released from institutions of the Massachusetts Department of Corrections.* Boston: Massachusetts Department of Corrections.

Carney, L.P. (1977). *Probation and parole: Legal and social dimensions.* New York: McGraw-Hill.

Carpenter, P., & Sugrue, D.P. (1984). Psychoeducation in an outpatient setting—Designing a heterogeneous format for a heterogeneous population of juvenile delinquents. *Adolescence, 19,* 113–122.

Carron, A.V. (1980). *Social psychology of sport.* Ithaca, NY: Mouvement.

Cartwright, D.S. (1975). The nature of gangs. In D.S. Cartwright, B. Tomson, & H. Schwartz (Eds.), *Gang delinquency.* Pacific Grove, CA: Brooks/Cole.

Cartwright, D.S., Howard, K., & Reuterman, N.A. (1970). Multivariate analysis of gang delinquency: II. Structural and dynamic properties of groups. *Multivariate Behavioral Research, 5,* 303–324.

Cartwright, D.S., Tomson, B., & Schwartz, H. (1975). *Gang delinquency.* Pacific Grove, CA: Brooks/Cole.

Cattell, R.B. (1948). Concepts and methods in the measurement of group syntality. *Psychological Review, 55,* 48–63.

Center for Studies of Crime and Delinquency. (1973). *Community based correctional program models and practices.* Washington, DC: National Institute of Mental Health.

Chandler, M. (1973). Egocentrism and antisocial behavior: The assessment and training of social perspective-taking skills. *Developmental Psychology, 9,* 326–332.

Chelladurai, P., & Saleh, S.D. (1978). Preferred leadership in sport. *Canadian Journal of Applied Sport Sciences, 3,* 85–97.

Chin, K. (1990). Chinese gangs and extortion. In C.R. Huff (Ed.), *Gangs in America.* Newbury Park, CA: Sage.

Christiansen, K.O. (1977). A review of studies of criminality among twins. In S.A. Mednick & K.O. Christiansen (Eds.), *Biosocial bases of criminal behavior.* New York: Wiley.

Christopherson, E.R., Arnold, C.M., Hill, D.W., & Quilitch, H.R. (1972). The home point system: Token reinforcement procedures for application by parents of children with behavior problems. *Journal of Applied Behavior Analysis, 5,* 485–497.

Clarke, R.V.G. (1977). Psychology and crime. *Bulletin of the British Psychological Society, 30,* 280–283.

Cleckley, H. (1964). *The mask of sanity.* St. Louis: Mosby.

Cloward, R.A., & Ohlin, L.E. (1960). *Delinquency and opportunity: A theory of delinquent gangs.* New York: Free Press.

Cobb, S. (1976). Social support as a moderator of life stress. *Psychosomatic Medicine, 38,* 300–314.

Cohen, A.K. (1955). *Delinquent boys: The culture of the gang.* New York: Free Press.

Cohen, A.K. (1966). The delinquency subculture. In R. Giallombardo (Ed.), *Juvenile delinquency.* New York: Wiley.

Cohen, A.K., & Short, J.F. (1958). Research in delinquent subcultures. *Journal of Social Issues, 14,* 20–37.

Cohen, B. (1969). The delinquency of gangs and spontaneous groups. In T. Sellin & M.E. Wolfgang (Eds.), *Delinquency: Selected topics.* New York: Wiley.

Cohen, H.L., & Filipczak, J.A. (1971). *A new learning environment.* San Francisco: Jossey-Bass.

Cohen, J. (1983). The relationship between friendship selection and peer influence. In J.L. Epstein & N. Karweit (Eds.), *Friends in school.* New York: Academic.

Cohen, L.E., & Land, K.C. (1987). Sociological positivism and the explanation of criminality. In F.R. Gottfredson & T. Hirschi (Eds.), *Positive criminology.* Newbury Park, CA: Sage.

Coleman, J.C. (1980). Friendship and the peer group in adolescence. In J. Adelson (Ed.), *Handbook of adolescent psychology.* New York: Wiley.

Collins, H.C. (1979). *Street gangs: Profiles for police.* New York: New York City Police Department.

Comstock, G. (1983). Media influences on aggression. In A.P. Goldstein (Ed.), *Prevention and control of aggression.* Elmsford, NY: Pergamon.

Conger, J.J., & Miller, W.C. (1966). *Personality, social class, and delinquency.* New York: Wiley.

Cook, P.J. (1980). Research in criminal deterrence: Laying the groundwork for the second decade. In N. Morris & M. Tonry (Eds.), *Crime and justice: An annual review of research.* Chicago: University of Chicago Press.

Cook, S.W. (1972). Motives in conceptual analysis of attitude-related behavior. In J. Brigham & T. Weissbach (Eds.), *Racial attitudes in America: Analyses and findings of social psychology.* New York: Harper & Row.

Cooper, J., & Fazio, R.H. (1979). The formation and persistence of attitudes that support intergroup conflict. In W.G. Austin & S. Worchel (Eds.), *The social psychology of intergroup relations.* Pacific Grove, CA: Brooks/Cole.

Corning, P.A., & Corning, C.H. (1972). Toward a general theory of violent aggression. *Social Science Information, 11,* 7–13.

Cortes, J.B., & Gatti, F.M. (1972). *Delinquency and crime.* New York: Seminar.

Coser, L.A. (1956). *The functions of social conflict.* Glencoe, IL: Free Press.

Craft, M., Stephenson, G., & Granger, C. (1964). A controlled trial of authoritarian and self-governing regimes with adolescent psychopaths. *American Journal of Orthopsychiatry, 34,* 543–554.

Crawford, P.L., Malamud, D.I., & Dumpson, J.R. (1950). *Working with teen-age gangs. A report on the Central Harlem Street Clubs Project.* New York: Welfare Council of New York City.

Crocker, D. (1955). A study of a problem of aggression. *Psychoanalytic Study of the Child, 10,* 300–335.

Cronbach, L.J., & Snow, R.E. (1977). *Aptitudes and instructional methods.* New York: Irvington.

Crowe, R.R. (1975). An adoptive study of psychopathy. In R.R. Fieve, D. Rosenthal, & H. Brill (Eds.), *Genetic research in psychiatry.* Baltimore: Johns Hopkins University Press.

Csikszentmihalyi, M., & Larsen, R. (1984). *Being adolescent: Conflict and growth in the teenage years.* New York: Basic.

Cuomo, M. (1987). *State of the state.* Albany, NY: Office of the Governor.

Dalgaard, O.S., & Kringlen, E. (1976). A Norwegian twin study of criminality. *British Journal of Criminology, 16,* 213–232.

Davis, A. (1944). Socialization and adolescent personality. In *Adolescence* (43rd Yearbook, National Society for Studies in Education). Chicago: University of Chicago Press.

DeLange, J.M., Lanham, S.L., & Barton, J.A. (1981). Social skills training for juvenile delinquents: Behavioral skill training and cognitive techniques. In D. Upper and S. Ross (Eds.), *Behavioral group therapy, 1981: An annual review* (Vol. 3). Champaign, IL: Research Press.

DeLeon, R.V. (1977). Averting violence in the gang community. *The Police Chief, 44,* 52–53.

Deur, J.L., & Parke, R.D. (1970). The effects of inconsistent punishment on aggression in children. *Developmental Psychology, 2,* 403–411.

Deutsch, M. (1973). *The resolution of conflict.* New Haven, CT: Yale University Press.

Deutsch, M., & Krauss, R.M. (1960). The effect of threat upon interpersonal bargaining. *Journal of Abnormal and Social Psychology, 61,* 181–189.

Diener, E. (1976). Effects of prior destructive behavior, anonymity, and group presence on deindividuation and aggression. *Journal of Personality and Social Psychology, 33,* 497–507.

Dion, K.L. (1973). Cohesiveness as a determinant of ingroup-outgroup bias. *Journal of Personality and Social Psychology, 28,* 163–171.

Dodge, K.A., & Murphy, R.R. (1984). The assessment of social competence in adolescents. In P. Karoly & J.J. Steffen (Eds.), *Advances in child behavior analysis and therapy* (Vol. 4). New York: Plenum.

Dugdale, R.L. (1942). *The Jukes: A study in crime, pauperism, disease, and heredity.* New York: Putnam.

Dumpson, J.R. (1949). An approach to antisocial street gangs. *Federal Probation, 13,* 22–29.

D'Zurilla, T.J., & Goldfried, M.R. (1971). Problem solving and behavior modification. *Journal of Abnormal Psychology, 78,* 107–126.

Edelman, B. (1981, May). Does New York need the Guardian Angels? *Police Magazine,* pp. 51–56.

Edelman, E., & Goldstein, A.P. (1984). Prescriptive relationship levels for juvenile delinquents in a psychotherapy analog. *Aggressive Behavior, 10,* 269–278.

Edgerton, R. (1988). Foreword. In J.D. Vigil, *Barrio gangs: Street life and identity in Southern California.* Austin: University of Texas Press.

Edman, I. (1919). *Human traits and their social significance.* New York: Houghton Mifflin.

Eissler, K.R. (1950). Ego-psychological implications of the psychoanalytic treatment of delinquents. *Psychoanalytic Study of the Child, 5,* 97–121.

Elardo, P., & Cooper, M. (1977). *AWARE: Activities for social development.* Reading, MA: Addison-Wesley.

Elderly abuse in America. (1990, May 1). *New York Times,* p. 28.

Elliott, D.S., Ageton, S.S., & Canter, R.J. (1979). An integrated theoretical perspective on juvenile delinquency. *Journal of Research in Crime and Delinquency, 16,* 3–27.

Elliott, D.S., Huizenga, D., & Ageton, S.S. (1985). *Explaining delinquency and drug use.* Newbury Park, CA: Sage.

Elliott, D.S., & Voss, H.L. (1974). *Delinquency and dropout.* Toronto: Lexington.

Ellis, H. (1914). *The criminal.* London: Scott.

Ellis, L. (1987). Neurohormonal bases of varying tendencies to learn delinquent and criminal behavior. In E.K. Morris & C.J. Braukmann (Eds.), *Behavioral approaches to crime and delinquency.* New York: Plenum.

Empey, L.T. (1969). Contemporary programs for convicted juvenile offenders: Problems of theory, practice and research. In D.J. Mulvihill & M.M. Tremis (Eds.), *Crimes of violence* (Vol. 13). Washington, DC: U.S. Government Printing Office.

Empey, L.T., & Erickson, M.L. (1972). *The Provo experiment: Evaluating community control of delinquency.* Lexington, MA: Lexington.

Epps, P., & Parnell, R.W. (1952). Physique and temperament of women delinquents compared with women undergraduates. *British Journal of Medical Psychology, 25,* 249–255.

Erikson, E.H. (1975). The problem of ego identity. In A.V. Esman (Ed.), *The psychology of adolescence.* New York: International Universities Press.

Eysenck, H.J. (1977). *Crime and personality.* London: Routledge & Kegan Paul.

Fagan, J.A., & Hartstone, E. (1984). Strategic planning in juvenile justice—Defining the toughest kids. In R.A. Mathias, P. DeMurray, & R.S. Allinson (Eds.), *Violent juvenile offenders.* San Francisco: National Council on Crime and Delinquency.

Fagan, J.A., Piper, E., & Moore, E. (1986). Violent delinquents and urban youths. *Criminology, 24,* 439–471.

Fahlberg, V. (1979). *Attachment and separation: Putting the pieces together* (DSS Publication No. 429). Lansing, MI: Michigan Department of Social Services.

Falbo, T. (1977). The multidimensional scaling of power strategies. *Journal of Personality and Social Psychology, 35,* 537–548.

Farrington, D.P., Gundry, G., & West, D.J. (1975). The familial transmission of criminality. *Medicine, Science and the Law, 15,* 177–186.

Federal Bureau of Investigation. (1989). *Uniform crime report, 1989.* Washington, DC: U.S. Government Printing Office.

Federation on Child Abuse and Neglect. (1990). *Fact sheet.* New York: National Committee for Prevention of Child Abuse.

Feindler, E.L., & Ecton, R. (1986). *Anger control training.* Elmsford, NY: Pergamon.

Feindler, E.L., Marriott, S.A., & Iwata, M. (1984). Group anger control training for junior high school delinquents. *Cognitive Therapy and Research, 8,* 299–311.

Feiring, C., & Lewis, M. (1989). The social networks of girls and boys from early through middle childhood. In D. Belle (Ed.), *Children's social networks and social supports.* New York: Wiley.

Feistman, E.G. (1966). *Comparative analysis of the Willowbrook-Harbor Intensive Services Program* (Research Report No. 28). Los Angeles: Los Angeles County Probation Department.

Feldman, M.P. (1977). *Criminal behavior: A psychological analysis.* London: Wiley.

Feldman, R.A., Caplinger, T.E., & Wodarski, J.S. (1983). *The St. Louis conundrum: The effective treatment of anti-social youths.* Englewood Cliffs, NJ: Prentice-Hall.

Feshbach, S. (1970). Aggression. In P.H. Mussen (Ed.), *Carmichael's manual of child psychology* (Vol. 2). New York: Wiley.

Feshbach, S., & Singer, R.D. (1971). *Television and aggression.* San Francisco: Jossey-Bass.

Festinger, L. (1954). A theory of social comparison processes. *Human Relations, 7,* 117–140.

Fiedler, F.E. (1967). *A theory of leadership effectiveness.* New York: McGraw-Hill.

Filipczak, J., Friedman, R.M., & Reese, S.C. (1979). PREP: Educational programming to prevent juvenile problems. In J.S. Stumphauzer (Ed.), *Progress in behavior therapy with delinquents.* Springfield, IL: Charles C Thomas.

Fischer, C.S. (1977). *Networks and places.* London: Free Press.

Fischer, C.S. (1982). *To dwell among friends.* Chicago: University of Chicago Press.

Fisher, J.C. (1976). Homicide in Detroit. *Criminology, 14,* 387–400.

Fo, W., & O'Donnell, C. (1974). The buddy system: Relationship and contingency conditions in a community intervention program for youth with nonprofessionals as behavior change agents. *Journal of Consulting and Clinical Psychology, 42,* 163–168.

Fo, W., & O'Donnell, C. (1975). The buddy system: Effect of community intervention on delinquent offenses. *Behavior Therapy, 6,* 522–524.

Foley, L.A. (1976). Personality and situational influences on changes in prejudice. *Journal of Personality and Social Psychology, 34,* 846–856.

Forsyth, D.R. (1983). *An introduction to group dynamics.* Pacific Grove, CA: Brooks/Cole.

Forsyth, D.R. (1990). *Group dynamics* (2nd ed.). Pacific Grove, CA: Brooks/Cole.

Fox, F.L. (1981). The family and the ex-offender: Potential for rehabilitation. In S.E. Martin, L.B. Sechrest, & R. Redner (Eds.), *New directions in the rehabilitation of criminal offenders.* Washington, DC: National Academy Press.

Fox, H.G. (1970). Gang youth and police: Live-in. *The Police Chief, 37,* 233–235.

Fox, J.R. (1985). Mission impossible? Social work practice with Black urban youth gangs. *Social Work, 30,* 25–31.

Foxx, C.L., Foxx, R.M., Jones, J.R., & Kiely, D. (1980). Twenty-four hour social isolation: A program for reducing the aggressive behavior of a psychotic-like retarded adult. *Behavior Modification, 4,* 130–144.

Foxx, R.M., & Azrin, N.H. (1972). Restitution: A method of eliminating aggressive-disruptive behavior of retarded and brain damaged patients. *Behaviour Research and Therapy, 10,* 15–27.

French, J.R.P., Jr., & Raven, B. (1959). The bases of social power. In D. Cartwright (Ed.), *Studies in social power.* Ann Arbor, MI: University of Michigan, Institute for Social Research.

Freud, S. (1961). *The complete works of Sigmund Freud.* London: Hogarth.

Friedlander, K. (1947). *The psychoanalytic approach to juvenile delinquency.* New York: International Universities Press.

Friedman, C.J., Mann, F., & Friedman, A.S. (1975). A profile of juvenile street gang members. *Adolescence, 40,* 563–607.

Furfey, P.H. (1926). *The gang age.* New York: Macmillan.

Furman, W. (1989). The development of children's social networks. In D. Belle (Ed.), *Children's social networks and social supports.* New York: Wiley.

Gannon, T.M. (1965). *The changing role of the street worker in the Council of Social and Athletic Clubs.* New York: New York City Youth Board Research Department.

Gannon, T.M. (1967). Emergence of the "defensive gang." *Federal Probation, 30,* 44–48.

Gardner, S. (1983). *Street gangs.* New York: Franklin Watts.

Garrett, C.J. (1985). Effects of residential treatment on adjudicated delinquents: A meta-analysis. *Journal of Research on Crime and Delinquency, 22,* 287–308.

Garrity, D. (1956). *The effects of length of incarceration upon parole adjustment and estimation of optimum sentence.* Unpublished doctoral dissertation, University of Washington, Seattle.

Gensheimer, L.K., Mayer, J.P., Gottschalk, R., & Davidson, W.S. (1986). Diverting youth from the Juvenile Justice System: A meta-analysis of intervention efficacy. In S.J. Apter & A.P. Goldstein (Eds.), *Youth violence.* Elmsford, NY: Pergamon.

Gibb, C.A. (1969). Leadership. In G. Lindzey & E. Aronson (Eds.), *The handbook of social psychology* (Vol. 4). Reading, MA: Addison-Wesley.

Gibb, J.R. (1961). Defensive level and influence potential in small groups. In L. Petrullo & B.M. Bass (Eds.), *Leadership and interpersonal behavior.* New York: Holt, Rinehart & Winston.

Gibb, J.R. (1973). Defensive communication. In W.G. Bennis, D.E. Berlew, E.H. Schein, & F.I. Steele (Eds.), *Interpersonal dynamics.* Homewood, IL: Dorsey.

Gibbens, T.C. (1963). *Psychiatric studies of Borstal lads.* London: Oxford University Press.

Gibbs, J.C. (1986). *Small group sociomoral treatment programs: Dilemmas for use with conduct-disordered or antisocial adolescents or preadolescents.* Unpublished manuscript: Ohio State University, Columbus.

Gil, D.G. (1970). *Violence against children.* Cambridge, MA: Harvard University Press.

Gillis, A.R., & Hagan, J. (1990). Delinquent samaritans: Network structures, social conflict and the willingness to intervene. *Journal of Research in Crime and Delinquency, 27,* 30–51.

Gladstone, H.P. (1962). A study of techniques of psychotherapy with youthful offenders. *Psychiatry, 25,* 147–159.

Glaser, D. (1956). Criminality theories and behavioral images. In D.R. Cressey & D.A. Ward (Eds.), *Delinquency, crime, and social process.* New York: Harper & Row.

Glaser, D. (1973, November). *The state of the art of criminal justice evaluation.* Paper presented at the meeting of the Association for Criminal Justice Research, Los Angeles.

Glaser, W. (1969). *Schools without failure.* New York: Harper & Row.

Glasgow, D.G. (1980). *The Black underclass: Poverty, unemployment, and entrapment of ghetto youth.* San Francisco: Jossey-Bass.

Glover, E. (1944). The diagnosis and treatment of delinquency. In L. Radzinowicz & J.W.C. Turner (Eds.), *Mental abnormality and crime.* London: Macmillan.

Glover, E. (1960). *The roots of crime.* New York: International Universities Press.

Glueck, S., & Glueck, E.T. (1950). *Unraveling juvenile delinquency.* Cambridge, MA: Harvard University Press.

Goddard, H.H. (1916). *The Kallikak family: A study in the heredity of feeblemindedness.* New York: Macmillan.

Goethals, G.R., & Darley, J.M. (1987). Social comparison theory: Self-evaluation and group life. In B. Mullen & G.R. Goethals (Eds.), *Theories of group behavior.* New York: Springer-Verlag.

Goins, S. (1977). The serious or violent juvenile offender—Is there a treatment response? In *The serious juvenile offender: Proceedings of a national symposium.* Washington, DC: U.S. Government Printing Office.

Gold, M. (1963). *Status forces in delinquent boys.* Ann Arbor: University of Michigan Press.

Gold, M. (1970). *Delinquent behavior in an American city.* Pacific Grove, CA: Brooks/Cole.

Gold, M., & Petronio, R.J. (1980). Delinquent behavior in adolescence. In J. Adelson (Ed.), *Handbook of adolescence.* New York: Wiley.

Goldstein, A.P. (Ed.). (1978). *Prescriptions for child mental health and education.* Elmsford, NY: Pergamon.

Goldstein, A.P. (1983). United States. In A.P. Goldstein & M.H. Segall (Eds.), *Aggression in global perspective.* Elmsford, NY: Pergamon.

Goldstein, A.P. (1988a). New directions in aggression reduction. *International Journal of Group Tensions, 18,* 286–313.

Goldstein, A.P. (1988b). *The Prepare Curriculum: Teaching prosocial competencies.* Champaign, IL: Research Press.

Goldstein, A.P. (1990). *Delinquents on delinquency.* Champaign, IL: Research Press.

Goldstein, A.P., Apter, S.J., & Harootunian, B. (1984). *School violence.* Englewood Cliffs, NJ: Prentice-Hall.

Goldstein, A.P., & Glick, B. (1987). *Aggression Replacement Training: A comprehensive intervention for aggressive youth.* Champaign, IL: Research Press.

Goldstein, A.P., Glick, B., Irwin, M.J., Pask-McCartney, C., & Rubama, I. (1989). *Reducing delinquency: Intervention in the community.* Elmsford, NY: Pergamon.

Goldstein, A.P., Heller, K., & Sechrest, L.B. (1966). *Psychotherapy and the psychology of behavior change.* New York: Wiley.

Goldstein, A.P., & Keller, H. (1987). *Aggressive behavior: Assessment and intervention.* Elmsford, NY: Pergamon.

Goldstein, A.P., & Segall, M. (1983). *Aggression in global perspective.* Elmsford, NY: Pergamon.

Goldstein, A.P., Sprafkin, R.P., Gershaw, N.J., & Klein, P. (1980). *Skillstreaming the adolescent: A structured learning approach to teaching prosocial skills.* Champaign, IL: Research Press.

Goldstein, A.P., & Stein, N. (1976). *Prescriptive psychotherapies.* Elmsford, NY: Pergamon.

Gonzalez, A. (1981). *Mexican/Chicano gangs in Los Angeles.* Unpublished doctoral dissertation, University of California, Berkeley.

Gordon, D.A., & Arbuthnot, J. (1987). Individual, group, and family interventions. In H.C. Quay (Ed.), *Handbook of juvenile delinquency.* New York: Wiley.

Goring, C. (1913). *The English convict: A statistical study.* London: Darling & Son.

Gott, R. (1989, May). *Juvenile gangs.* Paper presented at the Conference on Juvenile Crime, Eastern Kentucky University, Richmond.

Gottschalk, R., Davidson, W.S., Mayer, J.P., & Gensheimer, L.K. (1987). Community-based interventions. In H.C. Quay (Ed.), *Handbook of juvenile delinquency.* New York: Wiley.

Gough, H.G. (1948). A sociological theory of psychopathy. *American Journal of Sociology, 53,* 359–366.

Grant, J., & Grant, M.Q. (1959). A group dynamics approach to the treatment of nonconformists in the navy. *Annals of the American Academy of Political and Social Science, 322,* 126–135.

Gray, K.C., & Hutchison, H.C. (1964). The psychopathic personality: A survey of Canadian psychiatrists' opinions. *Canadian Psychiatric Association Journal, 9,* 452–461.

Greenwood, P.W. (1986). *Intervention strategies for chronic juvenile offenders.* New York: Greenwood.

Grendreau, P., & Ross, R.R. (1987). Revivification of rehabilitation: Evidence from the 1980s. *Justice Quarterly, 4,* 349–397.

Gross, A.M., & Levin, R.B. (1987). Learning. In V.B. VanHasselt & M. Hersen (Eds.), *Handbook of adolescent psychology.* Elmsford, NY: Pergamon.

Gurr, T.A. (1989). *Violence in America: Protest, rebellion, reform.* Newbury Park, CA: Sage.

Gutterman, E.S. (1963). *Effects of short-term psychiatric treatment* (Research Report No. 36). Sacramento: California Department of the Youth Authority.

Hagedorn, J. (1990). Back in the field again: Gang research in the nineties. In C.R. Huff (Ed.), *Gangs in America*. Newbury Park, CA: Sage.

Hagedorn, J., & Macon, P. (1988). *People and folks*. Chicago: Lake View.

Haire, T.D. (1979). Street gangs: Some suggested remedies for violence and vandalism. *The Police Chief, 46*, 54–55.

Hall, R.V., Axelrod, S., Foundopoulos, M., Shellman, J., Campbell, R.S., & Cranston, S.S. (1971). The effective use of punishment to modify behavior in the classroom. *Education Technology, 11*, 24–26.

Halpin, A.W., & Winer, J.B. (1952). *The leadership behavior of the airplane commander*. Columbus: Ohio State University Research Foundation.

Hammer, M., Gutwirth, L., & Phillips, S.L. (1982). Parenthood and social networks: A preliminary view. *Social Science and Medicine, 16*, 2091–2100.

Hamparian, D.M., Schuster, R., Dinitz, S., & Conrad, J.P. (1978). *The violent few: A study of dangerous juvenile offenders*. Lexington, MA: Lexington.

Hanson, B., Beschner, G., Walters, J.M., & Bovelle, E. (1985). *Life with heroin: Voices from the inner city*. Lexington, MA: Lexington.

Hardman, D.G. (1967). Historical perspectives on gang research. *Journal of Research in Crime and Delinquency, 4*, 5–27.

Hare, R.D. (1970). *Psychopathy: Theory and research*. New York: Wiley.

Hargardine, J.E. (1968). *The attention homes of Boulder, Colorado*. Washington, DC: U.S. Department of Health, Education and Welfare, Juvenile Delinquency and Youth Development Office.

Harlow, E., Weber, J.R., & Wilkins, L.T. (1971). *Community based correctional program models and practices*. Washington, DC: National Institute of Mental Health.

Harper, N.L., & Askling, L.R. (1980). Group communication and quality of task solution in a media production organization. *Communication Monographs, 47*, 77–100.

Harrison, R.M., & Mueller, P. (1964). *Clue hunting about group counseling and parole outcome*. Sacramento, CA: California Department of Corrections.

Havighurst, R.J. (1987). Adolescent culture and subculture. In V.B. VanHasselt & M. Hersen (Eds.), *Handbook of adolescent psychology*. Elmsford, NY: Pergamon.

Hawkins, J.D., & Weis, J.G. (1985). The social development model: An integrated approach to delinquency prevention. *Journal of Primary Prevention, 6*, 73–97.

Hawkins, R., & Tiedemann, G. (1975). *The creation of deviance: Interpersonal and organizational determinants*. Columbus, OH: Merrill.

Healy, W. (1915). *The individual delinquent*. Boston: Little, Brown.

Healy, W., & Bronner, A. (1936). *New light on delinquency and its treatment*. New Haven, CT: Yale University Press.

Helfer, R.E., & Kempe, C.H. (1976). *Child abuse and neglect*. Cambridge, MA: Ballinger.

Heller, K., Price, R.H., & Hogg, J.R. (1988). The role of social support in community and clinical intervention. In I.G. Sarason, B.R. Sarason, & G.R. Pierce (Eds.), *Social support: An interactional view*. New York: Wiley.

Heller, K., Swindle, R.W., & Dusenbury, L. (1986). Component social support processes: Comments and integration. *Journal of Consulting and Clinical Psychology, 54*, 466–470.

Helmreich, W.B. (1973). Race, sex and gangs. *Society, 11,* 44–50.

Hemphill, J.K., & Coons, A.E. (1957). Development of the Leader Behavior Description Questionnaire. In R.M. Stogdill & A.E. Coons (Eds.), *Leader behavior: Its description and measurement* (Research Monograph No. 88). Columbus, OH: Ohio State University, Bureau of Business Research.

Henderson, C.R. (1910). *Prison reform and criminal law.* New York: Charities Publication Committee.

Hewitt, J.P. (1970). *Social stratification and deviant behavior.* New York: Random House.

Hill, M.C., & Whiting, A.N. (1950). Some theoretical and methodological problems in community studies. *Social Forces, 29,* 117–124.

Hillery, G.A. (1955). Definitions of community: Areas of agreement. *Rural Sociology, 120,* 111–123.

Himelhoch, S. (1965). Delinquency and opportunity: An end and a beginning of theory. In L. Gouldner & M. Miller (Eds.), *Applied sociology.* New York: Free Press.

Hindelang, M. (1972). The relationship of self-reported delinquency to scales of the CPI and the MMPI. *Journal of Criminal Law, Criminology, and Police Science, 63,* 75–81.

Hirsch, B.J. (1980). Natural support systems and coping with major life changes. *American Journal of Community Psychology, 8,* 159–172.

Hirschi, T. (1969). *Causes of delinquency.* Berkeley: University of California Press.

Hogan, R., & Jones, W.H. (1983). A role-theoretical model of criminal conduct. In W.S. Laufer & J.M. Day (Eds.), *Personality theory, moral development, and criminal behavior.* Lexington, MA: Lexington.

Hollin, C.R. (1989). *Cognitive-behavioral interventions with young offenders.* Elmsford, NY: Pergamon.

Hollin, C.R., Huff, G.J., Clarkson, F., & Edmondson, A.C. (1986). Social skills training with young offenders in a Borstal: An evaluative study. *Journal of Community Psychology, 14,* 289–299.

Horowitz, R. (1983). *Honor and the American dream.* New Brunswick, NJ: Rutgers University Press.

Hoskins, R.G. (1941). *Endocrinology.* New York: Norton.

House, J.S. (1981). *Work stress and social support.* Reading, MA: Addison-Wesley.

House, J.S., Umberson, D., & Landis, K.R. (1988). Structures and processes of social support. *Annual Review of Sociology, 14,* 293–318.

House, R.J. (1971). A path goal theory of leader effectiveness. *Administrative Science Quarterly, 16,* 321–338.

Howard, A., & Scott, R.A. (1981). The study of minority groups in complex societies. In R.H. Monroe, R.L. Monroe, & B.B. Whiting (Eds.), *Handbook of cross-cultural human development.* New York: Garland.

Howitt, D., & Cumberbatch, G. (1975). *Mass media violence and society.* New York: Wiley.

Hudson, C.H. (1973). *Summary report: An experimental study of the differential effects of parole supervision for a group of adolescent boys and girls.* Minneapolis: Minnesota Department of Corrections.

Huff, C.R. (1989). Youth gangs and public policy. *Crime and delinquency, 35,* 524–537.

Hunt, D.E. (1972). Matching models for teacher training. In B.R. Joyce & M. Weil (Eds.), *Perspectives for reform in teacher education.* Englewood Cliffs, NJ: Prentice-Hall.

Hyman, H.H., & Singer, E. (Eds.). (1959). *Reference group theory and research.* New York: Free Press.

Illinois State Police. (1989, January). *Criminal Intelligence Bulletin* (No. 42). Springfield, IL: Author.

Ingram, G.L., Gerard, R.E., Quay, H.C., & Levinson, R.B. (1970). An experimental program for the psychopathic delinquent: Looking in the "correctional wastebasket." *Journal of Research in Crime and Delinquency, 7,* 24–30.

Jacobs, J.B. (1974). Street gangs behind bars. *Social Problems, 21,* 395–408.

Janis, I.L. (1972). *Victims of groupthink.* Boston: Houghton Mifflin.

Janis, I.L. (1979). *Preventing groupthink in policy planning groups.* Paper presented at the meeting of the International Society of Political Psychology, Washington, DC.

Jenkins, R.L., & Brown, W.K. (1988). *The abandonment of delinquent behavior.* New York: Praeger.

Jennings, W.S., Kilkenny, R., & Kohlberg, L. (1983). In W.S. Laufer & J.M. Day (Eds.), *Personality theory, moral development, and criminal behavior.* Lexington, MA: Lexington.

Jesness, C. (1965). *The Fricot Ranch Study.* Sacramento: California Department of the Youth Authority.

Jesness, C., Allison, T., McCormick, R., Wedge, R., & Young, M. (1975). *Cooperative Behavior Demonstration Project.* Sacramento: California Department of the Youth Authority.

Jetmore, L.F. (1988, November). Hartford street gangs: A new generation. *Law and Order,* pp. 63–67.

Johnson, A.M. (1949). Sanctions for super-ego lacunae. In K.R. Eissler (Ed.), *Searchlights on delinquency.* New York: International Universities Press.

Johnson, A.M. (1959). Juvenile delinquency. In S. Arieti (Ed.), *American handbook of psychiatry.* New York: Basic.

Johnson, A.M., & Szurek, S.A. (1952). The genesis of anti-social acting out in children and adults. *Psychoanalytic Quarterly, 21,* 323–343.

Johnson, B.M. (1965). The "failure" of a parole research project. *California Youth Authority Quarterly, 18,* 35–39.

Johnson, R.E. (1979). *Juvenile delinquency and its origins.* Cambridge: Cambridge University Press.

Jones, F.H., & Miller, W.H. (1974). The effective use of negative attention for reducing group disruption in special elementary school classrooms. *The Psychological Record, 24,* 435–448.

Jones, M. (1953). *The therapeutic community.* New York: Basic.

Jurjevich, R.M. (1968). *No water in my cup: Experiences and a controlled study of psychotherapy of delinquent girls.* New York: Libra.

Kahn, R., & Antonucci, T. (1980). Attachment, role, and social support. In P. Baltes & O. Brim (Eds.), *Life-span development and behavior*. New York: Academic.

Kaplan, D.E., & Dubro, A. (1986). *Yakuza: The explosive account of Japan's criminal underworld*. Reading, MA: Addison-Wesley.

Katz, R., & Tushman, M. (1979). Communication patterns, project performance, and task characteristics. *Organization Behavior and Group Performance, 23,* 139–162.

Kazdin, A.E. (1985). *Treatment of antisocial behavior in children and adolescents*. Homewood, IL: Dorsey.

Kazdin, A.E. (1987). *Conduct disorders in childhood and adolescence*. Newbury Park, CA: Sage.

Keiser, R.L. (1969). *The Vice Lords: Warriors of the streets*. New York: Holt, Rinehart & Winston.

Keith, C.R. (Ed.). (1984a). *The aggressive adolescent*. New York: Free Press.

Keith, C.R. (1984b). Individual psychotherapy and psychoanalysis with the aggressive adolescent: A historical review. In C.R. Keith (Ed.), *The aggressive adolescent*. New York: Free Press.

Keller, F.S. (1966). A personal course in psychology. In R. Ulrich, T. Stachnik, & J. Mabry (Eds.), *Control of human behavior*. Glenview, IL: Scott, Foresman.

Keller, S.I. (1968). *The urban neighborhood: A sociological perspective*. New York: Random House.

Kelley, H.H. (1959). Two functions of reference groups. In H.H. Hyman & E. Singer (Eds.), *Reference group theory and research*. New York: Free Press.

Kelley, H.H., & Thibaut, J.W. (1978). *Interpersonal relations: A theory of interdependence*. New York: Wiley.

Kelling, G.W. (1975). Leadership in the gang. In D.S. Cartwright, B. Tomson, & H. Schwartz (Eds.), *Gang delinquency*. Pacific Grove, CA: Brooks/Cole.

Kelly, J.A., & Hansen, D.J. (1987). Social interactions and adjustment. In V.B. VanHasselt & M. Hersen (Eds.), *Handbook of adolescent psychology*. Elmsford, NY: Pergamon.

Kempe, C.H., Silverman, F.N., Steele, B.B., Droegemueller, W., & Silver, H.K. (1962). The battered child syndrome. *Journal of the American Medical Association, 181,* 17–24.

Kentucky Child Welfare Research Foundation. (1967). *Community rehabilitation of the younger delinquent boy: Parkland non-residential group center*. Washington, DC: U.S. Department of Health, Education and Welfare.

Kiesler, D.J. (1969). A grid model for theory and research. In L.D. Eron & R. Callahan (Eds.), *The relation of theory to practice in psychotherapy*. Chicago: Aldine.

Kipnis, D. (1974). *The powerholders*. Chicago: University of Chicago Press.

Kipnis, D., Castell, P.J., Gergen, M., & Mauch, D. (1976). Metamorphic effects of power. *Journal of Applied Psychology, 61,* 127–135.

Kipnis, D., & Consentino, J. (1969). Use of leadership powers in industry. *Journal of Applied Psychology, 53,* 460–466.

Klausmeier, H.J., Rossmiller, R.A., & Sailey, M. (1977). *Individually guided elementary education*. New York: Academic.

Klein, M.W. (1968a). Impressions of juvenile gang members. *Adolescence, 3,* 53–78.

Klein, M.W. (1968b). *The Ladino Hills Project* (Final Report). Washington, DC: Office of Juvenile Delinquency and Youth Development.

Klein, M.W. (1971). *Street gangs and street workers.* Englewood Cliffs, NJ: Prentice-Hall.

Klein, M.W., & Crawford, L.Y. (1968). Groups, gangs and cohesiveness. In J.F. Short (Ed.), *Gang delinquency and delinquent subcultures.* New York: Harper & Row.

Klein, M.W., & Maxson, C.L. (1989). Street gang violence. In N.A. Weiner & N.W. Wolfgang (Eds.), *Violent crime, violent criminals.* Newbury Park, CA: Sage.

Klein, M.W., Maxson, C.L., & Cunningham, L. (1988). *Gang involvement in cocaine "rock" trafficking.* Los Angeles: University of Southern California, Social Science Research Institute.

Kleiner, R.J., Holger, R.S., & Lanahan, J. (1975). A study of Black youth groups: Implications for research, action, and the role of the investigator. *Human Organization, 34,* 391–393.

Knight, D. (1969). *The Marshall Program—Assessment of a short-term institutional treatment program* (Research Report No. 56). Sacramento: California Department of the Youth Authority.

Knight, D. (1970). *The Marshall Program—Assessment of a short-term institutional treatment program: Part 2. Amenability to confrontive peer-group treatment* (Research Report No. 59). Sacramento: California Department of the Youth Authority.

Kobrin, S. (1959). The Chicago Area Project: A twenty-five year assessment. *Annals of the American Academy of Political and Social Science, 322,* 136–151.

Kobrin, S., & Klein, M.W. (1983). *Community treatment of juvenile offenders: The DSO experiments.* Newbury Park, CA: Sage.

Kobrin, S., Puntil, J., & Peluso, E. (1968). Criteria of status among street groups. In J.F. Short (Ed.), *Gang delinquency and delinquent subcultures.* New York: Harper & Row.

Kochman, T. (1981). *Black and White styles in conflict.* Chicago: University of Chicago Press.

Kohlberg, L. (1969). Stage and sequence: The cognitive-developmental approach to socialization. In D.A. Goslin (Ed.), *Handbook of socialization theory and research.* Chicago: Rand McNally.

Kohlberg, L. (Ed.). (1973). *Collected papers on moral development and moral education.* Cambridge, MA: Harvard University, Center for Moral Education.

Kornhauser, R. (1978). *Social sources of delinquency.* Chicago: University of Chicago Press.

Kozeny, E. (1962). Experimentelle Untersuchungen zur Ausdruckskundemittel photographisch-statistischer Methode. [Experimental research on the use of the photographic-statistical method in the study of physiognomic expression]. *Archive für die gesamte Psychologie, 114,* 55–71.

Krantz, H. (1936). *Lebensschicksale krimineller Zwillinge.* [Life patterns of criminal twins]. Berlin: Springer-Verlag.

Kratcoski, P.C., & Kratcoski, M.A. (1975). Changing patterns in the delinquent activities of boys and girls: A self-reported delinquency analysis. *Adolescence, 10,* 83–91.

Kraus, J. (1974). The deterrent effect of fines and probation on male juvenile offenders. *Australian and New Zealand Journal of Criminology, 7,*231–240.

Krisberg, B. (1974). Gang youth and hustling: The psychology of survival. *Issues in Criminology, 9,* 243–255.

Krohn, M.D., Massey, J.L., & Skinner, W.F. (1987). A sociological theory of crime and delinquency: Social learning theory. In E.K. Morris & C.J. Braukmann (Eds.), *Behavioral approaches to crime and delinquency.* New York: Plenum.

Kulik, J.A., Stein, K.B., & Sarbin, T.R. (1968). Disclosure of delinquent behavior under conditions of anonymity and nonanonymity. *Journal of Consulting and Clinical Psychology, 32,* 506–509.

Landesco, J. (1932). Crime and the failure of institutions in Chicago's immigrant areas. *Journal of Criminal Law and Criminology, 23,* 238–248.

Lane, M.P. (1989, July). Inmate gangs. *Corrections Today,* pp. 98–99, 126–128.

Lange, J. (1928). *Crime as destiny.* London: George Allen & Unwin.

Latane, B., Williams, K., & Harkins, S. (1979). Many hands make light the work: The causes and consequences of social loafing. *Journal of Personality and Social Psychology, 37,* 822–832.

Laufer, W.S., & Day, J.M. (Eds.). (1983). *Personality theory, moral development, and criminal behavior.* Lexington, MA: Lexington.

Lawler, E.J., & Thompson, M.E. (1979). Subordinate response to a leader's cooptation strategy as a function of type of coalition power. *Representative Research in Social Psychology, 9,* 69–80.

LeBon, G. (1895). *The crowd.* London: Ernest Benn.

Lefkowitz, M.M., Eron, L.D., Walder, L.O., & Huessman, L.R. (1977). *Growing up to be violent.* Elmsford, NY: Pergamon.

Lemert, E.M. (1967). *Human deviance, social problems, and social control.* Englewood Cliffs, NJ: Prentice-Hall.

Lerner, H. (1987). Psychodynamic models. In V.B. VanHasselt & M. Hersen (Eds.), *Handbook of adolescent psychology.* Elmsford, NY: Pergamon.

Levin, G.K., Trabka, S., & Kahn, E.M. (1984). Group therapy with aggressive and delinquent adolescents. In C.R. Keith (Ed.), *The aggressive adolescent.* New York: Free Press.

Levinson, R.B., & Kitchener, H.L. (1964). *Demonstration counseling project.* Washington, DC: National Training School for Boys.

Levy, D.M. (1932). On the problem of delinquency. *American Journal of Orthopsychiatry, 2,* 197–207.

Lewin, K. (1951). *Field theory and social science.* New York: Harper.

Lewin, K., Lippitt, R., & White, R.K. (1939). Patterns of aggressive behavior in experimentally created "social climates." *Journal of Social Psychology, 10,* 271–299.

Ley, D. (1976). The street gang in its milieu. In G. Gapport & H.M. Rose (Eds.), *Social economy of cities.* Newbury Park, CA: Sage.

Leyens, J.P., & Parke, R.D. (1975). Aggressive slides can induce a weapons effect. *European Journal of Social Psychology, 5,* 229–236.

Liebert, R.M., Neale, J.M., & Davidson, E.S. (1973). *The early window: Effects of television on children and youth.* Elmsford, NY: Pergamon.

Lin, N. (1986). Conceptualizing social support. In N. Lin, A. Dean, & W. Ensel (Eds.), *Social support, life events and depression.* Orlando: Academic.

Linden, R. (1978). Myths of middle-class delinquency. *Youth & Society, 9,* 407–432.

Lindgren, J.G. (1987). Social policy and the prevention of delinquency. In J.D. Burchard & N.S. Burchard (Eds.), *Prevention of delinquent behavior.* Newbury Park, CA: Sage.

Lindskold, S. (1978). Trust development, the GRIT proposal, and the effects of conciliatory acts on conflict and cooperation. *Psychological Bulletin, 85,* 772–793.

Lindskold, S. (1979). Conciliation with simultaneous or sequential interaction. *Journal of Conflict Resolution, 23,* 704–714.

Linville, P.W., & Jones, E.E. (1980). Polarized appraisals of out-group members. *Journal of Personality and Social Psychology, 38,* 689–703.

Little, V.L., & Kendall, D.C. (1979). Cognitive-behavioral interventions with delinquents: Problem solving, role-taking and self-control. In P.C. Kendall & S.D. Hollon (Eds.), *Cognitive-behavioral interventions: Theory, research, and procedures.* New York: Academic.

Loeber, R., & Dishion, T. (1983). Early predictors of male delinquency: A review. *Psychological Bulletin, 94,* 68–99.

Lombroso, C. (1911). *Crime, its causes and remedies.* Boston: Little, Brown.

Lord, R.G. (1977). Functional leadership behavior: Measurement and relation to social power and leadership perceptions. *Administrative Science Quarterly, 22,* 114–133.

Los Angeles Unified School District. (1989). *GREAT: Gang resistance education and training.* Los Angeles: Office of Instruction.

Lucore, P. (1975). Cohesiveness in the gang. In D.S. Cartwright, B. Tomson, & H. Schwartz (Eds.), *Gang delinquency.* Pacific Grove, CA: Brooks/Cole.

Lundman, R.J. (1984). *Prevention and control of delinquency.* New York: Oxford University Press.

Lundman, R.J., Sykes, R.E., & Clark, J.P. (1978). Police control of juveniles: A replication. *Journal of Research in Crime and Delinquency, 15,* 74–91.

MacIver, R.M., & Page, C.H. (1949). *Society.* New York: Rinehart.

Magaro, P.A. (1969). A prescriptive treatment model based on social class and premorbid adjustment. *Psychotherapy: Theory, Research and Practice, 6,* 57–70.

Magdid, K., & McKelvey, C.A. (1987). *High risk: Children without a conscience.* New York: Bantam.

Marcia, J.E. (1980). Identity in adolescence. In J. Adelson (Ed.), *Handbook of adolescence.* New York: Wiley.

Mark, V.H., & Erwin, F.R. (1970). *Violence and the brain.* New York: Harper & Row.

Martin, P.L., & Foxx, R.M. (1973). Victim control of the aggression of an institutionalized retardate. *Journal of Behavior Therapy and Experimental Psychiatry, 4,* 161–165.

Martin, S.E., Sechrest, L.B., & Redner, R. (1981). *New directions in the rehabilitation of criminal offenders.* Washington, DC: National Academy Press.

Martinson, R. (1974, Spring). What works? Questions and answers about prison reform. *The Public Interest,* pp. 22–54.

Matson, J.L., Stephens, R.M., & Horne, A.M. (1978). Overcorrection and extinction-reinforcement as rapid methods of eliminating the disruptive behaviors of relatively normal children. *Behavioral Engineering, 4,* 89–94.

Mattick, H.W., & Caplan, N.S. (1962). *Chicago Youth Development Project: The Chicago Boys Club.* Ann Arbor, MI: Institute for Social Research.

Matza, D. (1964). *Delinquency and drift.* New York: Wiley.

Maxson, C.L., Gordon, M.A., & Klein, M.W. (1985). Differences between gang and nongang homicides. *Criminology, 23,* 209–221.

Maxson, C.L., & Klein, M.W. (1983). Gangs, why we couldn't stay away. In J.R. Kleugel (Ed.), *Evaluating juvenile justice.* Newbury Park, CA: Sage.

McClelland, D.C. (1975). *Power: The inner experience.* New York: Irvington.

McCord, W., & McCord, J. (1959). *Origins of crime: A new evaluation of the Cambridge-Somerville study.* New York: Columbia University Press.

McCord, W., & McCord, J. (1964). *The psychopath: An essay on the criminal mind.* Princeton, NJ: Van Nostrand.

McCorkle, L., Elias, A., & Bixby, F. (1958). *The Highfields story: A unique experiment in the treatment of juvenile delinquency.* New York: Holt.

McCullough, J.P., Huntsinger, G.M., & Nay, W.R. (1977). Case study: Self-control treatment of aggression in a 16-year-old male. *Journal of Consulting and Clinical Psychology, 45,* 322–331.

McDougall, W. (1908). *An introduction to social psychology.* London: Methuen.

McKinney, K.C. (1988, September). Juvenile gangs: Crime and drug trafficking. *Juvenile Justice Bulletin,* pp. 1–4.

McMillan, D.W., & Chavis, D.M. (1986). Sense of community: A definition and theory. *Journal of Community Psychology, 14,* 6–23.

Mead, G.H. (1934). *Mind, self and society.* Chicago: University of Chicago Press.

Mednick, S.A. (1977). A biosocial theory of the learning of law-abiding behavior. In S.A. Mednick & K.O. Christiansen (Eds.), *Biosocial bases of criminal behavior.* New York: Wiley.

Megargee, E.J., & Bohn, M.J., Jr. (1979). *Classifying criminal offenders: A new system based on the MMPI.* Newbury Park, CA: Sage.

Meier, R. (1976). The new criminology: Continuity in criminological theory. *Journal of Criminal Law and Criminology, 67,* 461–469.

Meltzer, M. (1984). *The Chinese Americans.* New York: Crowell.

Merrill-Palmer Institute. (1971). *The Detroit Foster Homes Project.* Unpublished manuscript, Merrill-Palmer Institute, Detroit.

Merton, R.K. (1938). Social structure and anomie. *American Sociological Review, 3,* 672–682.

Metfessel, M., & Lovell, C. (1942). Recent literature on individual correlates of crime. *Psychological Bulletin, 39,* 133–142.

Miller, W.B. (1958). Lower class culture as a generating milieu of gang delinquency. *Journal of Social Issues, 14,* 5–19.

Miller, W.B. (1970). Youth gangs in the urban crisis era. In J.F. Short (Ed.), *Delinquency, crime and society.* Chicago: University of Chicago Press.

Miller, W.B. (1974). American youth gangs: Past and present. In A. Blumberg (Ed.), *Current perspectives on criminal behavior.* New York: Knopf.

Miller, W.B. (1975). *Violence by youth gangs and youth groups as a crime problem in major American cities.* Washington, DC: National Institute for Juvenile Justice and Delinquency Prevention.

Miller, W.B. (1980). Gangs, groups, and serious youth crime. In D. Shicker & D.H. Kelly (Eds.), *Critical issues in juvenile delinquency.* Lexington, MA: Lexington.

Miller, W.B. (1982). *Crime by youth gangs and groups in the United States.* Washington, DC: National Institute for Juvenile Justice and Delinquency Prevention.

Miller, W.B. (1990). Why the United States has failed to solve its youth gang problem. In C.R. Huff (Ed.), *Gangs in America.* Newbury Park, CA: Sage.

Miller, W.B., Geertz, H., & Cutter, H.S.G. (1968). Aggression in a boys' street-corner group. In J.F. Short (Ed.), *Gang delinquency and delinquent subcultures.* New York: Harper & Row.

Mirande, A. (1987). *Gringo justice.* Notre Dame, IN: University of Notre Dame Press.

Monahan, J. (1981). *The clinical prediction of violent behavior.* Rockville, MD: National Institute of Mental Health.

Monroe, R. (1970). *Episodic behavioral disorder: A psychodynamic and neurological analysis.* Cambridge: Harvard University Press.

Monroe, S., & Goldman, P. (1988). *Brothers: Black and poor—A true story of courage and survival.* New York: Morrow.

Montagu, A. (1941). The biologist looks at crime. *The Annals, 218,* 53–55.

Moore, J.W., Garcia, R., Garcia, C., Cerda, L., & Valencia, F. (1978). *Homeboys, gangs, drugs, and prison in the barrios of Los Angeles.* Philadelphia: Temple University Press.

Moore, J.W., Vigil, D., & Garcia, R. (1983). Residence and territoriality in Chicano gangs. *Social Problems, 31,* 182–194.

Morales, A. (1981). *Treatment of Hispanic gang members.* Los Angeles: University of California, Neuropsychiatric Institute.

Moreno, J.L. (1960). *The sociometry reader.* Glencoe, IL: Free Press.

Morris, E.K., & Braukmann, C.J. (Eds.). (1987). *Behavioral approaches to crime and delinquency.* New York: Plenum.

Mullen, B. (1987). Introduction: The study of group behavior. In B. Mullen & G.R. Goethals (Eds.), *Theories of group behavior.* New York: Springer-Verlag.

Mulvey, E.P., & LaRosa, J.F. (1986). Delinquency cessation and adolescent development: Preliminary data. *American Journal of Orthopsychiatry, 56,* 212–224.

Mulvihill, D.J., Tumin, M.M., & Curtis, L.A. (1969). *Crimes of violence.* Washington, DC: National Commission on the Causes and Prevention of Violence.

Murray, H.A. (1938). *Explorations in personality.* New York: Oxford.

Muuss, R.E. (1975). *Theories of adolescence.* New York: Random House.

National Coalition on Television Violence. (1990, July-September). *NCTV News* (Vol. 2).

Needle, J.A., & Stapleton, W.V. (1982). *Police handling of youth gangs.* Washington, DC: National Juvenile Justice Assessment Center.

Nelson, L. (1948). *Rural sociology.* New York: American Book.

Nettler, G. (1974). *Explaining crime.* New York: McGraw-Hill.

New York City Police Department. (1988). *Gang activity in New York City.* New York: New York City Police Department, Gang Intelligence Unit.

New York City Youth Board. (1960). *Reaching the fighting gang.* New York: Author.

New York State Division for Youth. (1990). *Reaffirming prevention: Report of the Task Force on Juvenile Gangs.* Albany, NY: Author.

Nietzel, M.T. (1979). *Crime and its modification.* Elmsford, NY: Pergamon.

Nietzel, M.T., Guthrie, P.R., & Susman, D.T. (1990). Utilization of community and social support resources. In F.H. Kanfer & A.P. Goldstein (Eds.), *Helping people change.* Elmsford, NY: Pergamon.

Nietzel, M.T., & Himelein, M.J. (1987). Probation and parole. In E.K. Morris & C.J. Braukmann (Eds.), *Behavioral approaches to crime and delinquency.* New York: Plenum.

Northern California Service League. (1968). *Final report of the San Francisco Rehabilitation Project for Offenders.* San Francisco: Author.

Novaco, R.W. (1975). *Anger control: The development and evaluation of an experimental treatment.* Lexington, MA: Heath.

Nye, F.I. (1958). *Family relationships and delinquent behavior.* New York: Wiley.

O'Leary, K.D., & Becker, W.C. (1967). Behavior modification of an adjustment class: A token reinforcement program. *Exceptional Children, 33,* 637–642.

O'Leary, K.D., Kaufman, K.F., Kass, R.E., & Drabman, R.S. (1970). The effects of loud and soft reprimands on the behavior of disruptive students. *Exceptional Children, 37,* 145–155.

Osborn, S.G., & West, D.J. (1979). Conviction records of fathers and sons compared. *British Journal of Criminology, 19,* 120–133.

Osgood, C.E. (1979). GRIT for MBFR: A proposal for unfreezing force-level postures in Europe. *Peace Research Review, 8,* 77–92.

Oskamp, S., & Hartry, A. (1968). A factor-analytic study of the double standard in attitudes toward U.S. and Russian actions. *Behavioral Science, 13,* 178–188.

Palmer, T.B. (1973). Matching worker and client in corrections. *Social Work, 18,* 95–103.

Palmer, T.B. (1976). Martinson revisited. *Journal of Research in Crime and Delinquency, 12,* 133–152.

Patterson, G.R. (1982). *Coercive family process.* Eugene, OR: Castalia.

Patterson, G.R., Cobb, J.A., & Ray, R.S. (1973). A social engineering technology for retraining the families of aggressive boys. In H.E. Adams & I.P. Unikel (Eds.), *Issues and trends in behavior therapy.* Springfield, IL: Charles C Thomas.

Philadelphia Police Department Preventive Patrol Unit. (1987). *Youth gangs: Problem and response.* Washington, DC: Office of Juvenile Justice and Delinquency Prevention.

Philibosian, R.H. (1986). *State Task Force on Youth Gang Violence.* Sacramento: California Council on Criminal Justice.

Phillips, E.L. (1968). Achievement Place: Token reinforcement procedures in a home style rehabilitation setting for pre-delinquent boys. *Journal of Applied Behavior Analysis, 7,* 207–215.

Piliavin, J., & Briar, S. (1964). Police encounters with juveniles. *American Journal of Sociology, 70,* 206–214.

Pilnick, S. (1967). *Collegefields: From delinquency to freedom.* Newark, NJ: Newark State College.

Pines, M. (1979, March). Superkids. *Psychology Today,* pp. 53–63.

Platt, J.J., & Prout, M.F. (1987). Cognitive-behavioral theory and interventions for crime and delinquency. In E.K. Morris and C.J. Braukmann (Eds.), *Behavioral approaches to crime and delinquency.* New York: Plenum.

Pollock, V., Mednick, S.A., & Gabrielli, W.F. (1983). Crime causation: Biological theories. In S.H. Kadish (Ed.), *Encyclopedia of crime and justice* (Vol. 1). New York: Free Press.

Pond, E. (1970). *The Los Angeles Community Delinquency Control Project: An experiment in the rehabilitation of delinquents in an urban community* (Research Report No. 60). Sacramento: California Department of the Youth Authority.

Post, G.C., Hicks, R.A., & Monfort, M.F. (1968). Day care program for delinquents: A new treatment approach. *Crime and Delinquency, 14,* 353–359.

Powell, M. (1955). Age and sex differences in degree of conflict within certain areas of psychological adjustment. *Psychological Monographs, 69* (Whole No. 387).

Prentice-Dunn, S., & Rogers, R.W. (1980). Effects of deindividuating situation cues and aggressive models on subjective deindividuation and aggression. *Journal of Personality and Social Psychology, 39,* 104–113.

President's Commission on Law Enforcement and Administration of Justice. (1967). *Juvenile delinquency and youth crime.* Washington, DC: U.S. Government Printing Office.

President's Commission on Organized Crime. (1985). *Organized Crime of Asian Origin.* Washington, DC: U.S. Government Printing Office.

Proshansky, H.M., Fabian, A.K., & Kaminoff, R. (1983). Place-identity: Physical world socialization of the self. *Journal of Environmental Psychology, 3,* 57–83.

Pruitt, D.G. (1971). Choice shifts in group discussion: An introductory review. *Journal of Personality and Social Psychology, 20,* 339–360.

Puffer, J.A. (1912). *The boy and his gang.* Boston: Houghton Mifflin.

Quay, H.C. (1965). Psychopathic personality as pathological stimulation-seeking. *American Journal of Psychiatry, 122,* 180–183.

Quay, H.C. (1977). Psychopathic behavior: Reflections on its nature, origins, and treatment. In I. Uzgiris & F. Weizmann (Eds.), *The structuring of experience.* New York: Plenum.

Quicker, J.C. (1983a). *Homegirls: Characterizing Chicana gangs.* San Pedro, CA: International Universities Press.

Quicker, J.C. (1983b). *Seven decades of gangs.* Sacramento: State of California Commission on Crime Control and Violence Prevention.

Quinney, R. (1974). *Critique of legal order: Crime control in capitalist society.* Boston: Little, Brown.

Rafferty, F.T., & Bertcher, H. (1963). Gang formation in vitro. *Journal of Nervous and Mental Disease, 137,* 76–81.

Ramirez, M. (1983). *Psychology of the Americas.* Elmsford, NY: Pergamon.

Raven, B.H., & Kruglanski, A.W. (1970). Conflict and power. In P. Swingle (Ed.), *The structure of conflict.* New York: Academic.

Reckless, W.C. (1961). *The crime problem.* New York: Appleton-Century-Crofts.

Redl, F. (1945). The psychology of gang formation and the treatment of juvenile delinquents. In *Psychoanalytic study of the child* (Vol. 1). New York: International Universities Press.

Redl, F., & Wineman, D. (1957). *The aggressive child.* Glencoe, IL: Free Press.

Redner, R., Snellman, L., & Davidson, W.S. (1983). Juvenile delinquency. In R.J. Morris & T.R. Kratochwill (Eds.), *The practice of child therapy.* Elmsford, NY: Pergamon.

Reicher, S. (1982). The determination of collective behavior. In H. Tajfel (Ed.), *Social identity and intergroup relations.* Cambridge, MA: Cambridge University Press.

Reiss, A.J., & Rhodes, A.L. (1964). Status deprivation and delinquent behavior. *The Sociological Quarterly, 4,* 135–149.

Reuterman, N.A. (1975). Formal theories of gangs. In D. Cartwright, B. Tomson, & H. Schwartz (Eds.), *Gang delinquency.* Pacific Grove, CA: Brooks/Cole.

Richards, M., & Peterson, A.C. (1987). Biological theoretical models. In V.B. VanHasselt & M. Hersen (Eds.), *Handbook of adolescent psychology.* Elmsford, NY: Pergamon.

Rivlin, L.G. (1987). The neighborhood, personal identity, and group affiliations. In I. Altman & E. Zube (Eds.), *Neighborhood and community environments.* New York: Plenum.

Roberts, H.B. (1987). *The inner world of the Black juvenile delinquent.* Hillsdale, NJ: Erlbaum.

Robins, L.N., & Lewis, R.G. (1966). The role of the antisocial family in school completion and delinquency: A three-generation study. *Sociological Quarterly, 7,* 500–514.

Robins, L.N., West, P.A., & Herjanic, B.L. (1975). Arrests and delinquency in two generations: A study of black urban families and their children. *Journal of Child Psychology and Psychiatry, 16,* 125–140.

Rogers, E.M., & Shoemaker, F.F. (1971). *Communication of innovations.* New York: Free Press.

Romig, D.A. (1978). *Justice for our children: An examination of juvenile delinquency rehabilitation programs.* Lexington, MA: Lexington.

Rosenbaum, A. (1979). Wife abuse: Characteristics of the participants and etiological considerations. Unpublished doctoral dissertation, State University of New York at Stony Brook.

Rosenthal, D. (1970). *Genetics of psychopathology.* New York: McGraw-Hill.

Ross, H.L., & Glasser, E.M. (1973). Making it out of the ghetto. *Professional Psychology, 4,* 347–356.

Ross, R.R., & Fabiano, E.A. (1985). *Time to think: A cognitive model of delinquency prevention and offender rehabilitation.* Johnson City, TN: Institute of Social Sciences and Arts.

Ruben, M. (1957). Delinquency, a defense against loss of objects and reality. *Psychoanalytic Study of the Child, 12,* 335–349.

Rutter, M. (1971). Parent-child separation: Psychological effects on the child. *Journal of Child Psychology and Psychiatry, 12,* 233–260.

Rutter, M. (1980). *Changing youth in a changing society.* Cambridge, MA: Harvard University Press.

Rutter, M., & Giller, H. (1983). *Juvenile delinquency: Trends and perspectives.* New York: Guilford.

Ryan, A.H., & Kahn, A. (1970). Own-group bias: The effects of individual competence and group outcome. *Proceedings of the Iowa Academy of Science, 77,* 302–307.

Sampson, R.V. (1965). *Equality and power.* London: Heinemann.

San Diego Association of State Governments. (1982). *Juvenile violence and gang-related crime.* San Diego: Author.

San Diego County Probation Department. (1971). *Research and evaluation of the first year of operations of the San Diego County Juvenile Narcotics Project.* San Diego: Author.

Sandler, I.N., Miller, P., Short, J., & Wolchik, S.A. (1989). Social support as a protective factor for children in stress. In D. Belle (Ed.), *Children's social networks and social supports.* New York: Wiley.

Sarason, I.J., & Ganzer, V.J. (1973). Modeling and group discussion in the rehabilitation of juvenile delinquents. *Journal of Counseling Psychology, 20,* 442–449.

Sarason, S.B. (1974). *The psychological sense of community.* San Francisco: Jossey-Bass.

Sarnecki, J. (1985). *Delinquent networks.* Stockholm: National Swedish Council for Crime Prevention.

Savitz, L.D., Rosen, L., & Lalli, M. (1980). Delinquency and gang membership as related to victimization. *Victimology, 5,* 152–160.

Sawin, D.B., & Parke, R.D. (1979). The effects of interagent inconsistent discipline on children's aggressive behavior. *Journal of Experimental Child Psychology, 28,* 528–535.

Schachter, S. (1959). *The psychology of affiliation.* Palo Alto, CA: Stanford University Press.

Schachter, S., Ellertson, N., McBride, D., & Gregory, D. (1951). An experimental study of cohesiveness and productivity. *Human Relations, 4,* 229–238.

Schlapp, M.G., & Smith, E.H. (1928). *The new criminology.* New York: Boni & Liveright.

School crime rates continue to rise. (1990, May 24). *New York Times,* p. 31.

School violence increases. (1990, May 17). *San Francisco Chronicle,* p. 1.

Schuessler, K.F., & Cressey, D.R. (1950). Personality characteristics of criminals. *American Journal of Sociology, 55,* 476–484.

Schur, E. (1971). *Labeling deviant behavior: Its sociological implications.* New York: Random House.

Schutz, W.C. (1967). *FIRO*. New York: Holt, Rinehart & Winston.

Schwartz, B.N., & Disch, R. (1970). *White racism*. New York: Dell.

Schwitzgebel, R.L. (1967). Short term operant conditioning of adolescent offenders on socially relevant variables. *Journal of Abnormal Psychology, 72*, 134–142.

Schwitzgebel, R.L., & Kolb, D.A. (1964). Inducing behavior change in adolescent delinquents. *Behaviour Research and Therapy, 1*, 297–304.

Sealy, A., & Banks, C. (1971). Social maturity, training, experience, and recidivism amongst British Borstal boys. *British Journal of Criminology, 11*, 245–264.

Seaman, D. (1979). *A geography of the lifeworld*. New York: St. Martin's.

Seckel, J. (1975). *Assessment of Preston Family Drug Treatment Project*. Sacramento: California Department of the Youth Authority.

Shannon, L.W. (1988). *Criminal career continuity*. New York: Human Sciences.

Shaw, C.R. (1966). *The jack-roller: A delinquent boy's own story*. Chicago: University of Chicago Press. (Original work published 1930)

Shaw, C.R., & McKay, H.D. (1942). *Juvenile delinquency and urban areas: A study of rates of delinquency in relation to differential characteristics of local communities in American cities*. Chicago: University of Chicago Press.

Shaw, M.E. (1964). Communication networks. In L. Berkowitz (Ed.), *Advances in experimental social psychology* (Vol. 1). New York: Academic.

Shaw, M.E. (1981). *Group dynamics: The psychology of small group behavior*. New York: McGraw-Hill.

Sheldon, W.H. (1942). *The varieties of temperament*. New York: Harper.

Sheldon, W.H. (1949). *Varieties of delinquent youth*. New York: Harper.

Sherif, M., Harvey, O.J., White, B.J., Hood, W.R., & Sherif, C.W. (1961). *Intergroup conflict and cooperation: The Robbers Cave Experiment*. Norman, OK: Institute of Group Relations.

Sherif, M., & Sherif, C.W. (1953). *Groups in harmony and tension*. New York: Harper & Row.

Sherif, M., & Sherif, C.W. (1967). Group processes and collective interaction in delinquency activities. *Journal of Research in Crime and Delinquency, 4*, 43–62.

Shibutani, T. (1959). Reference groups as perspectives. In H.H. Hyman & E. Singer (Eds.), *Reference group theory and research*. New York: Free Press.

Shinn, M., Lehmann, S., & Wong, N.W. (1984). Social interaction and social support. *Journal of Social Issues, 40*, 55–76.

Short, J.F. (1974). Youth gangs and society: Micro- and macrosociological processes. *The Sociological Quarterly, 15*, 3–19.

Short, J.F. (1990). New wine in old bottles? Change and continuity in American gangs. In C.R. Huff (Ed.), *Gangs in America*. Newbury Park, CA: Sage.

Short, J.F., & Nye, F.I. (1957). Reported behavior as a criterion of deviant behavior. *Social Problems, 5*, 207–213.

Short, J.F., & Strodtbeck, F.L. (1965). *Group process and gang delinquency*. Chicago: University of Chicago Press.

Shumaker, S.A., & Brownell, A. (1984). Toward a theory of social support: Closing conceptual gaps. *Journal of Social Issues, 40*, 11–36.

Silverstein, B., & Krate, R. (1975). *Children of the dark ghetto.* New York: Praeger.

Simon, W., & Gagnon, J.H. (1976). The anomie of affluence: A post-Mertonian conception. *American Journal of Sociology, 82,* 356–378.

Singer, J.E., Brush, C.A., & Lublin, S.C. (1965). Some aspects of deindividuation: Identification and conformity. *Journal of Experimental Social Psychology, 1,* 356–378.

Skogan, W.G. (1989). Social change and the future of violent crime. In T.R. Gurr (Ed.), *Violence in America: Vol. 1. The history of crime.* Newbury Park, CA: Sage.

Slack, C.W. (1960). Experimenter-subject psychotherapy: A new method of introductory intensive office treatment for unreachable cases. *Mental Hygiene, 44,* 238–256.

Slavson, S.R. (1964). *A textbook of analytic group psychotherapy.* New York: International Universities Press.

Sliwa, C. (1987). The Guardian Angels. In B. Berkowitz (Ed.), *Local heroes.* Lexington, MA: Lexington.

Smart, R. (1965). Social group membership, leadership, and birth order. *Journal of Social Psychology, 67,* 221–225.

Snow, C.P. (1961). Either-or. *Progressive, 25,* 24–25.

Snyder, J.J. (1977). Reinforcement analysis of problem and nonproblem families. *Journal of Abnormal Psychology, 86,* 528–535.

Snyder, J.J., & Patterson, G.R. (1987). Family interaction and delinquent behavior. In H.C. Quay (Ed.), *Handbook of juvenile delinquency.* New York: Wiley.

Snyder, J.J., & White, M.H. (1979). The use of cognitive self-instruction in the treatment of behaviorally disturbed adolescents. *Behavior Therapy, 10,* 227–235.

Sowles, R.C., & Gill, J.H. (1970). Institutional and community adjustment of delinquents following counseling. *Journal of Consulting and Clinical Psychology, 34,* 398–402.

Spergel, I.A. (1964). *Racketville, Slumtown, and Haulberg.* Chicago: University of Chicago Press.

Spergel, I.A. (1965). *Street gang work: Theory and practice.* Reading, MA: Addison-Wesley.

Spergel, I.A. (1985). *The violent gang problem in Chicago.* Chicago: University of Chicago, School of Social Service Administration.

Spergel, I.A. (1989). *Survey of youth gang problems and programs in 45 cities and 6 states.* Washington, DC: Office of Juvenile Justice and Delinquency Prevention.

Spergel, I.A., Ross, R.E., Curry, G.D., & Chance, R. (1989). *Youth gangs: Problem and response.* Washington, DC: Office of Juvenile Justice and Delinquency Prevention.

Stein, N., & Bogin, D. (1978). Individual child psychotherapy. In A.P. Goldstein (Ed.), *Prescriptions for child mental health and education.* Elmsford, NY: Pergamon.

Steiner, I.D. (1972). *Group process and productivity.* New York: Academic.

Steiner, I.D. (1976). Task-performing groups. In J.W. Thibaut, J.T. Spence, & R.C. Carson (Eds.), *Contemporary topics in social psychology.* Morristown, NJ: General Learning.

Stephenson, R., & Scarpitti, F. (1968). A study of probation effectiveness. *The Journal of Criminal Law, Criminology and Police Science, 59,* 361–369.

Strauss, M.A. (1977–1978). Wife beating: How common and why? *Victimology, 2,* 443–458.

Strickland, L.H. (1958). Surveillance and trust. *Journal of Personality, 26,* 206–215.

Strodtbeck, F.L., Short, J.F., & Kolegar, E. (1962). The analysis of self-descriptions by members of delinquent gangs. *Sociological Quarterly, 3,* 331–356.

Stuart, R.B., Jayaratne, S., & Tripoldi, T. (1976). Changing adolescent deviant behavior through reprogramming the behavior of parents and teachers. *Canadian Journal of Behavioral Science, 8,* 132–144.

Stumphauzer, J.S., Aiken, T.W., & Veloz, E.V. (1977). East Side story: Behavioral analysis of a high juvenile crime community. *Behavior Disorders, 2,* 76–84.

Stumphauzer, J.S., Veloz, E.V., & Aiken, T.W. (1981). Violence by street gangs: East Side story? In R.B. Stuart (Ed.), *Violent behavior: Social learning approaches to prediction, management and treatment.* New York: Bruner/Mazel.

Sullivan, M.L. (1989). *Getting paid: Youth crime and work in the inner city.* Ithaca, NY: Cornell University Press.

Sutherland, E.H. (1937). *Principles of criminology.* Philadelphia: Lippincott.

Sutherland, E.H. (1947). *Principles of criminology.* Philadelphia: Lippincott.

Sutherland, E.H., & Cressey, D.R. (1974). *Criminology.* New York: Lippincott.

Suttles, G.D. (1972). *The social construction of communities.* Chicago: University of Chicago Press.

Sykes, G.M., & Matza, D. (1957). Techniques of neutralization: A theory of delinquency. *American Sociological Review, 22,* 664–670.

Tajfel, H. (1981). *Human groups and social categories.* Cambridge, MA: Cambridge University Press.

Tajfel, H., & Turner, J.C. (1986). The social identity theory of intergroup behavior. In S. Worchel & W.G. Austen (Eds.), *Psychology of intergroup relations.* New York: Nelson-Hall.

Tannenbaum, F. (1938). *Crime and the community.* Boston: Ginn.

Tappan, P. (1960). *Crime, justice and correction.* New York: McGraw-Hill.

Taylor, C.S. (1990). Gang imperialism. In C.R. Huff (Ed.), *Gangs in America.* Newbury Park, CA: Sage.

Taylor, T., & Watt, D.C. (1977). The relationship of deviant symptoms and behavior in a normal population to subsequent delinquency and maladjustment. *Psychological Medicine, 7,* 163–169.

Tennenbaum, D.J. (1977). Personality and criminality: A summary and implications of the literature. *Journal of Criminal Justice, 5,* 225–235.

Terrance, M. (1971). *Positive Action for Youth (PAY).* Flint, MI: Flint Board of Education, Mott Crime and Delinquency Prevention Program.

Thibaut, J.W., & Kelley, H.H. (1959). *The social psychology of groups.* New York: Wiley.

Thoits, P.A. (1982). Conceptual, methodological and theoretical problems in studying social support as a buffer against life stress. *Journal of Health and Social Behavior, 23,* 145–159.

Thompson, D.W., & Jason, L.A. (1988). Street gangs and preventive interventions. *Criminal Justice and Behavior, 15,* 323–333.

Thornburg, H. (1972). A comparative study of sex information sources. *Journal of School Health, 42,* 88–91.

Thornton, G. (1939). The ability to judge crimes from photographs of criminals. *Journal of Abnormal and Social Psychology, 34,* 378–383.

Thrasher, F.M. (1963). *The gang.* Chicago: University of Chicago Press. (Original work published 1927)

Toch, H. (1969). *Violent men.* Chicago: Aldine.

Tognacci, L. (1975). Pressures toward uniformity in delinquent gangs. In D.S. Cartwright, B. Tomson, & H. Schwartz (Eds.), *Gang delinquency.* Pacific Grove, CA: Brooks/Cole.

Torchia, J.R. (1980, December). Ocean Township Youth Volunteer Corps. *Law and Order,* pp. 12–15.

Tracy, P.E. (1979). *Subcultural delinquency: A comparison of the incidence and seriousness of gang and nongang member offensivity.* Philadelphia: University of Pennsylvania, Center for Studies in Criminology and Criminal Law.

Trasler, G. (1987). Biogenetic factors. In H.C. Quay (Ed.), *Handbook of juvenile delinquency.* New York: Wiley.

Trojanowicz, R.C., & Morash, M. (1987). *Juvenile delinquency: Concepts and control.* Englewood Cliffs, NJ: Prentice-Hall.

Tuckman, B.W. (1965). Developmental sequences in small groups. *Psychological Bulletin, 63,* 384–399.

Tuckman, B.W., & Jensen, M.A.C. (1977). Stages of small group development revisited. *Group and Organization, 2,* 419–427.

Turner, C.W., Simons, L.S., Berkowitz, L., & Frodi, A. (1977). The stimulating and inhibiting effects of weapons on aggressive behavior. *Aggressive Behavior, 3,* 355–378.

Turner, J.C. (1987). *Rediscovering the social group: A self-categorization theory.* New York: Basil Blackwell.

Turner, R.H., & Killian, L.M. (1972). *Collective behavior.* Englewood Cliffs, NJ: Prentice-Hall.

Tyler, V., & Brown, G. (1968). Token reinforcement of academic performance with institutionalized delinquent boys. *Journal of Educational Psychology, 59,* 164–168.

Unger, D.G., & Wandersman, A. (1985). The importance of neighbors: The social, cognitive, and affective components of neighboring. *American Journal of Community Psychology, 13,* 139–169.

U.S. Department of Justice. (1977). *Project New Pride.* Washington, DC: National Institute of Law Enforcement and Criminal Justice.

Vanden Haeg, E. (1975). *Punishing criminals: Concerning a very old and painful question.* New York: Basic.

Vaux, A. (1988). *Social support.* New York: Praeger.

Vigil, J.D. (1983). Chicano gangs: One response to Mexican urban adaptation in the Los Angeles area. *Urban Anthropology, 12,* 45–75.

Vigil, J.D. (1988). *Barrio gangs: Street life and identity in southern California.* Austin: University of Texas Press.

Vigil, J.D., & Long, J.M. (1990). Emic and etic perspectives on gang culture: The Chicano case. In C.R. Huff (Ed.), *Gangs in America.* Newbury Park, CA: Sage.

Vigil, J.D., & Yun, S.C. (1990). Vietnamese youth gangs in southern California. In C.R. Huff (Ed.), *Gangs in America.* Newbury Park, CA: Sage.

Vorrath, H., & Brendtro, L.K. (1974). *Positive peer culture.* Chicago: Aldine.

Voss, H.L. (1963). Ethnic differentials in delinquency in Honolulu. *Journal of Criminal Law, Criminology, and Police Science, 54,* 322–327.

Vroom, V.H., & Yetton, P.W. (1973). *Leadership and decision making.* Pittsburgh: University of Pittsburgh Press.

Waldo, G.P., & Dinitz, S. (1967). Personality attributes of the criminal: An analysis of research studies, 1950–65. *Journal of Research in Crime and Delinquency, 4,* 185–202.

Wallach, M.A., Kogan, N., & Bem, D.J. (1962). Group influence on individual risk taking. *Journal of Abnormal and Social Psychology, 65,* 75–86.

Warren, M.Q. (1974). *Classification for treatment.* Paper presented at a seminar on the classification of criminal behavior, National Institute of Law Enforcement and Criminal Justice, Washington, DC.

Warren, M.Q. (1983). Applications of interpersonal-maturity theory to offender populations. In W.S. Laufer & J.M. Day (Eds.), *Personality theory, moral development, and criminal behavior.* Lexington, MA: Lexington.

Warren, R.L. (1963). *The community in America.* Chicago: Rand McNally.

Wattenberg, W.W., & Balistrieri, J.J. (1950). Gang membership and juvenile misconduct. *American Sociological Review, 15,* 181–186.

Wegmann, T.G., & Smith, D.W. (1963). Incidence of Klinefelter's syndrome among juvenile delinquents and felons. *Lancet, 1,* 274.

Weisner, T.S. (1989). Cultural and universal aspects of social support for children. In D. Belle (Ed.), *Children's social networks and social supports.* New York: Wiley.

Weiss, R.S. (1974). The provisions of social relations. In Z. Rubin (Ed.), *Doing unto others.* Englewood Cliffs, NJ: Prentice-Hall.

Werner, E.E., & Smith, R.S. (1982). *Vulnerable but invincible.* New York: McGraw-Hill.

West, D.J. (1967). *The young offender.* Harmondsworth, England: Penguin.

West, D.J., & Farrington, D.P. (1977). *The delinquent way of life.* London: Heinemann.

White, G.D., Nielson, G., & Johnson, S.M. (1972). Timeout duration and the suppression of deviant behavior in children. *Journal of Applied Behavior Analysis, 5,* 111–120.

White, J.L. (1984). *The psychology of Blacks.* Englewood Cliffs, NJ: Prentice-Hall.

White, R.K. (1970). *Nobody wanted war: Misperception in Vietnam and other wars.* New York: Doubleday.

White, R.K. (1977). Misperception in the Arab-Israeli conflict. *Journal of Social Issues, 33,* 190–221.

White, R.K., & Lippitt, R. (1968). Leader behavior and member reaction in three "social climates." In D. Cartwright & A. Zander (Eds.), *Group dynamics: Research and theory.* New York: Harper & Row.

Wilder, D.A. (1986). Cognitive factors affecting the success of intergroup contact. In S. Worchel & W.G. Austin (Eds.), *Psychology of intergroup relations.* Chicago: Nelson-Hall.

Wilkins, L.T., & Gottfredson, D.M. (1969). *Research, demonstration and social action.* Davis, CA: National Council on Crime and Delinquency.

Williams, D., & Akamatsu, J. (1978). Cognitive self-guidance training with juvenile delinquents: Applicability and generalization. *Cognitive Therapy and Research, 2,* 205–208.

Williams, T. (1989). *The cocaine kids.* Reading, MA: Addison-Wesley.

Williams, T., & Kornblum, W. (1985). *Growing up poor.* Lexington, MA: Heath.

Willis-Kistler, P. (1988, November). Fighting gangs with recreation. *P & R,* pp. 45–49.

Willman, M.T., & Snortum, J.R. (1982). A police program for employment of youth gang members. *International Journal of Offender Therapy and Comparative Criminology, 26,* 207–214.

Wilson, E.O. (1975). *Sociology: The new synthesis.* Cambridge, MA: Belknap.

Wilson, H. (1980). Parental supervision: A neglected aspect of delinquency. *British Journal of Criminology, 20,* 203–235.

Wilson, J.Q., & Hernnstein, R.J. (1985). *Crime and human nature.* New York: Simon & Schuster.

Wilson, R.W. (1970). *Learning to be Chinese.* Cambridge, MA: The MIT Press.

Wilson, W., & Miller, N. (1961). Shifts in evaluations of participants following intergroup competition. *Journal of Abnormal and Social Psychology, 63,* 428–431.

Witkin, H.A., Mednick, S.A., Schulsinger, F., Bakkestrom, E., Christiansen, K.O., Goodenough, D.R., Hirschhorn, K., Lundsteen, C., Owen, D.R., Philip, J., Rubin, D.B., & Stocking, M. (1976). Criminality, aggression and intelligence among XYY and XXY men. *Science, 193,* 547.

Wolfgang, M., Figlio, R., & Sellin, T. (1972). *Delinquency in a birth cohort.* Chicago: University of Chicago Press.

Woodson, R.L. (1981). *A summons to life: Mediating structures and the prevention of youth crime.* Cambridge, MA: Ballinger.

Wright, F. (1985). Transition processes: Healthy versus pathological in youth groups. *International Journal of Offender Therapy and Comparative Criminology, 29,* 159–170.

Wright, W.E., & Dixon, M.C. (1977). Community prevention and treatment of juvenile delinquency: A review of evaluation studies. *Journal of Research in Crime and Delinquency, 14,* 35–67.

Wrong, D.H. (1979). *Power.* New York: Harper & Row.

Yablonsky, L. (1959). The delinquent gang as a near group. *Social Problems, 7,* 108–117.

Yablonsky, L. (1967). *The violent gang.* New York: Penguin.

Yochelson, S., & Samenow, S.E. (1976). *The criminal personality.* New York: Jason Aronson.

Zander, A., Cohen, A.R., & Stotland, E. (1959). Power and relations among the professions. In D. Cartwright (Ed.), *Studies in social power.* Ann Arbor, MI: University of Michigan, Institute for Social Research.

Zillman, D., Bryant, J., Cantor, J.R., & Day, K.D. (1975). Irrelevance of mitigating circumstances in retaliatory behavior at high levels of excitation. *Journal of Research in Personality, 9,* 282–293.

Zimbardo, P.G. (1969). The human choice. In W.J. Arnold & D. Levine (Eds.), *Nebraska Symposium on Motivation.* Lincoln: University of Nebraska Press.

Zimring, F. (1977). Determinants of the death rate from robbery. *Journal of Legal Studies, 6,* 317–332.

Author Index

Subject Index

About the Author

Arnold P. Goldstein, PhD, joined the clinical psychology section of Syracuse University's Psychology Department in 1963 and both taught there and directed its Psychotherapy Center until 1980. In 1981, he founded the Center for Research on Aggression, which he currently directs. He joined Syracuse University's Division of Special Education in 1985. Dr. Goldstein has a career-long interest, as both researcher and practitioner, in difficult-to-reach clients. Since 1980, his main research and psychoeducational focus has been juvenile offenders and child-abusing parents. He is the developer of psychoeducational programs and curricula designed to teach prosocial behaviors to chronically antisocial persons. Dr. Goldstein's many books include, among others, *Aggression Replacement Training: A Comprehensive Intervention for Aggressive Youth; Changing the Abusive Parent; The Prepare Curriculum: Teaching Prosocial Competencies; Refusal Skills: Preventing Drug Use in Adolescents; Skillstreaming the Adolescent: A Structured Learning Approach to Teaching Prosocial Skills;* and *Delinquents on Delinquency.*